Mereness' Essentials of psychiatric nursing
Learning and activity guide

Mereness'
Essentials of psychiatric nursing

LEARNING AND ACTIVITY GUIDE

Carol Ruth Lofstedt, R.N., M.A.

Professor of Nursing,
Bronx Community College,
Bronx, New York

SECOND EDITION
with *Foreword by* **Cecelia Monat Taylor**
Illustrations by **Meri Bourgard**

The C. V. Mosby Company

St. Louis • Toronto • Princeton   1986

MOSBY

A TRADITION OF PUBLISHING EXCELLENCE

editor: Nancy L. Mullins
assistant editor: Maureen Slaten
manuscript editor: CRACOM Corporation
cover design: John Rokusek
book design and production: CRACOM Corporation

SECOND EDITION

Copyright © 1986 by The C.V. Mosby Company

Previous edition copyrighted 1982

Printed in the United States of America

International Standard Book Number 0-8016-3087-8

The C.V. Mosby Company
11830 Westline Industrial Drive, St. Louis, Missouri 63146

C/VH/VH   9 8 7 6 5 4 3 2 1   01/B/076

To **all nursing students**—
yesterday's, today's, and tomorrow's,
who are challenged and rewarded by the care of the mentally ill,
and who make the teaching of psychiatric nursing so worthwhile.

foreword

The publication of this learning and activity guide is the culmination of many years of thought and work. As early as 1976, Dr. Dorothy A. Mereness and I were confronted with preparing the tenth edition of *Essentials of Psychiatric Nursing* and came to the conclusion that there was more material to be presented than was appropriate or economically feasible for a textbook. Students and faculty had consistently requested more case material and study questions to accompany each chapter of the book. Consequently, we began to envision a separate workbook that would focus primarily on application of the theoretical material presented in the text.

Simultaneously, but unbeknown to us, Carol Lofstedt had identified a similar problem as she taught psychiatric nursing to associate degree students at Bronx Community College. The limitation of time forced her to confine lectures to the most basic material; the nature of the clinical learning experiences dictated that students be limited to an in-depth experience with only one or, at most, a few clients. Consequently, she felt that while the course provided the students with a valuable introduction to psychiatric nursing, its scope was necessarily narrow. In an effort to broaden the students' exposure to psychiatric nursing as well as to increase their interest, Carol began to develop exercises to accompany lectures. These exercises were designed to be completed by the student out of class and largely consisted of word games.

Over the years the response of those students who participated in these exercises was uniformly enthusiastic. As a result, Carol believed that the exercises had the potential for being a valuable teaching-learning tool for others, and she prepared a representative manuscript that she took with her to the 1980 ANA Convention in Houston, Texas, in the hope of interesting a publisher in issuing a manual of this type.

It was at this convention that Carol and I renewed our acquaintance (we had been classmates many years ago at New York

University in the graduate program in psychiatric-mental health nursing directed by Dr. Mereness), and we discussed at length our current activities. I was planning the eleventh edition of *Essentials of Psychiatric Nursing* and, as just described, Carol was engrossed in the development of learning activities to supplement and enhance basic instruction in psychiatric nursing. Thus after a gestation period of 4 years, a learning and activity guide to accompany the textbook was born.

The learning and activity guide is designed to be used with *Mereness' Essentials of Psychiatric Nursing,* and the material in the guide is carefully coordinated with the text. Both Carol and I believe that the use of this manual by beginning students of psychiatric nursing will greatly enrich their understanding and appreciation of the area.

Cecelia Monat Taylor

preface

In June 1980 I participated in a discussion in Philadelphia with Dorothy A. Mereness and Cecelia M. Taylor, co-authors of the ninth and tenth editions of *Essentials of Psychiatric Nursing.* The purpose of the meeting was to begin preparation of the eleventh edition of the textbook and, in response to requests by the readers, to consider the development of a student workbook to accompany the latest revision. The first edition of the learning and activity guide resulted from that June meeting. This second edition is the result of continued reader responsiveness.

Although the second edition of the learning and activity guide could be used with other psychiatric nursing textbooks, it is essentially designed to accompany *Mereness' Essentials of Psychiatric Nursing,* twelfth edition, by Dr. Cecelia M. Taylor. First, the guide subscribes to the belief set forth in the text that all nurses need a sound theoretical foundation to give purposeful and concerned care to emotionally ill persons. It also recognizes that knowledge once considered unique to psychiatric nursing has relevance to all areas of nursing. Second, there are six sections and twenty-six chapters in the guide, each one articulating with the content in the six sections and twenty-six chapters in the text. The exercises in the guide reenforce selected material covered in the text.

Section I looks at the context of psychiatric nursing practice: the mental health delivery system and the mental health team. The exercises in this section focus the reader on treatment measures used through the centuries, with the greatest emphasis being placed on current methods. In addition, the roles of the mental health team members, especially nursing roles, are identified and explored.

Section II introduces concepts basic to the practice of psychiatric nursing. A new chapter and related exercises on systems theory and stress and adaptation have been added to this edition and provide a conceptual framework from which the nurse may operate. In addition, Section II explores the evolution of personality from infancy to old age from intrapsychic, interpersonal, and cultural perspectives. Anxiety, its development, its effect on functioning, and the mental mechanisms used to defend against anxiety are also covered. Finally, the nature of mental health and the factors contributing to the development and prevention of mental illness are included in this section. Exercises in these four chapters provide the reader with opportunities to use these basic concepts. New case situations have been added to help facilitate the application of these concepts. In addition, the need for the nurse to develop self-awareness is first introduced in Section II, as several exercises encourage readers to look at themselves and their reactions.

Section III focuses on the tools used by the nurse in the practice of psychiatric nursing: self-awareness, communication skills, interpersonal interventions, psychotropic agents, manipulation of the environment, and the nursing process. The content and exercises in these six chapters in Section III are basic to the remaining chapters and exercises in the guide and will be threaded throughout. This is particularly true of self-awareness, communication skills, and the nursing process. The reader should find the index (a new addition to the learning and activity guide) helpful in locating additional exercises illustrating the use of these tools. Exercises in Section III continue to use case situations to aid in applications. The chapter on psychotropic agents has been strengthened by focusing on medications exclusviely. A drug card format has been introduced into the exercises in this chapter to encourage the reader to begin to build a file of medications. Several exercises give examples of therapeutic and non-therapeutic communications discussed in the text, identify characteristics of nursing interventions, review nursing measures used to intervene therapeutically with clients in one-to-one interactions, identify the various phases of the nursing process, and provide the reader with opportunities to begin writing nursing care plans.

Section IV focuses on the consumers of psychiatric nursing: adults, adolescents, the physically ill and elderly, whose behavioral patterns have become dysfunctional. Exercises in this section make extensive use of case situations. Dysfunctional behaviors, theoretical concepts basic to an understanding of these dysfunctions, and the stages of dying are some of the new content areas focused on in this section. In addition, several exercises throughout the chapters review materials covered earlier in the text/guide, including defense mechanisms, communication skills, ego functions, and self-awareness. The major emphasis of the exercises in Section IV, however, is on the nursing process and its application to the consumers of psychiatric nursing. Numerous opportunities are provided to the reader to write nursing diagnoses and develop care plans specific to client situations.

Section V covers interventions used in crisis states, group situations, and families. Basic to crisis intervention is the effective use of the interview and more direct communication skills. This has been included in one of the exercises. In addition, the reader will find exercises that look at group roles, interactions, and characteristics, as well as family functions, dynamics, types, and characteristics.

Section VI looks at legal and other issues affecting the practice of psychiatric nursing. Exercises in this final section review client rights and their nursing implications. They also encourage the reader to identify and discuss issues affecting the care of the mentally ill and the current practice and future of psychiatric nursing.

This learning and activity guide is designed to meet the educational needs of the beginning psychiatric nursing student. It should also be useful to the graduate nurse who desires to review specific information on the care of emotionally ill clients as well as develop increased general understanding of interpersonal relationships with all clients. The guide has been developed on two basic principles: first, learning occurs best when the student is actively, rather than passively, involved in the learning process, and second, that learning should be pleasurable.

All the chapters in this second edition of the learning and activity guide are introduced with a brief overview, contain a statement of purpose, and identify a series of objectives to be achieved by completing the exercises in the chapter. These introductory overviews as well as the narratives that accompany some of the exercises emphasize material covered in the text and occasionally introduce new content. This has been done to create interest, to clarify, and to provide a foundation for exercises requiring additional information. This narrative is meant to supplement and enhance, not replace, the content presented in the text. The objectives structure the presentation of the exercises, which have been selected for emphasis and follow the content of the text. Exercises vary in style, scope, and depth throughout the guide. At reader request, the number of case situations has increased. Although the contents of both the text and the guide are organized in a logical, sequential fashion, no assumption is made that all the chapters will be read and, if read, will necessarily be read in the order in which they are presented. Therefore no effort has been made to develop exercises that are progressively more difficult in the final sections of the guide.

Although the first edition of the guide contained test items related to the text's content and the guide's exercises, the number, nature, and location of these items have been changed in the second edition. Almost all the items are new, they are all multiple choice in form, and, most significantly, they are located at the end of each chapter rather than at the end of each section. This change from the first edition acknowledges that chapters need to stand alone and that readers may wish to test out their understandings before proceeding to another chapter.

Each of the six sections concludes with several word games. The word games are, for the most part, entirely new. Persons familiar with word puzzles will probably recognize most of these game types, even though some of the names may be unfamiliar and there may be some variations in the forms. In addition to the word search, fill-in, crosshatch, and quote-a-crostic puzzles included in the first edition, several logic problems have been added to reinforce problem-solving techniques inherent in the nursing process. All the word games attempt to utilize terminology and reinforce content in a given section. Quote-a-crostics introduce the reader to quotations from fictional or nonfictional works consistent with the content of the section in which they appear. Once these puzzles are solved, the quotations, their sources, and authors will be revealed, and the reader may be encouraged to read further in these works.

The Appendix has been expanded in the second edition of the guide to include not only the answers to the test items and solutions to the word games but also the responses to the exercises. These have been added at the request of readers. The author continues to advocate that the text be read first. The exercises should be completed next, either independently or discussed in small groups. Finally, the reader's responses can then be compared with the responses in the Appendix and discrepancies checked out with the text.

As mentioned earlier, an index has been included in this edition of the learning and activity guide. It essentially identifies the content of the exercises in the chapters. It should be helpful to anyone who wishes additional practice in selected areas that are threaded throughout the guide, such as communication, nursing process, and self-awareness. A number of illustrations by Meri Bourgard have increased the attractiveness of the guide.

The author wishes to acknowledge all the friends, family members, and colleagues who expressed interest in the progress of the manuscript. Special thanks are extended to my friend and colleague, Dr. Mae Pepper, Associate Professor and Chairperson, Department of Nursing, Mercy College, Dobbs Ferry, New York, for her encouragement and support throughout various stages of the development of the manuscript.

Carol Ruth Lofstedt

contents

Mereness' Essentials of psychiatric nursing
Learning and activity guide

section I

the context of psychiatric nursing practice

chapter 1

the mental health delivery system

INTRODUCTION

Care of the mentally ill has not always been humane. Although the mentally ill have sometimes been revered and treated with sympathy, acceptance, and compassion, more often than not they have been misunderstood, ridiculed, rejected, exploited, condemned, and, at times, even put to death because of their bizarre behavior. Prior to the American Civil War, the moral treatment approach was popular in certain sections of the United States. It emphasized humane, individualized care of the mentally ill in homelike surroundings. As the number of persons requiring care for mental problems increased, moral treatment was replaced by custodial care. Custodial care emphasized providing a protective environment for control of deviant behaviors that were disrupting and disturbing to the families of mentally ill persons and to the communities from which they came. Treatment was not a major concern. Mental illness was viewed as a stigma and the mentally ill were seen as sources of embarrassment to be hidden away and often forgotten. Large mental institutions, some housing thousands of persons, grew up, often in remote, rural areas. Little effort was made to help hospitalized patients and their families maintain ties. Isolation from family and community encouraged hospitalized individuals to adapt to and accept institutionalization and resist efforts to be returned to the community.

In the 1950s the development and use of psychotropic agents, specifically antipsychotic medications, contributed significantly to a change in the care of the mentally ill. Hospitalized persons once thought to be incurable were found to be treatable. Psychotropic medications helped patients control their behavior and become more receptive to other treatments, thus paving the way for the community mental health movement of the 1960s.

The community mental health movement returned patients to their families and to the community at large, reducing the size of mental hospitals. Although the community mental health move-

3

ment continued to provide comprehensive treatment and follow-up care of clients, there was a shift in emphasis to prevention of mental illness, which was believed to be a more cost-effective method of meeting the mental health needs of the public. Social change within the communities served was promoted, research into the cause and treatment of mental disorders encouraged, consultation and educational services to community agencies provided, and evaluation of ongoing programs implemented.

These community-based treatment measures were considered revolutionary at the time they were first instituted in the mid-1960s because they departed from the previous system of institution-based care of the mentally ill. In reality, however, the concept of community mental health had a precedent in Gheel, Belgium, where a model community treatment program for the mentally ill had existed for centuries. The present community mental health movement has incorporated some of the values and treatment philosophy of the Gheel colony.

"An appreciation of the history of the treatment of the mentally ill can aid in the understanding of the contemporary systems of mental health delivery."* The purpose of this chapter is to review selected social, medical, and nursing events of the past that have contributed to the evolution of the mental health delivery system as it exists today.

OBJECTIVES

1. To identify treatment methods used in the care of the mentally ill from prerecorded history to the present.
2. To review the general goals of a comprehensive community mental health program.
3. To describe the clinical implications that have evolved from the treatment measures utilized in community mental health care centers.
4. To identify some of the coping skills that could be taught to markedly impaired mentally ill individuals in order to help them meet their needs and become more autonomous members of society.

*From Taylor, C.M.: Mereness' essentials of psychiatric nursing, ed. 12, St. Louis, 1986, The C.V. Mosby Co., chapter 1.

1 From prerecorded history to the present day, the mentally ill have been exposed to a wide variety of attitudes and treatment methods. Listed below are 15 treatment methods and 7 eras in history. Identify the era in which each treatment method predominated by placing a check in the box in the appropriate column. The first one has been filled in to help you get started.

	Eras in history						
Treatment methods	Prerecorded	Egypt-Greek civ.	Middle Ages	15th cent.	16-18th cent.	19th cent.	20th cent.
The mentally ill were:							
1. Exorcised of evil spirits.	☐	☐	☑	☐	☐	☐	☐
2. Put in penal institutions, almshouses.	☐	☐	☐	☐	☐	☐	☐
3. Provided with milieu therapy and open-door policies.	☐	☐	☐	☐	☐	☐	☐
4. Abandoned in the wilderness.	☐	☐	☐	☐	☐	☐	☐
5. Treated with tribal rites.	☐	☐	☐	☐	☐	☐	☐
6. Cared for in communities—not institutions.	☐	☐	☐	☐	☐	☐	☐
7. Introduced to psychotropic agents.	☐	☐	☐	☐	☐	☐	☐
8. Purged, bled, and whipped.	☐	☐	☐	☐	☐	☐	☐
9. Cared for humanely in sanatoriums.	☐	☐	☐	☐	☐	☐	☐
10. Burned at the stake as witches.	☐	☐	☐	☐	☐	☐	☐
11. Provided with custodial care.	☐	☐	☐	☐	☐	☐	☐
12. Treated with fresh air, sunshine, and diverting activities.	☐	☐	☐	☐	☐	☐	☐
13. Starved, chained, and flogged.	☐	☐	☐	☐	☐	☐	☐
14. Housed in large, remote, self-supporting institutions.	☐	☐	☐	☐	☐	☐	☐
15. Exposed to reforms in care following the mental hygiene movement.	☐	☐	☐	☐	☐	☐	☐

2 List 4 general goals or characteristics of a comprehensive community mental health program.

1. _____

2. _____

3. _____

4. _____

3 Listed below are 5 approaches used by community mental health centers in caring for the mentally ill. In the space provided, describe the clinical implications that have evolved from each approach. An example has been provided to help you get started.

Treatment approaches	Clinical implications
1. Use group rather than one-to-one relationships in caring for clients.	Acquire a knowledge of group process and skills in intervening in a variety of group settings such as family therapy, group therapy, therapeutic communities, and crisis intervention.
2. Involve indigenous workers and other community people in the care of clients, utilizing their awareness of the hopes, interests, and concerns of clients and their first-hand knowledge of the clients' language, culture, and social situation.	
3. Develop a collaborative team approach in giving care to clients.	
4. Work in the community helping parents, teachers, law-enforcement persons, public health nurses, etc., to promote the prevention of mental illness.	
5. Cooperate with families, schools, churches, hospitals, recreational and housing facilities, as well as other community-based services to improve the social system being served.	

4 In order to better serve the markedly impaired mentally ill, treatment goals need to emphasize action, while treatment measures need to focus on helping the individual cope in tangible ways with problems of everyday life. Read the following situation and in the space provided identify specific coping skills that could be taught to Harry Harlow to help him meet his needs and become a more autonomous member of the community.

SITUATION: Until recently, Harry Harlow, a 45-year-old man, lived with his elderly parents. He completed high school and at times during his adult years worked for brief periods as an elevator operator, janitor's helper, delivery man, and dog walker. In general, however, he lived a reclusive life. He had no friends and when his parents entertained, Harry remained in his room watching television or staring out the window. Although he was able to carry out his physical care, he relied on his mother to tell him when to bathe and shave and decide what he was to wear, etc. He responded well to direction but took no initiative for his own care or for care of his home. His conversation was limited, exhibiting his indecisiveness: "What should I do now?" "Where should I go?" Upon the sudden deaths of his parents in a car accident, Harry was left financially secure, but alone and unable to care for himself. He lost weight for lack of adequate food, and his clothing and hygiene deteriorated markedly. Neighbors noted that he smelled bad. He was hospitalized.

Needs	Specific coping skills
1. Activities of daily living	
2. Vocational skills	
3. Use of leisure time	
4. Social and interpersonal skills	

TEST ITEMS

DIRECTIONS: Select the *best* response. (Answers appear in the Appendix.)

1 What was the locus of mental health care during the Egyptian and Greek Civilizations?

   a The family.   **c** The almshouse.

   b The temple.   **d** The penal institution.

2 The technique of "exorcising" evil spirits and demons from the mentally ill was performed by:

   a Laying on of hands.   **c** Whipping.

   b Burning at the stake.   **d** Bleeding.

3 Where was the first community-based care of the mentally ill said to have been located?

   a Bicêtre, France.   **c** Hartford, Connecticut.

   b Williamsburg, Virginia.   **d** Gheel, Belgium.

4 The "Father of American Psychiatry" was:

   a Benjamin Franklin.   **c** Benjamin Rush.

   b William Menninger.   **d** Horace Mann.

5 The syndrome of institutionalization refers to which one of the following?

   a Hospitalizing individuals against their will.

   b Maintaining individuals in hospitals until they are ready for discharge.

   c Promoting adaptation to hospitalization to the extent that individuals resist discharge.

   d Keeping individuals in institutions past the time when treatment is indicated.

6 Clifford Beers and his book *A Mind That Found Itself* impacted on the care of the mentally ill by:

   a Revealing the psychodynamics of mental illness.

   b Supporting the formation of community mental health centers.

   c Demonstrating a need for psychotropic drugs in the care of psychotic persons.

   d Bringing about reforms in the state hospital system of mental health care.

7 The Mental Health Act of 1946 was primarily responsible for funding the:

   a Development of community mental health centers.

   b Development of multidisciplinary psychiatric treatment teams.

    c Research and testing of psychotropic medications.

    d Construction of hospitals to accommodate increasing numbers of psychiatric patients.

8 Who was Martha Mitchell?

    a Reformer in the care of the mentally ill.

    b Fund-raiser responsible for funding new treatment programs.

    c Nurse-educator on the President's Commission on Mental Health.

    d Founder of the mental hygiene movement.

9 Which one of the following goal statements is *not* a goal of comprehensive community mental health centers?

    a To serve the residents of a catchment area.

    b To provide all clients with one-to-one therapy.

    c To assist the community in improving its level of mental health.

    d To help hospitalized individuals maintain ties with the community.

10 The *most* cost-effective way to meet the mental health needs of the public is through programs with a priority goal of:

    a Prevention.   **c** Research.

    b Treatment.   **d** Rehabilitation.

11 Indigenous personnel working in community mental health centers usually are:

    a Law-enforcement officers.

    b Nonprofessional neighborhood residents.

    c Psychiatric nursing consultants.

    d Professional community leaders.

12 Role blurring is *best* defined as the:

    a Ambiguous statement of therapist job descriptions.

    b Allocation of responsibilities to team members.

    c Unclear explanation of professional responsibilities.

    d Interdisciplinary blending of functions and responsibilities.

13 Which one of the following community mental health care services is provided when staff serve as resources to the professional and indigenous community people working with persons with emotional problems in the courts, schools, churches, public health agencies, and recreational departments?

    a Consultation-education.

b Outpatient service.

c Rehabilitative services.

d Research-evaluation.

14 Which one of the following factors has probably had the greatest impact on decreasing the size of public mental hospital populations?

    a Administration of psychotropic medications.

    b Acceleration of discharges from hospitals.

    c Restriction of admissions into hospitals.

    d Implementation of follow-up care.

15 To more effectively serve the markedly impaired mental patient, the community mental health movement needs to emphasize which one of the following activities?

    a Helping clients share their feelings.

    b Teaching clients basic coping skills.

    c Encouraging clients to discuss their fantasies.

    d Rewarding clients for use of appropriate behaviors.

the mental health team

INTRODUCTION

"Four health care professions are considered to constitute the core mental health disciplines—psychiatric nursing, psychiatry, clinical psychology, and psychiatric social work. They all emerged as specialties within their respective professions during the last half of the nineteenth century at the time when behaviorally disturbed persons were generally viewed as being ill rather than as being possessed by demons or being morally corrupt."* In addition to this core of professions, other disciplines grew up to balance out the mental health team. Activity therapists, each trained in their own specialties, shared a common belief that clients could be helped if they were involved in activities that focused them on objects and events outside themselves.

The nurse who works in a mental health setting assumes a variety of different roles in order to meet patient needs: creator of a therapeutic environment, socializing agent, counselor, teacher, mother surrogate, therapist, and technical nurse. These roles often overlap and the nurse assumes more than one role simultaneously as nursing activities are implemented. For example, when intervening in a physical dispute between two clients, the nurse takes on the role of mother surrogate (setting limits on impulsive, irrational behaviors), the role of teacher (demonstrating more appropriate ways of dealing with feelings), and the roles of counselor and therapist (encouraging and listening to the circumstances surrounding the original incident).

In addition, some of these nursing roles overlap with those of other team members. For example, the nurse in the role of socializing agent may at times use some of the tools and carry out some of the activities of the recreational therapist. The nurse in the roles of counselor and therapist is an empathic listener as are the psychiatrist, psychologist, social worker, psychiatric nurse, and activity therapists with whom the patient has developed

*From Taylor, C.M.: Mereness' essentials of psychiatric nursing, ed. 12, St. Louis, 1986, The C.V. Mosby Co., chapter 2.

other meaningful relationships. It is essential for an effective team relationship that all members recognize this blurring of roles and work collaboratively rather than competitively to meet the needs of the client.

The purpose of this chapter is to review the roles and functions of the members of the interdisciplinary mental health team.

OBJECTIVES

1. To identify the roles and functions of the members of the mental health team.
2. To describe client behaviors anticipated as results of actions taken by nurses as they assume various nursing roles.

EXERCISES

1 Listed below are 10 roles and functions of the members of the mental health team. Identify which roles/functions are characteristic of each team member by placing a check in the box in the appropriate column. Keep in mind that blurring sometimes occurs and a role/function may be carried out by more than one team member. The first one has been filled in to help you get started.

Roles and functions	Team members				
	Clinical psychologist	Psychiatric social worker	Psychiatrist	Psychiatric nurse	Activity therapist
1. Prescribes medications and administers somatic treatments.	□	□	☑	□	□
2. Assumes a variety of roles in meeting patient needs.	□	□	□	□	□
3. Assesses client's familial, social, and environmental background.	□	□	□	□	□
4. Provides nonverbal means for clients to express themselves.	□	□	□	□	□
5. Makes a medical diagnosis.	□	□	□	□	□
6. Strives to meet both emotional and physiological needs of clients.	□	□	□	□	□
7. Uses projective techniques to make psychiatric diagnosis.	□	□	□	□	□
8. Provides work and recreational experiences for patients.	□	□	□	□	□
9. Emphasizes the concept of object relations in planning programs.	□	□	□	□	□
10. Uses a variety of tools to meet the needs of emotionally ill clients.	□	□	□	□	□

2 Read the following situation that exemplifies the multiple roles of the nurse. Each example has been italicized and numbered. Place the number of the example opposite the role it illustrates. A role may be illustrated more than once; an example may illustrate more than one role. The first example has been filled in to help you get started.

Roles of the nurse
a Creator of a therapeutic environment __(1)_____
b Socializing agent _____ e Therapist _____
c Technical nurse _____ f Counselor __(1)_____
d Mother surrogate _____ g Teacher _____

SITUATION: Roberta, 15-year-old girl, was admitted to the psychiatric unit. She arrived on the ward at 5 PM wearing soiled and torn clothing. Her hair was unwashed and matted, and she volunteered she had not bathed in two weeks. *(1) Sue Hall, a staff nurse, greeted Roberta and introduced herself. She invited Robert to sit down and listened quietly as the patient anxiously asked, "Where am I? What are you going to do to me?" (2) The nurse responded, "You are on a psychiatric ward. It is almost time for supper and I'd like to help you bathe and put on clean clothing before you go into eat."* Roberta grew somewhat calmer and accepted the nurse's offer of help. When she was dressed, Roberta was shown into the dining room and seated at a table with two other patients and Sue. *(3) The nurse introduced everyone and then focused on a neutral topic in an effort to encourage conversation.*

(4) After supper Sue gave Roberta a tour of the ward. She was shown her room, which she was to share with another patient. Roberta noticed that there were personal belongings in the room and expressed surprise that this was allowed. Following this brief orientation, *(5) Sue checked Roberta's vital signs as part of a routine physical examination.* During the assessment procedure, Roberta began to talk about some of her immediate concerns: "They think I'm crazy just because I've been living on the streets." *(6) "You've got no home to go to?" asked the nurse.* "None I want to go to," said Roberta. "What do you mean?" asked Sue. Roberta replied, "My mother is a tramp and my father . . . ." " Go on," encouraged Sue. "Well," continued Roberta, "he beats me." "Beats you?" asked Sue. "Yeah, beats me . . . and that's not all . . . . But I really don't want to talk about it now," Roberta concluded. *(7) The nurse nodded and said, "OK. Perhaps you'll feel more like talking later. Sometimes it helps to talk about what worries you."* "What worries me now is being here. I don't

belong here with all these crazies," said Roberts. *(8) "Have you ever been on a psych ward before?" asked Sue.* "Yes, I OD'd a couple years back and after they brought me 'round they sent me up to Psycho. It was the pits." "How long were you there?" asked Sue. "A week, but it seemed like forever." *The patient and nurse continued to talk, Sue encouraging Roberta to express her feelings. (9) She avoided giving advice or making personal judgments* and *(10) helped Roberta begin to think about some alternative solutions to her problems. (11) Sue also told Roberta that she would be sharing some of Roberta's concerns with the other staff members so they could all be in a better position to help her.*

The psychiatrist saw Roberta briefly and promised to meet with her again the following day. In response to her apparent anxiety he ordered a psychotropic agent for her which *(12) Sue administered.* In response to Roberta's questions, *(13) Sue elaborated on the purpose of the medication and briefly alerted her to possible side effects.* Following the admission procedure, Sue brought Roberta into the dayroom where patients were variously engaged in watching television, reading, playing games, or talking with staff members. A few patients sat by themselves and appeared to be deep in their own thoughts. Roberta expressed interest in joining the card-playing group and learning the game. *(14) Sue introduced Roberta to the members and asked them to explain the game to her. (15) Sue Hall then retired to the nurses' station and wrote a summary admission note in Roberta's chart.*

3 The roles of the nurse, the purposes of each, and selective nursing actions have been outlined in the following grid. In the space provided fill in the anticipated results in terms of hoped-for changes in client behaviors. An example has been provided to help you get started.

Roles of nurse	Purposes	Nursing actions	Anticipated results
1. Technical nurse	Achieve specific goals of procedure and treatment. Provide opportunity for relatedness and development of trust as client experiences caring activities.	Carry out technical aspects of nursing care—administer medication, take vital signs, give treatments, report, and record.	Trusting feelings develop as the client experiences nurse's genuine interest and concern while carrying out technical aspects of care.
2. Creator of a therapeutic environment	Develop warm, accepting atmosphere and feelings of security which are necessary for change to occur.	Respond in an honest, sincere, caring, friendly manner; communicate expectation that client can change.	
3. Socializing agent	Facilitate relatedness among clients in supportive group situations.	Encourage common social and work activities in groups—conversation, singing, ward chores, arts and crafts, eating, and games.	
4. Teacher	Help client learn to participate in more socially acceptable, satisfying living activities with increasing autonomy.	Demonstrate, orient, and instruct in activities of daily living; set limits.	
5. Mother surrogate	Provide warm, accepting, mothering relationship Nurture. Meet dependency needs.	Temporarily assume mothering activities for clients too ill to take responsibility—bathing, feeding, dressing, toileting, and limit setting.	
6. Nurse therapist	Help client cope with problems of daily living.	Collaborate with others on health care team. Develop and implement treatment plan. Establish nurse-client relationship.	
7. Counselor	Communicate caring. Sort out reality-oriented problems with which nurse can deal; channel other problems to therapist.	Provide helpful, realistic reassurance—respond with consistency, sitting with client and listening in an empathic way.	

DIRECTIONS: Select the *best* response. (Answers appear in the Appendix.)

1 Which one of the following was *not* included in the core of mental health disciplines?

   a Nursing.   **c** Social work.

   b Psychiatry.   **d** Activity therapy.

2 The first school of nursing in a psychiatric setting was established in the United States at:

   a McLean Hospital, Massachusetts.

   b Bellevue Hospital, New York.

   c Boston's Psychopathic Hospital, Massachusetts.

   d St. Elizabeth's Hospital, Washington, D.C.

3 The specialty of psychiatry was first given significant attention after which one of the following wars?

   a Spanish American War.   **c** World War II.

   b World War I.   **d** Korean War.

4 Which one of the following members was *not* included in the traditional clinic team?

   a Nurse.   **c** Psychologist.

   b Social worker.   **d** Psychiatrist.

5 Arranging for groups of hospitalized persons to attend community functions such as plays, concerts, and sports events is included in which one of the following treatment modalities?

   a Educational theapy.   **c** Music therapy.

   b Recreational therapy.   **d** Drama therapy.

6 Which one of the following activity therapies is the oldest?

   a Recreational therapy.

   b Rehabilitative counseling.

   c Music therapy.

   d Occupational therapy.

7 The role of the occupational therapist was first assumed by:

   a Indigenous personnel.   **c** Attendants.

   b Social workers.   **d** Nurses.

8 The psychiatrist's unique function is that of:

   a Diagnosing mental disorders.

   b Assessing environmental factors contributing to dysfunctional behavior.

   c Prescribing medications and administering somatic treatments.

   d Promoting mental health among individuals.

9 Clinical psychologists are prepared to do *all but which one* of the following activities?

    a Diagnose mental illness.

    b Treat emotionally ill persons.

    c Utilize projective techniques.

    d Administer somatic therapies to clients.

10 The goals of activity therapies in a mental health setting include which one of the following?

    a To provide the client with a structured work-related program.

    b To assist in diagnostic and personality evaluations of the client.

    c To facilitate the client's return to society at large.

    d All of the above.

11 Which one of the following roles of the nurse facilitates relatedness among clients in group situations?

    a Teacher.   **c** Counselor.

    b Therapist.   **d** Socializing agent.

12 Which one of the following nursing roles is utilized by John Henry, a nurse working in a psychiatric setting, when he role models for his clients by dressing appropriately?

    a Technical nurse role.   **c** Teacher role.

    b Therapist role.   **d** Counselor role.

13 Arthur Burry, an aggressive, impulsive client, needs help to control his behavior. When nurses set limits on his aggressive behavior they are assuming the role of:

    a Socializing agent.   **c** Therapist.

    b Mother surrogate.   **d** Technical nurse.

14 Which nursing role is illustrated by the nurse who administers psychotropic medications as ordered by the physician?

    a Technical nurse role.   **c** Mother surrogate.

    b Therapist.   **d** Counselor.

15 Which one of the following functions is used by *all* members of the mental health team in their client contacts?

    a Assumes a clear-cut identifiable role in meeting client needs.

    b Provides nonverbal means for clients to express themselves.

    c Uses a variety of tools to meet the needs of emotionally ill clients.

    d Strives to meet both emotional and physical needs of clients.

1 Crosshatch

DIRECTIONS: Fit the words listed below into the proper boxes. The words read left to right or top to bottom, one letter per box. REFORMS has been entered to give you a starting point. (Solution appears in the Appendix.)

3 letters
ADL
ART
DIX

4 letters
CARE
MANN
MEDS
RUSH
TEAM

5 letters
BEERS
COPES
DANCE
DRAMA
FREUD
GHEEL
GOALS
MUSIC
NURSE
PINEL
REHAB
ROLES
STAFF

6 letters
ASYLUM
BEDLAM
CHAINS
CLIENT
CRISIS
FAMILY
GROUPS
HEALTH
HUMANE
INSANE

7 letters
BICÊTRE
CENTERS
DEVIANT
EMPATHY
NURSING
✔ REFORMS
THERAPY

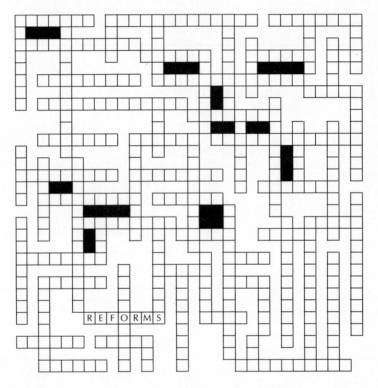

8 letters
ADVOCATE
BLURRING
FLOGGING
NURTURES
OPEN-DOOR
SECURITY
TRAINING

9 letters
AFFLICTED
ALMSHOUSE
ATTITUDES
BACK WARDS
CUSTODIAL
DIAGNOSIS
EDUCATION
RECORDING
SURROGATE
TREATMENT

10 letters
COUNSELING
EXORCISING
PREVENTION
PROFESSION
SOCIAL WORK

11 letters
REASSURANCE
SPECIALTIES

12 letters
INSTITUTIONS
WALK-IN CLINIC

13 letters
CATCHMENT AREA
COLLABORATION
MENTAL HYGIENE
MILIEU THERAPY
PSYCHOTROPICS
REVOLVING DOOR
UNDERSTANDING

2 Logic problem

DIRECTIONS: Sue, June, Marion, Walter, and David are five clients who come to the Community Mental Health Center and participate in a variety of therapeutic activities on different days of the week. Using the clues and the grid provided below, match the clients with the appropriate program and day they attend their programs.

Clues:

a David attends OT 3 days before Sue goes to her program.
b Group Therapy is held on Thursday.
c Walter participates in an ADL program with the nurse.
d June had attended both Group Therapy and RT in the past, but is now in a different program.
e Sue's choice of program was limited by the fact that she could not come to the CMHC on Mondays, Wednesdays, or Fridays.
f Marion goes to her program on Wednesday.
g RT is held the day after Music Therapy.

Use an X in the boxes as you rule out a day or program for each client, an O when you identify a day or program you think is appropriate for the client. For example, in the grid, Marion has an O filled in for Wednesday (since she attends the program on that day—clue No. f) and Xs for all the other days (since, by process of elimination, she would not be in programs on any other day).

Grid:

	Clients	Therapies					Days of the week				
		OT	GT	ADL	RT	MT	M	T	W	Th	F
Clients	Sue										
	June										
	Marion						X	X	O	X	X
	Walter										
	David										
Days of the week	Mon										
	Tues										
	Wed										
	Thur										
	Fri										

section II

concepts basic to
psychiatric nursing

chapter 3

general systems theory and stress and adaptation

a conceptual framework

INTRODUCTION

"In order for nurses to practice efficiently and effectively, they must do so within the context of a conceptual framework. The purpose of a conceptual framework is to organize information in a manner that enables the practitioner to plan, implement, and evaluate nursing care."* The conceptual framework utilized in this text is comprised of the general systems theory and the stress and adaptation theory.

General systems theory looks at the world as a complex of interrelated parts or systems. Every individual is a system unto

*From Taylor, C.M.: Mereness' essentials of psychiatric nursing, ed. 12, St. Louis, 1986, The C.V. Mosby Co., chapter 3.

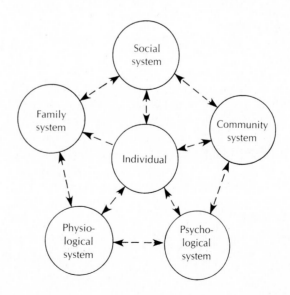

himself, consisting of a variety of subsystems that are affected by and affecting each other. Systems may be open or closed. In a closed system the components are in relative isolation and there is little interchange between the component parts and the environment. Human beings generally belong to open systems or relatively open systems, in which there is communication between the component parts of the system. The diagram on p. 23 illustrates an open system, showing the interrelationships and two-way communication that exist between the subsystems.

In a closed or relatively closed system the communication between the subsystems may be limited or nonexistent. In the following diagram an individual maintains relatedness with several subsystems, but has isolated himself from his family system.

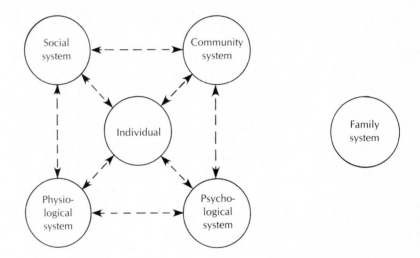

The second conceptual framework utilized in this text is the stress and adaptation theory. This theory helps provide an understanding of the effect of stress on an individual. Stress refers to tension. Adaptation, in the general sense, refers to the individual's response, either positive or negative, to stress or tension. In its positive form it is often motivating and growth promoting; in its negative form it can be disrupting and interfere with health. Events or experiences that create stress are called stressors. They may be either developmental or situational. Developmental stressors are usually associated with challenges and tasks encountered while progressing through the stages of the life cycle. These stressors can be anticipated. Situational stressors, on the other hand, are not predictable. They occur suddenly and unexpectedly, with little or no warning.

The purpose of this chapter is to review several basic concepts associated with the general systems theory and the theory of stress and adaptation as foundations for nursing practice.

OBJECTIVES

1. To identify the subsystems or component parts associated with several representative systems.
2. To differentiate between examples of developmental and situational stressors.
3. To categorize behavioral examples of relatively open or relatively closed human systems.
4. To identify resources associated with various systems and subsystems that can be available to aid adaptations to stressors.

EXERCISES

1 In planning a holistic approach to client care, the nurse uses a knowledge of general systems theory and recognizes that the client is made up of multiple systems and subsystems. Listed below are 15 examples of subsystems. Categorize each one in terms of the system or systems it represents by placing a check in the appropriate box or boxes in the systems columns. The first one has been filled in to help you get started.

Subsystems	Systems				
	Family	Social	Community	Physiological	Psychological
1. Gastrointestinal network	☐	☐	☐	☑	☐
2. Parents	☐	☐	☐	☐	☐
3. Culture	☐	☐	☐	☐	☐
4. Schools and churches	☐	☐	☐	☐	☐
5. Cardiovascular network	☐	☐	☐	☐	☐
6. Brothers and sisters	☐	☐	☐	☐	☐
7. Human needs	☐	☐	☐	☐	☐
8. Friends	☐	☐	☐	☐	☐
9. Hospitals and clinics	☐	☐	☐	☐	☐
10. Religion	☐	☐	☐	☐	☐
11. In-laws	☐	☐	☐	☐	☐
12. Feelings	☐	☐	☐	☐	☐
13. Respiratory network	☐	☐	☐	☐	☐
14. Norms and values	☐	☐	☐	☐	☐
15. Social clubs	☐	☐	☐	☐	☐

2 Events and experiences that create stress are called stressors. Those that can be anticipated and are predictable are developmental in nature; those that are unexpected and unpredictable are situational stressors. In this exercise classify each of the following events as either developmental or situational stressors by placing a check in the box in the appropriate column. The first one has been filled in to help you get started.

Events	Stressors	
	Developmental	Situational
1. Onset of diabetic symptoms.	☐	☑
2. Birth of a new baby.	☐	☐
3. Radical mastectomy.	☐	☐
4. Adolescent's rapid growth and physical changes.	☐	☐
5. Retirement from a job.	☐	☐
6. Vacation and leisure time.	☐	☐
7. Loss of possessions in a fire.	☐	☐
8. Divorce action.	☐	☐
9. Daughter marries and moves out of state.	☐	☐
10. Onset of menopausal symptoms.	☐	☐
11. Death of elderly parent.	☐	☐
12. Winning large sum of money in sweepstakes.	☐	☐
13. Adolescent son joining the army.	☐	☐
14. Promotion and raise in salary at work.	☐	☐
15. Death of spouse from chronic illness.	☐	☐

3 Human beings generally belong to relatively open human systems. The greater the number of systems to which one is related and the greater the degree of communication between these systems, the greater the resources an individual has available when faced with developmental and situational stressors.

In the grid below are listed 15 behavioral examples that illustrate either relatively open or closed human systems.

a Categorize each behavior as either open or closed by placing a check in the box in the appropriate column.

b In the space provided, identify at least one resource (subsystem) to which communication has either been cut off or extended in each behavioral example.

The first one has been filled in to help you get started.

Behavioral examples	Relatively		Resources or subsystems
	Open system	Closed system	
1. Attends local church	☑	☐	Clergy, church members
2. Participates in civic organizations	☐	☐	_____
3. Ignores communications from school counselor	☐	☐	_____
4. Lives alone and does not socialize with others	☐	☐	_____
5. Volunteers to fund-raise in neighborhood	☐	☐	_____
6. Dies at home alone, undiscovered for 3 weeks	☐	☐	_____
7. Allows house to deteriorate rather than seek help	☐	☐	_____
8. Baby-sits for neighborhood children	☐	☐	_____
9. Prepares a stew for a sick relative	☐	☐	_____
10. Has an unlisted telephone and discourages callers	☐	☐	_____
11. Denies dizziness when changing positions	☐	☐	_____
12. Participates in library program to read to children and the elderly	☐	☐	_____
13. Attends and participates in PTA meetings	☐	☐	_____
14. Avails self of free monthly blood pressure	☐	☐	_____
15. Seeks out medical advice for unexplained hoarseness	☐	☐	_____

TEST ITEMS

DIRECTIONS: Select the *best* response. (Answers appear in the Appendix.)

1 General systems theory was first written about in 1968 by:
- **a** Ludwig von Bertalanffy.
- **b** Kurt Lewin.
- **c** Walter Cannon.
- **d** Hans Selye.

2 According to the general systems theory, the only true system is the:
- **a** Family.
- **b** Community.
- **c** Individual.
- **d** Universe.

3 The elements or components of a system are called:
- **a** Boundaries.
- **b** Subsystems.
- **c** Complexes.
- **d** Frameworks.

4 The process by which a system is continuously regulating itself in order to attain a steady state in *most* correctly known as:
- **a** Entropy.
- **b** Adaptation.
- **c** Wholeness.
- **d** Homeokinesis.

5 Relatively closed systems are *most* characterized by which one of the following?
- **a** Boundary permeability.
- **b** Exchange of matter with the environment.
- **c** Movement toward integration and growth.
- **d** Energy bound in maintaining a steady state.

6 Which one of the following behavioral examples *best* illustrates relatively closed human systems?
- **a** Baking cakes for the school bazaar.
- **b** Contributing to charitable organizations.
- **c** Living alone with three cats.
- **d** Acknowledging neighbors and relatives perfunctorily.

7 Which one of the following examples of feedback is *least* effective?
- **a** Rewarding a bright student's exceptional achievements with high grades.
- **b** Acknowledging a weak student's maximum efforts with positive feedback.
- **c** Responding to a bright student's minimal efforts with criticism.
- **d** Responding to a weak student's maximum efforts with negative feedback.

8 A stressor may be *most* correctly defined as an event that:

   a Causes tension.

   b Promotes growth.

   c Is predictable and avoidable.

   d Gives input to the human system.

9 Which one of the following is an example of a developmental stressor?

   a Promotion at work.

   b Loss of limb in an accident.

   c Death of aging, ailing grandparent.

   d Unmarried daughter becoming pregnant.

10 Which one of the following is an example of a situational stressor?

   a Son joining army and leaving home.

   b Father retiring from work.

   c Aged grandparents dying in automobile accident.

   d Wife experiencing menopausal symptoms.

11 The condition resulting when the input to the human system is disrupting is *most* correctly called:

   a Stress.   **c** Negentrophy.

   b Adaptation.   **d** Homeokinesis.

12 *All but which one* of the following statements reflects nursing goals within the framework of the general systems theory and the theory of stress and adaptation?

   a To protect the human system from all stressors.

   b To increase the human system's energy potential to deal with stressors.

   c To enhance the human system's ability to adapt to stressors.

   d To decrease the potency of stressors.

chapter 4

personality

its structure and development

INTRODUCTION

Personality is the reflection of the physical, mental, and sociocultural characteristics that uniquely combine to contribute to each person's individuality. The development of personality is a dynamic process, involving an interplay of innate biological forces, interpersonal experiences, and cultural expectations beginning at conception and continuing into maturity. An understanding of this dynamic process is essential for the nurse to take an active role in prevention of, and intervention in, dysfunctional behaviors. Whether this action is to educate parents in better child-rearing practices or to help a person with a personality defect enhance his or her self-concept, the nurse who understands and accepts the dynamic nature of personality development will communicate the expectation that people can change and grow in a positive direction. In addition, "while the understanding of personality development is integral to the practice of psychiatric nursing, it is also essential to the general practice of nursing since nursing interventions must be geared to the developmental level of the recipient if they are to be effective."*

The purpose of this chapter is to explore the evolution of personality from infancy to maturity from three theoretical frameworks: Freud's intrapsychic theory, Sullivan's interpersonal theory, and Erikson's cultural theory.

OBJECTIVES

1. To list the characteristics of the conscious, preconscious, and unconscious and the id, ego, and superego.
2. To categorize behavior as it reflects the functioning of the parts of the personality.

---

*From Taylor, C.M.: Mereness' essentials of psychiatric nursing, ed. 12, St. Louis, 1986, The C.V. Mosby Co., chapter 4.

3. To identify the areas of the body involved with psychosexual development and the libidinal pleasures associated with each.
4. To differentiate between the needs for satisfaction and security.
5. To describe the interpersonal learnings that occur in each developmental era.
6. To evaluate the effect selected reflected appraisals have on the development of the self-concept.
7. To match behavioral examples with the positive or negative developmental outcomes they illustrate.

EXERCISES

1 Freud described the mind topographically from two points of view: the levels of consciousness and the structure of the personality. Neither one can be observed directly, but their existence can be inferred through behavior.

a Freud's three levels of consciousness have been compared to an iceberg in terms of the availability of material stored in the conscious, preconscious (subconscious), and unconscious. As with the iceberg, the deeper the level of consciousness, the less available is the content stored there. List in the space provided two characteristics of each of these three levels of consciousness. One characteristic has been filled in to help you get started.

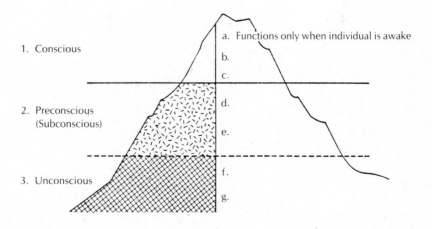

1. Conscious

2. Preconscious (Subconscious)

3. Unconscious

a. Functions only when individual is awake
b.
c.
d.
e.
f.
g.

b The three parts of the personality are the id, ego, and super-ego. It is thought that the id is innate and that the ego and superego develop subsequently as the individual comes in contact with the environment. In the following situation the three parts of the personality are illustrated by 15 behaviors that have been italicized and numbered. At the end of the situation complete the following two exercises:

1. Categorize each behavior as it reflects either id, ego, or superego functioning, by placing its number in the space provided. Each part of the personality will be illustrated by several different behavioral examples.
2. Briefly list four or five characteristics of the id, ego, and superego in the space provided.

Several pieces of data have been filled in to help you get started.

SITUATION: Franklyn is a computer programmer. As a teenager *(1) he preferred working with his personal computer to socializing with his peers. (2) He had very high expectations* and *(3) experienced great frustration when he failed to meet the standards he set for himself.* At such times *(4) he became irritable and was prone to bursts of temper.* A childhood diabetic and overweight, *(5) he would overeat when stressed* even though *(6) he was well aware that this aggravated his physical problems.*

When Franklyn completed high school, *(7) he pursued his goal to become more knowledgeable in the use of computers. (8) He explored available funding, applying for and receiving a scholarship that helped put him through college. (9) He was an excellent scholar and graduated at the top of his class.* Upon graduation he was immediately hired by a software company to develop educational programs.

(10) He is skilled in his work and known for his meticulous attention to detail. Although respected by his colleagues for his expertise and frequently consulted by them, he is not particularly well liked. *(11) He is very self-centered, demanding, short tempered, and has little patience with others' limitations.* In nonwork situations, Franklyn is particularly ill at ease with people. *(12) When stressed, he continues to have difficulty controlling his tendency to overeat. In addition, he sometimes drinks alcohol to excess.*

When under the influence of alcohol his behavior changes dramatically. *(13) He tells inappropriate jokes, flirts with the women present, and argues unreasonably with the other men.* The day following such occasions, *(14) he is able to recall his behavior* and *(15) experiences tremendous feelings of guilt.*

	Parts of the personality		
	Id	Ego	Superego
1. Behaviors		(1),	
2. Characteristics of parts of the personality	Impulsive,	Reality-oriented,	Moralistic,

2 Freud's theory of personality development is called the psychosexual theory. It is based on the hypothesis that libidinal, or sexual, energy shifts from one part of the body to another as the individual matures physiologically.

For each stage of psychosexual personality development identify the area of the body that is invested with libidinal energy and give one activity that an individual at that stage of development would consider pleasurable. An example has been provided to help you get started.

Psychosexual stage	Area of the body	Pleasurable activities
1. Oral	Mouth	Sucking thumb (In the oral stage an infant finds thumb sucking pleasurable.)
2. Anal		
3. Phallic		
4. Latency		
5. Genital		

3 Interpersonal theory identifies two goals of all human behavior, the fulfillment of the need for satisfaction and the need for security.

a Differentiate between these two needs and give three methods or conditions that might gratify these needs.

b Briefly explain the relationship between fulfilling the needs for satisfaction and security and the development of the self-concept.

4 Identify and briefly describe the interpersonal learnings that occur during each of Sullivan's developmental eras. An example has been provided to help you get started.

Developmental era	Interpersonal learnings	Description
1. Infancy	The self-concept is learned.	The child's development of the self begins in infancy and is associated with the feeding process. If satisfaction and security are experienced during feeding, a "good-me" self-concept develops; if tension and anxiety are experienced during feeding, a "bad-me" self-concept develops.
2. Early childhood		
3. Later childhood		
4. Juvenile era		
5. Pre-adolescence		
6. Early adolescence		
7. Later adolescence		

5 According to Sullivan's interpersonal theory, the significant other in the child's early developmental years is the mothering one. This person may be either male or female and may or may not be the biological parent. The significant other is the person who nurtures the child in these developmental years. The

35

mothering one communicates verbal and nonverbal messages to the child about his value and worth. These messages, or mirror images, are called reflected appraisals and are largely responsible for the way the child comes to see himself. By the time the child reaches the age of 6, other persons begin to take on greater importance in his life, gradually replacing the mothering one as the most significant figure. These persons, including the father, chums, teachers, and peers, may communicate additional messages about value and worth, either reinforcing or revising the child's original concept of self.

a Listed below are 12 examples of reflected appraisals that might be observed in interactions between the mothering one and the child. Categorize each appraisal in terms of the effect each might have on the child's development of the self-concept (good-me, bad-me, not-me), placing a check in the box or boxes in the appropriate column(s). The first one has been filled in to help you get started.

Reflected appraisals	Self-concept		
	Good-me	Bad-me	Not-me
1. Follows through on promises made to child.	☑	☐	☐
2. Insists on meeting child's needs even after autonomy is demonstrated.	☐	☐	☐
3. Criticizes child unfairly.	☐	☐	☐
4. Holds child tenderly and lovingly.	☐	☐	☐
5. Communicates extreme levels of anxiety to child.	☐	☐	☐
6. Interferes with child's efforts to socialize with peers.	☐	☐	☐
7. Meets child's needs in return for child's love.	☐	☐	☐
8. Responds to child's efforts with praise.	☐	☐	☐
9. Respects child's individuality, opinions, wishes.	☐	☐	☐
10. Acts unpredictably in meeting child's needs.	☐	☐	☐
11. Treats child with extreme indifference.	☐	☐	☐
12. Shares pleasure and pride in child's growth.	☐	☐	☐

b In the grid on p. 37 are listed 12 commonly observed adult behaviors. Each one reflects the adult's personification of self and may be said to be the outcome of consistent exposure to reflected appraisals experienced in infancy and childhood, such as those described in exercise 5a. Categorize each adult behavior in terms of the self-concept each reflects (good-me, bad-me, not-me), by placing a check in the box in the appropriate column. The first one has been filled in to help you get started.

	Self-concept		
Adult behaviors	**Good-me**	**Bad-me**	**Not-me**
1. Expresses misgivings about one's abilities.	☐	☑	☐
2. Listens with interest to what others have to say.	☐	☐	☐
3. Responds defensively to criticism.	☐	☐	☐
4. Awakens from a terrorizing nightmare.	☐	☐	☐
5. Responds shyly when meeting new people.	☐	☐	☐
6. Dissociates all-paralyzing interpersonal anxiety.	☐	☐	☐
7. Questions the reliability of others.	☐	☐	☐
8. Accepts earned praise without discomfort.	☐	☐	☐
9. Expresses trust and confidence in others.	☐	☐	☐
10. Feels comfortable with expressions of tenderness.	☐	☐	☐
11. Boasts about own accomplishments.	☐	☐	☐
12. Dissociates oneself from overwhelming experiences.	☐	☐	☐

6 Erikson's theory of personality development identifies eight ego qualities that emerge from each of Eight Ages of Man. Their emergence at a given time indicates the individual's ability to follow a social timetable for the mastery of certain basic achievements. These age-related and culturally determined achievements have become known as developmental tasks. Each task must be completed, at least in part, before the next one is achieved. Each task builds on previous ones. Difficulties mastering one task contribute to difficulties mastering subsequent ones. Mastery is affected by the nature of the interpersonal relationships a person experiences as each age is negotiated. If the experiences are essentially supportive and positive, the outcomes will also tend to be positive. On the other hand, if the experiences are rejecting and negative, the result will usually be negative. These results or outcomes, positive or negative, are expressed behaviorally. This developmental process is a dynamic one. It was not Erikson's intent to communicate that a task once adopted was secure for all time. New experiences, positive or negative, effect changes in the outcomes. This theory is particularly meaningful to nursing because it supports the nurse's efforts to provide clients with interpersonal experiences more positive than those they had previously known. In so doing, the nurse helps clients in the mastery of developmental tasks with which they had difficulty. Success or failure at negotiation of Erikson's eight stages and tasks is reflected in adult verbal and nonverbal behavior. Listed below are the positive and negative outcomes for each stage and verbal responses illustrating each outcome. Match each verbal response to the outcome it best exemplifies by filling in the blanks provided. An outcome will be used only once. An example has been provided to help you get started.

Positive and negative outcomes

a AUTONOMY	**e** GUILT	**i** INITIATIVE	**m** ROLE CONFUSION
b DESPAIR	**f** IDENTITY	**j** INTIMACY	**n** SHAME AND DOUBT
c EGO INTEGRITY	**g** INDUSTRY	**k** ISOLATION	**o** STAGNATION
d GENERATIVITY	**h** INFERIORITY	**l** MISTRUST	**p** TRUST

Verbal responses	Outcomes
1. "I'm such a dummy when it comes to electronics. I could never learn to use a computer."	1. _Inferiority_
2. "Sure, you can borrow my lecture notes. I'll need them Friday to review for the next quiz."	2. _____
3. "I'm not certain I can. I'll ask my husband. He makes all the decisions in our house."	3. _____
4. "I just enjoy being with you—listening to you, seeing you smile, hearing you laugh. . . ."	4. _____
5. "I hate my job but I can't leave it and give up the security it provides me."	5. _____
6. "I teach art in high school and in my spare time I paint portraits."	6. _____
7. "Why do you keep asking me so many questions? What are you going to do with this information?"	7. _____
8. "I get a lot of satisfaction from doing my job thoroughly and well."	8. _____
9. "Leave me alone. I don't mean to appear rude but I am a very private person."	9. _____
10. "Thanks, I appreciate the offer. But I can do it myself."	10. _____
11. "I'm so sorry. I'll never forgive myself for not being there when you needed me."	11. _____
12. "I have emphysema and my activities are limited, but there is still a lot I can do and enjoy."	12. _____
13. " 'Today is the first day of the rest of my life.' Where am I going? What am I going to do?"	13. _____
14. "My name is Carol. I am a nurse educator."	14. _____
15. "My husband's dead. My children don't bother with me anymore. I've got nothing to live for."	15. _____
16. "I volunteer to ask the tenants in my building to join our committee."	16. _____

DIRECTIONS: Select the *best* response. (Answers appear in the Appendix.)

1 The aggregate of the physical and mental qualities of the individual as these interact in characteristic fashion with the environment is a definition of:

   a Behavior.   **c** Sexuality.

   b Identity.   **d** Personality.

2 A pioneer in the exploration of personality development from an intrapsychic theoretical framework was:

   a Clifford Beers.   **c** Sigmund Freud.

   b Harry Stack Sullivan.   **d** Erik Erikson.

3 Freud's topographical description of the psyche includes which one of the following?

   a Levels of consciousness.   **c** Ego qualities.

   b Stages of development.   **d** Defense mechanisms.

4 The part of the mind that only functions when the individual is awake is the:

   a Unconscious.   **c** Subconscious.

   b Conscious.   **d** Preconscious.

5 *All but which one* of the following statements is true about the unconscious?

   a It directs rational, thoughtful responses.

   b It is the storehouse for inaccessible material.

   c It manifests its existence through dreams.

   d It is the largest part of the mind.

6 The ego is the part of the personality that:

   a Provides the source of libidinal energy.

   b Operates on the basis of the pleasure principle.

   c Mediates between the other parts of the personality.

   d Incorporates moralistic standards of behavior.

7 According to Sullivan, all human behavior is directed to meeting the needs for satisfaction and security. Which one of the following reflects the need for satisfaction?

   a Status.   **c** Self-esteem.

   b Intimacy.   **d** Sex.

8 According to Erikson, if the individual experiences severe inconsistency and anxiety in the stage of infancy, he will develop which one of the following behavioral outcomes?

   a Mistrust.   **c** Guilt.

   b Shame.   **d** Inferiority.

9 According to interpersonal theory, severe emotional problems in adults are said to result from which one of the following experiences in the early developmental years?

a Inconsistencies and anxiety-laden relationships with the biological mother.

b Dissociating and anxiety-generating relationships with the significant other.

c Negative reflected appraisals communicated empathically by the significant other.

d Failure on the part of the biological mother to consistently meet the need for satisfaction.

10 The behaviors characteristically observed in children during the second stage of development essentially reflect a struggle for which one of the following?

a Identity.   **c** Power.

b Lust.   **d** Intimacy.

11 Failure to resolve the oedipal conflict satisfactorily can result in which one of the following negative behavioral outcomes?

a Mistrust.   **c** Doubt.

b Shame.   **d** Guilt.

12 The chum relationship is *most* intense during which one of the following stages of personality development?

a Juvenile era.   **c** Early adolescence.

b Preadolescence.   **d** Late adolescence.

13 According to Erikson, an adult's ability to develop an intimate relationship with another adult of the opposite sex is largely dependent on which one of the following?

a Meeting a warm and caring individual.

b Experiencing the support of significant others.

c Feeling physical and emotional well-being.

d Mastering previous developmental tasks satisfactorily.

14 The purpose of the life review during maturity is to:

a Identify and master unmet developmental tasks.

b Accept the inevitability of death.

c Redo one's life to achieve fulfillment.

d Reconcile the futility of old age.

15 When an individual looks forward to retirement and recalls the past with pleasure, he is experiencing which of the following ego qualities?

a Identity.   **c** Generativity.

b Intimacy.   **d** Integrity.

chapter 5

anxiety

one response to stress

INTRODUCTION

Anxiety and fear are subjective experiences involving unpleasant tension and uneasiness. Fear occurs when an identifiable stressor threatens the existence of the system. The "fight or flight" response is automatically activated to provide an outlet for the physiological and psychological tension associated with fear. Anxiety, on the other hand, occurs in response to an unknown stressor associated with an unconscious intrapsychic conflict or an actual or anticipated threatening interpersonal experience. It is a universal emotion, felt in varying degrees of intensity and duration and generally perceived as negative. Mild anxiety, although still uncomfortable, is manageable and can be a stimulating and motivating force bringing about change, growth, productivity, and creativity. It can be the force that drives one to study, inspires one to produce a work of art, or moves one to seek a solution to a problem. However, as the degree of anxiety increases, effective functioning decreases. In addition, since the feelings of fear and anxiety cannot be readily differentiated, the "fight or flight" response is also activated when anxiety is experienced. However, since the source of the anxiety is unknown, this automatic response is ineffective in releasing the tension and, as a result, anxiety increases. Signs and symptoms of anxiety manifest themselves physiologically, alerting the individual to the impending threat.

No one can remain in a state of anxiety indefinitely. Various adaptations may be used to relieve tension and help individuals regain homeokinesis. Adaptive measures termed coping mechanisms may be consciously called upon to help deal with stress and anxiety. The most effective long-term coping measure is problem-solving. But people may also use less effective short-term coping measures when deciding to walk, talk, joke, laugh, eat, drink, bite their nails, chew gum, doodle, smoke or engage in sexual activities, including masturbation. Another adaptation to anxiety is the use of ego defense mechanisms. These defenses, such as sublimation, rationalization, isolation, regression, reaction-formation, and denial, to name just a few, may also be used in conjunction with another ego defense, repression, to control anxiety and to keep the conflicts contributing to the anxiety out of consciousness. Finally, another adaptation is the use of the security operations of apathy, somnolent detachment, preoccupation and selective inattention to deal with interpersonal anxiety and threats to the self-concept. Neither ego defenses nor security operations are very effective for long-term adaptation because they do not encourage the individual to deal with stress and anxiety in reality-based ways.

"Since anxiety is a basic factor in the development and manifestation of human behavior, it is necessary for the nurse to acquire an in-depth understanding of its characteristics, origin, and the usual adaptations to it."* The purpose of this chapter is to increase understanding of anxiety, its development, and the adaptations to it. As nurses reflect on personal stressors that contribute to the development of anxiety, they develop a greater appreciation of anxiety in others and the effect stress and anxiety have on the ability of an individual to function effectively.

*From Taylor, C.M.: Mereness' essentials of psychiatric nursing, ed. 12, St. Louis, 1986, The C.V. Mosby Co., Chapter 5.

OBJECTIVES

1. To differentiate between intrapsychic and interpersonal perceptions of anxiety.
2. To reflect on one's personal responses to stressors that contribute to the development of anxiety.
3. To differentiate among coping measures, ego defense mechanisms, and security operations.

EXERCISES

1 Listed below are 10 statements about anxiety that reflect the intrapsychic theory of Sigmund Freud or the interpersonal theory of Harry Stack Sullivan. In this exercise classify each statement as intrapsychic and/or interpersonal by placing a check in the boxes in the appropriate columns. The first one has been filled in to help you get started.

	Intrapsychic	Interpersonal
Anxiety is:		
1. Experienced in relationships with others.	☐	☑
2. Associated with experiences involving separation.	☐	☐
3. Manifested in responses to disapproval from significant others.	☐	☐
4. The result of unconscious conflict between the id and superego.	☐	☐
5. Experienced when the need for security is not met.	☐	☐
6. Controlled by adaptive measures called ego defenses.	☐	☐
7. Communicated in an empathic manner.	☐	☐
8. The result of a threat to biological integrity.	☐	☐
9. Controlled by adaptive measures called security operations.	☐	☐
10. Threatening to the self-concept.	☐	☐

2 Self-awareness

a When anxiety becomes excessive, it interferes with functioning. According to Freudian theory, psychic energy is used to deal with anxiety-producing conflicts to keep them out of consciousness. As more and more energy is used by the ego to maintain repression, less energy is available for life's other activities.

In the following exercise a partial list of ego functions has been identified. In the space provided reflect on your own past responses to stressors and describe the effect anxiety had on your functioning. For each of the identified ego functions give a personal example of normal or enhanced functioning as well as disrupted functioning when anxiety was high. An example has been provided to help you get started.

Ego functions	Normal or enhanced functioning	Disrupted functioning
1. Evaluation of reality: Differentiation of real world from fantasy or dream world, insight, judgment.	I awoke from a dream and was aware it was a dream. I reflected on it with little anxiety.	I awoke in a panic, feeling frightened by a dream. For a moment I was confused and did not realize I had been dreaming.
2. Use of cognitive abilities: Memory, thinking, learning, comprehension.		
3. Problem-solving: Identification of a problem and a reasonable solution.		
4. Control of instinctual drives: Postponement of pleasure; appropriate expression of sexual and aggressive feelings.		
5. Development of relationships with others.		

b According to Sullivan, anxiety is a distressing feeling accompanied by somatic experiences as well as emotional sensations of impending doom. Furthermore, anxiety is interpersonal in nature, occurring as a result of one or more of the following phenomenon: (1) negative reflected appraisals and feelings of disapproval from real of fantasied significant others, (2) unmet satisfaction and/or security needs, and (3) empathized anxiety.

In the following exercise describe a personal experience that illustrates each of Sullivan's theoretical considerations about anxiety.

Theoretical considerations about anxiety	Personal experiences
1. Somatic symptoms: Describe any physical symptoms you experienced during an anxiety-provoking situation.	
2. Emotional sensations: Describe any feelings you experienced during an anxiety-provoking situation.	
3. Negative reflected appraisals: Describe a situation in which you experienced disapproval from a significant person and the effect it had on you	
4. Unmet satisfaction and/or security needs: Describe a situation in which your need for satisfaction and/or security was threatened.	
5. Empathized anxiety: Describe a situation in which you were not anxious until you picked up, or empathized, anxiety in another person.	

3 The following exercise consists of a situation in which 24 behavioral examples are given to illustrate adaptations to anxiety. Reflect on each behavior and differentiate among coping measures, ego defense mechanisms, and security operations by writing in the number of the behavior and the name of the mental mechanism in the appropriate column. A list of mental mechanisms illustrated in the situation is provided. The first example has been filled in to help you get started.

Mental mechanisms

a Apathy
b Denial
c Displacement
d Drinking
e Eating
f Isolation
g Pacing
h Pleading sick
i Preoccupation
j Problem-solving
k Projection
l Rationalization
m Reaction-formation

n Regression
o Repression
p Selective inattention
q Smoking
r Somnolent detachment
s Sublimation
t Suppression
u Symbolization/condensation
v Talking
w Undoing
x Walking

SITUATION: Arthur Gould spent a restless night. Finally he got out of bed and went downstairs *(1) where he paced the floor* and *(2) smoked continuously. (3) Deep in his own thoughts, going over his speech and presentation, (4) he did not hear the clock strike three or, somewhat later, his wife Jennie entered the room to inquire about him.* For the next 30 minutes Arthur sat in the kitchen and *(5) talked with his wife, sharing his doubts and concerns about the coming day with her. (6) "I'm worried about Bill,"* he said, speaking about his partner. *"I hope he doesn't let me down."* Arthur reviewed his speech and presentation with Jennie and soon seemed more relaxed. He returned to bed and slept several more hours.

At breakfast Arthur was unusually *(7) irritable, snapping impatiently and unreasonably at Jennie and his two children.* He readied himself to leave the house for the office. Jennie offered to drive him to the train but he refused, saying that *(8) walking might help relax him.* On the train he sat by himself thinking, *(9) "So what if I don't make this deal. It won't be the end of the world. I can always get another account."* As he thought about the approaching business day and his scheduled presentation, Arthur was unaware *(10) that he had his hands thrust deep in his pockets, nervously fingering a four-leaf clover charm and a rabbit's foot, which he kept with him for good luck.*

On the surface Arthur seemed like a good-natured man. *(11) He was overly polite, always smiling and joking. His jokes, however, were usually a little sarcastic and hostile.* When Arthur and Bill were underbid and the account was picked up by another company, Arthur responded with characteristic sharp humor that antagonized his colleagues. Arthur and Bill left the office and went out for lunch. Arthur *(12) ate* and *(13) drank too much.* The two men discussed their future with the firm. Bill was very realistic and listed several reasons why he felt their prospects were not good. *(14) Arthur, on the other hand, refused to face the possibility that his job was in jeopardy.* Returning to the office Arthur found it difficult to concentrate on his work. *(15) He made a concerted, conscious effort to put his disappointment behind him and to focus his attention on other matters, but with little success.*

On the way home from work Arthur stopped at the gym where he was a member and *(16) played a little handball.* He felt somewhat better. *(17) He also went to a store and bought flowers for his wife and candy for the children. (18) Although not consciously aware that his actions that morning had been unreasonable,* he felt a need to make up to his family for his behavior.

(19) The next day Arthur awoke feeling ill. He complained to Jennie of a headache, upset stomach, aches and pains, and general malaise. He called in sick and spent the day in bed. When Bill called him that morning, Arthur refused to talk with him and *(20) went to sleep.* Later that day *(21) he called Jennie every 5 minutes, demanding to be waited on in a whining tone of voice and insisting on being served his favorite foods.*

Arthur felt better the following day. At breakfast *(22) he could describe the disappointing event without experiencing the painful feeling associated with it. (23) He also verbalized indifference at having lost the account.* When Jennie raised the question about his future with the firm, Arthur acknowledged that it was possible he could lose his job. *(24) He then went on to share with his wife several plans he was considering should his employment be terminated.*

Adaptations to anxiety		
Coping measures	Ego defense mechanisms	Security operations
1-g Pacing		

TEST ITEMS

DIRECTIONS: Select the *best* response. (Answers appear in the Appendix.)

1 Which one of the following is *more* true of anxiety functioning as an adaptation rather than as a stressor?

  a Signals the system that homeokinesis is not being maintained.

  b Puts the system into a state of stress.

  c Sees anxiety as a desirable and pleasurable emotion.

  d Compounds rather than relieves the original stress.

2 The emotion of fear is *most* effectively dealt with by:

  a Ego defense mechanisms.　　**c** Security operations.

  b Fight or flight responses.　　**d** Coping measures.

3 The irrational state that occurs in response to extreme anxiety is called:

  a Fear.　　　　　　　　　　**c** Tension.

  b Conflict.　　　　　　　　**d** Panic.

4 Which one of the following events did Freud consider prototypical of separation anxiety?

  a Birth process.

  b Going to school for the first time.

  c Moving out of the home.

  d Loss of a loved one through death.

5 According to intrapsychic theory, anxiety primarily results when which one of the following occurs?

  a Ego functions emerge into consciousness.
  b Superego fails to mediate between the id and the ego.
  c Id and the superego are in conflict.
  d Ego and id fail to control superego conflict.

6 Which one of the following mothering activities carried out with an infant would *best* meet the child's satisfaction needs?

  a Holding.   **c** Rocking.
  b Feeding.   **d** Singing.

7 The purpose of mental mechanisms is to do *all but which one* of the following?

  a Make intrapsychic conflicts conscious so they may be dealt with.
  b Provide the system with a means to regain homeokinesis.
  c Protect the individual from threatening aspects of reality.
  d Help maintain the individual's biological integrity.

8 Coping mechanisms *differ* from other mental mechanisms in that they are:

  a Used to reduce tension.   **c** Reality-oriented.
  b Always unconscious.   **d** Used to relieve anxiety.

9 Making up for a failure or deficiency by emphasizing an asset is a definition of which one of the following ego defense mechanisms?

  a Identification.   **c** Denial.
  b Reaction-formation.   **d** Compensation.

10 Persons who hoard every little thing, much as they withheld their feces in the anal stage of development, are using which one of the following ego defenses?

  a Sublimation.   **c** Undoing.
  b Fixation.   **d** Introjection.

11 Which one of the following ego defenses is operating when a psychotic person replaces his identity with that of another person?

  a Identification.   **c** Denial.
  b Reaction-formation.   **d** Introjection.

12 The morning after overhearing her parents talking about getting a divorce and arguing over her custody, Sue Ellen awoke and was unable to hear. Physical examination revealed that there was no organic reason for her deafness. Sue Ellen is probably using which adaptive measure to deal with the stress of her parents' impending separation?

   a Reaction-formation.   **c** Conversion.

   b Selective inattention.   **d** Apathy.

13 The security operation of apathy is similar to which one of the following ego defenses?

   a Isolation.   **c** Suppression.

   b Repression.   **d** Denial.

14 Sheila is a patient on a psychiatric ward. She sits in the corner of the dayroom staring into space, deep in her own thoughts, twirling her hair with her fingers. She is using which one of the following security operations?

   a Selective inattention.   **c** Apathy.

   b Somnolent detachment. **d** Preoccupation.

15 Which one of the following coping measures would be *most* effective in dealing with stress and anxiety on a long-term basis?

   a Pleading illness.   **c** Eating.

   b Problem-solving.   **d** Exercising.

chapter 6

the determinants of mental health and mental illness

INTRODUCTION

"Human beings have been concerned about aberrant behavior since the beginning of time, although the definition of aberrance and its causes have differed markedly over the centuries. In contrast, interest in and understanding of the manifestations and determinants of mental health are very recent."* Coping with stress, relating to others in relative comfort, recognizing one's strengths and weaknesses, perceiving reality with minimal distortion, mastering the challenges of the environment, and determining realistic goals are a few of the attributes of mental health. Although it is now generally accepted that mental illness is more than the opposite of mental health and that mental health is not merely the absence of mental illness, certainly the presence or absence of any one or more of these characteristics is a reflection of a person's emotional state at a given time. Just as the mentally healthy person is not ever totally free of conflict and occasionally responds dysfunctionally to stress, so too is the mentally ill individual not completely without attributes of mental health. To illustrate this point, I recall two situations. The first situation involved a person who was considered mentally healthy; the second situation involved a person who was hospitalized with an incapacitating mental illness.

The first person was a woman who had married in her teens and raised a family. She was a loving wife and mother, active in her church and community. She responded to the crises associated with each developmental era of life with good humor and sound judgment. When her children were older and grew more independent, she looked back on her life with satisfaction, but she also looked to the future with anticipation. With her family's emotional support, she returned to school, earned a college de-

*From Taylor, C.M.: Mereness' essentials of psychiatric nursing, ed. 12, St. Louis, 1986, The C.V. Mosby Co., Chapter 6.

gree, and eventually was employed in a local business. Certainly this woman manifested many of the attributes of mental health.

Then, during a family vacation, her husband and children perished in a hotel fire. She stopped working, turned away from her friends, experienced unrealistic guilt for having survived, and was temporarily unable to meet her own needs. At this point in time she demonstrated several characteristics of mental illness.

The second situation involved a man who had been hospitalized for many years with a severe thought disturbance. He was withdrawn, mute, and unresponsive to others. Although he seemed totally unaware of people and events in his environment, he one day intervened helpfully and unexpectedly when another client suddenly and irrationally lost control of himself. After helping the staff control this client, the man returned to his withdrawn state. In a brief span of time this mentally ill man exhibited some of the attributes of mental health identified earlier. He accurately assessed the reality of the situation and the need for immediate action. He rose to the challenge of the occasion and responded appropriately.

The nurse must be aware of the dynamic, ever-changing relationship between mental health and mental illness. An understanding of what constitutes health and illness, and an appreciation of their fluidity, becomes the foundation for therapeutic intervention with clients. The nurse as a significnt helping person has the opportunity to promote health and to intervene in illness.

The purpose of this chapter is to review the characteristics of mental health, identify the factors contributing to mental illness, and consider preventive measures that might be taken to deter the development of mental illness. This knowledge will contribute to understanding intervention in dysfunctional responses as discussed in subsequent chapters.

OBJECTIVES

1. To analyze a hypothetical situation in terms of commonly accepted mental health attributes.
2. To assess a hypothetical client's total life experience in terms of the development of mental illness.
3. To list measures that can be used in the prevention of mental illness.
4. To reflect on one's ability to deal with stress.

1 Mental health is a dynamic rather than an absolute state. Unlike physical health, which can be measured scientifically to some degree with evaluations of height, weight, vital signs, urine and blood analysis, mental health cannot be measured so precisely. However, in spite of this limitation, there are characteristics of mental health upon which an assessment of a person's mental status may be based. The following exercise consists of a situation in which 16 behavioral examples are given to illustrate commonly accepted attributes of mental health. Each behavior has been italicized and numbered. Read the situation and place the number of each example opposite the mental health attribute it illustrates. An attribute may be illustrated more than once; a behavior may illustrate more than one attribute. The first example has been filled in to help you get started.

Attributes of mental health
a Setting realistic goals _____   **e** Coping with stress __(1)__
b Relating in comfort _____   **f** Mastering challenges _____
c Recognizing assets _____   **g** Recognizing limitations ___
d Perceiving reality with minimal distortion _____

SITUATION: Three-year-old Sammy Silver was playing in the front yard on a balmy spring morning the day he disappeared. His mother, Jenny Silver, had left him briefly to answer the telephone. When she returned, Sammy was nowhere to be seen. *(1) Jenny remained calm and searched the immediate area with the help of her friends.* When one of her friends reminded Jenny that several children had disappeared in the area in recent weeks, and that perhaps she should call her husband and the police, Jenny refused to do so saying, "I'm sure it's nothing like that. There is no need for alarm. Sammy must be here somewhere." When several hours of search proved futile, and Jenny still would not call Jack, her husband, a neighbor alerted him to the situation.

(2) The Silvers had been married for 10 years when Sammy was born. (3) Jenny had miscarried in the fifth year of their marriage and, in spite of her disappointment, was able to accept the loss of the baby and *(4) to begin planning to have another child as soon as possible.*

Jack and Jenny met in high school, where *(5) Jenny was very popular with both peers and teachers. She also enjoyed the company of younger children. (6) She tutored students in the lower grades and discovered that she had an innate ability to communicate with others. (7) Jenny decided to pursue teaching as a career.* Jack, on the other hand, had been more of an introvert in high school. Although he was *(8) exceptionally bright and had many interests, such as photography and music,* he was generally uncomfortable in social situations and avoided most extracurricular activites. *(9) Although they had dated seriously during their senior year and discussed marriage, they decided to postpone getting married until they both had completed their college educations and were established in their respective careers. (10) Jack's father had died after a long illness while Jack was still in high school, and the family's financial means were severely strained. Jack worked after school and during the summer to help support his mother and younger sister. (11) He knew he would be unable to complete college and continue to help his family if he married Jenny.*

Jack studied architecture and, when he completed his studies, *(12) selected a job in which he could work independently. He knew he would be more comfortable in such a situation rather than in one that demanded a great deal of contact with other people.* His work was greatly admired and he was *(13) given increasing opportunities to demonstrate his skill and to progress upward in the firm. (14) Jenny earned her teaching certificate as she had planned. (15) She had not anticipated, however, the scarcity of teaching positions and her inability to get a permanent teaching job. However, she accepted substitute teaching positions, tutored, and had a variety of nonteaching jobs until she eventually found a permanent teaching position. (16) When Sammy was born, she gave up her position to devote herself to a full-time mothering role.*

2 In arriving at an understanding of mental illness, the nurse needs to study the client's total life experience.

   a In the following situation 16 behaviors/experiences have been italicized and numbered. Read and assess each one in terms of the genetic, physiological, intrapersonal, interpersonal, or cultural influences on the individual's development of dysfunctional responses. Place a check in the box or boxes in the appropriate column(s). The first one has been filled in to help you get started.

Situation	Genetic	Physiological	Intrapersonal	Interpersonal	Cultural
(1) Ralph was an unwanted child. Bernice, his mother, was (2) mentally retarded and a drug addict. She supported her addiction through prostitution and the sale of drugs. (3) Ralph was exposed to both drug abuse and venereal disease before he was born. Ralph never knew his father. Bernice said (4) he was "crazy" and told Ralph that he was locked up in a hospital for the criminally insane when he tried to kill her years ago. (5) Bernice often scolded Ralph and told him he was just like his father, and if he did not behave, he would be "put away too." (6) Bernice resented Ralph. She believed that he interfered with her work and often told him so. She left him alone for long periods of time in the room they shared, often (7) hungry and without food. When she brought clients home to be entertained, (8) she locked Ralph in a dark closet and threatened him with physical abuse if he made any noise. (9) Ralph was very fearful of the closet and escaped into fantasy in order to cope with the stressful situation. (10) During the first 6 years of his life, Ralph was cared for by many different people besides his mother. Their responses to him varied from apathy to overt hostility. His mother was in and out of jails, hospitals, and mental institutions. (11) In addition to her drug abuse and mental retardation, she had a history of schizophrenia. Bernice died from an overdose when Ralph was 7. He was placed in a series of foster homes in the ghetto community where he had been born. He continued to experience both physical and emotional neglect and (12) grew to have a very low opinion of himself. (13) In his community he was exposed to many social deprivations, including poverty, overcrowding, dirt, violence, and widespread use of alcohol and drugs. He began to attend school and was (14) rejected by his peers. (15) He sought to defend himself by assuming a bully role, picking on children smaller than himself. He was expelled from school when it was discovered that he was using and selling drugs to the other children. Eventually Ralph was arrested for mugging elderly people as a means of supporting his drug habit. (16) He rationalized his behavior by saying he only robbed the rich who had "too much money anyway."	(1) ☐ (2) ☐ (3) ☐ (4) ☐ (5) ☐ (6) ☐ (7) ☐ (8) ☐ (9) ☐ (10) ☐ (11) ☐ (12) ☐ (13) ☐ (14) ☐ (15) ☐ (16) ☐	☐ ☐ ☐ ☐ ☐ ☐ ☐ ☐ ☐ ☐ ☐ ☐ ☐ ☐ ☐ ☐	☐ ☐ ☐ ☐ ☐ ☐ ☐ ☐ ☐ ☐ ☐ ☐ ☐ ☐ ☐ ☐	☑ ☐ ☐ ☐ ☐ ☐ ☐ ☐ ☐ ☐ ☐ ☐ ☐ ☐ ☐ ☐	☐ ☐ ☐ ☐ ☐ ☐ ☐ ☐ ☐ ☐ ☐ ☐ ☐ ☐ ☐ ☐

b List 5 measures that might have been taken during Ralph's formative years to contribute to his developing a less dysfunctional life-style.

1. _____
2. _____
3. _____
4. _____
5. _____

3 Self-awareness: The ability to effectively deal with stress is influenced by several factors: personality strengths, membership in support groups, exposure to and handling of past crises, and expectations of others of how one will deal with crisis. In this exercise assess how well prepared you are to cope with stress by reflecting on the following questions. There are no right or wrong answers. The exercise is intended to open up some insights into your areas of strength as well as your areas of weakness, so that you may build on one and change the other. As a part of this exercise you may wish to share and discuss your perceptions with others with whom you feel comfortable.

g Do you think other people see you as capable, somewhat capable, helpless, etc., in handling stressful occurrences? Do they look to you for help when they are having trouble coping? How do you feel about other people asking you for help? you contact/see them? Who initiates most of the contacts?

d Who are your work/school associates? Do you feel you can count on them for support in work/school situations? Are you available to them if they need help? Do they know this?

e To what groups do you belong? How often are you in contact with these groups? What is your role in these groups? Do you experience satisfaction from membership in these groups? Are there other groups to which you would like to belong? Are your aspirations realistic?

f What was the most recent stressful event in your life? How did you handle it? Did you feel that you had to cope with it alone, or could you turn to others for help? Were you satisfied with your actions, with the outcome? Would you respond differently now? How? Why?

g Do you think other people see you as capable, somewhat capable, helpless, etc., in handling stressful occurrences? Do they look to you for help when they are having trouble coping? How do you feel about other people asking you for help?

TEST ITEMS

DIRECTIONS: Select the *best* response. (Answers appear in the Appendix.)

1 Characteristics of mental health are *most* accurately described as:

  a Culturally determined.

  b Clearly differentiated from characteristics of mental illness.

  c Relatively stable in each individual.

  d Measured as precisely as characteristics of physical health.

2 Which one of the following is *not* an attribute of mental health?

  a Environmental mastery.

  b Freedom from stressful anxiety.

  c Balance of psychological functions.

  d Ability to love and be loved by others.

3 Which one of the following is the *best* indicator of an individual's mental health?

  a Analysis of biochemical content of blood and other body fluids.

  b Measurement of the intelligence quotient (IQ).

  c Assessment of strengths and limitations in relation to social norms.

  d Ratio of coping mechanisms to defense mechanisms in current use.

4 The *most* significant factor in determining one's ability to maintain emotional equilibrium in the face of severe stress is one's:

  a Ethnic and religious background.

  b Genetic and biochemical makeup.

  c Membership in an emotionally supportive group.

  d Degree of self-awareness.

5 Another way of stating that emotionally mature individuals have developed the capacity for independent thinking and action is to say they have achieved self-:

  a Acceptance.   **c** Awareness.

  b Determinism.   **d** Love.

6 The *best* route to developing an understanding of mental illness is to study an individual's:

  a Genetic makeup.   **c** Total life experience.

  b Intrapersonal responses.   **d** Interpersonal associations.

7 Intrapersonal factors that may serve as determinants of mental illness include which one of the following?

  a Biological constitution.   **c** Intellectual ability.

  b Relationships with others. **d** Thoughts and feelings.

8 Prevention of mental illness is difficult primarily because:

  a The goals of mental health experts are ambiguous.

  b Staff are insufficient to meet the needs of society.

  c A clear definition of mental illness does not exist.

  d People fail to participate in prevention programs.

9 *All but which one* of the following might be useful in the prevention of mental illness?

  a Physical health management.

  b Genetic counseling.

  c Teaching effective parenting behaviors.

  d Widespread use of psychotropic medications.

10 When 3-year-old Sammy Silver disappeared from his yard, his mother continued her futile search and refused to call the police for help saying, "There is no need for alarm. Sammy must be here somewhere," she may be said to have been:

  a Coping with stress in a mature way.

  b Experiencing a distorted perception of reality.

  c Mastering a challenge courageously.

  d Responding with immobility to overwhelming anxiety.

11 Although Jack Silver was very intelligent and talented, he was very uncomfortable in most social situations. When he selected a job, he chose one in which he could work independently and limit his contacts with business associates. Jack's decision reflects *all but which one* of the following attributes of mental health?

  a Mastering a challenge.

  b Recognizing limitations.

  c Coping with stress.

  d Perceiving reality with minimal distortion.

12 Ralph, a drug addict, supported his addiction by robbing elderly, wealthy people. He justified his behavior by saying, "They're rich. They have too much money anyway." He is exhibiting which one of the following ego defense mechanisms?

  a Projection.   **c** Undoing.

  b Rationalization. **d** Displacement.

section II word games

1 Word search

DIRECTIONS: Listed below are 51 words hidden in the puzzle grid. They may be read up or down, forward or backward, or diagonally, but always in a straight line. Some words may overlap and some letters in the grid may be used more than once. All the letters in the grid will not be used. Circle each word as you locate it. The first word has been circled. (Solution appears in the Appendix.

```
M E N T A L I L L N E S S E I R A D N U O B E D I
I S O L A T I O N E G O I D E A L L S T E M O D N
S E I T I L A U Q O G E R E Y T E I X N A S O P T
T O S M S I S S I C R A N S S A S O H H E U T S E
R I N G A Q U N O I T A N G A T S A S U B O R M R
U F E A R N U Q J U I N F E R I O R I T Y A I E P
S H T E L A Y V E M S K P H O K L W E T R S A T E
T L I U G H O D E S S M C I E N E R G Y O E P S R
M I S O T H I L M A T T E R T Y S N U B R L S Y S
H T L A E H L A T N E M P S Y C I O N E M F E S O
A R P G H R L D R A I N T R A P S Y C H I C D E N
P A N I C N O A Y L I N O M O W O R O L D O W G A
E O J A B S O P S N I C I C O R U T N D E N I A L
N I C S M O X T S I N F A N C Y J E S F E C O E E
I D A U M N R A M O O Y C N E T A L C U O E F L E
S C H U A U T T S E S N E F E D G H I O R P A D S
E C N E L A V I B M A U T O N O M Y O P H T E D S
N C I T S I L O H Y R O L E C O N F U S I O N I T
V S X I O N R N N O I T A M I L B U S N V Y P M I
Y T R E B U P R O J E C T I O N O I S S E R P E R
```

✔ ADAPTATION
AMBIVALENCE
ANAL
ANXIETY
APATHY
AUTONOMY
BOUNDARIES
CHUMS
COPING
DEFENSES
DENIAL
DESPAIR
DOUBT
DYNAMISM
EGO IDEAL
EGO QUALITIES
ENERGY
FEAR
GUILT
HOLISTIC
INFANCY
INFERIORITY
INTERPERSONAL
INTRAPSYCHIC
ISOLATION
LATENCY
LOSS

LUST
MATTER
MENTAL HEALTH
MENTAL ILLNESS
MIDDLE AGE
MISTRUST
NARCISSISM
NOT ME

PANIC
PENIS ENVY
PROJECTION
PUBERTY
REPRESSION
ROLE CONFUSION
SELF CONCEPT
SHAME

STAGNATION
STRESS
SUBLIMATION
SYSTEMS
TASK
TENSION
TRUST
UNCONSCIOUS

2 Fill-in: Ego defenses

DIRECTIONS: Using the definitions provided, fill in the wordlist with selected *ego defenses* discussed in the text. (Solution appears in the Appendix.

DEFINITIONS

A Making up for a failure or deficiency by emphasizing an asset

B Reverting to activities or behaviors more typical of an earlier era

C Using a seemingly neutral object to represent one with a conflictual aspect

D Involuntarily refusing to acknowledge reality

E Expressing conflicts through physical symptoms in body parts innervated by sensory or motor nervous system

F Halting development at a point in time

G Unconsciously refusing to accept a feeling, thought, or impulse and attributing it to someone else

H Justifying behavior, attitudes, and feelings with excuses

I Discharging emotions associated with one subject or person on an entirely different one

J Involuntarily excluding wishes, impulses, memories, and feelings from awareness

K Excluding from consciousness feelings associated with a painful experience while at the same time recalling the experience

WORD LIST

_ _ _ _ E _ _ _ _ _ _ _ _

_ _ G _ _ _ _ _ _ _

_ _ _ _ O _ _ _ _ _ _ _ _ _

D _ _ _ _ _ _

_ _ _ _ E _ _ _ _ _

F _ _ _ _ _ _ _

_ _ _ _ E _ _ _ _ _

_ _ _ _ _ N _ _ _ _ _ _ _ _

_ _ S _ _ _ _ _ _ _ _ _ _

_ _ _ _ E _ _ _ _ _

_ S _ _ _ _ _ _ _ _

3 Quote-a-crostic

DIRECTIONS: Using cues on the left, fill in the words in the list on the right. Transfer each letter in the word list to the corresponding numbered square in the puzzle grid. Shaded squares in the grid represent the ends of words. Work back and forth between grid and word list until both are completed. (Note the letters and consecutive numbers that have been entered in the grid to help in location of words.) The completed grid will be a quotation relevant to Section II of the text. The source of the quote and its author are spelled out in the boxed-in letters in the word list. The first word in the list has been filled in to help you get started. (Solution appears in the Appendix.)

Cues

A Health

B Male client

C Freud: _____:: Erikson: Locomotor-Genital Stage (two words)

D Developmental and situational

E Quality of an ego that arbitrates effectively between id and superego

F Chum

G Systems theory concept

H _____ systems _____ (two words)

I Very physical interpersonal conflict

J Type of input (two words)

K Basic ingredient in Freud's biologically based theories; reflection of Sullivan's need for satisfaction.

L Negotiator of Erikson's task of ego integrity (two words)

M Psychologist who identified criteria for mental health

Word list

W	E	L	L	N	E	S	S
146	30	13	108	68	37	87	135

717 11

174 20 169 76 72 84 32

42 10 153 98 151

31 145 29 110 99 83 139 81 54

63 164 12 43 154 163 156 168

137 111 161 35 125 141

127 109 95 77 118 39 46

64 101 52 16 183 80 93

123 165 61 69 44 6

55 129 41 138 62

36 97 48 117 179 124 60 147

15 71 2 67 78 166 88 115

142 177 96

49 85 182 155   34 19 152 73 133 176

112 21 150 128 105 47

61

The grid (cell number and letter):

Row 1: 1 U, 2 J, 3 Q, 4 R, 5 P, 6 H, ■, 7 U, 8 W, 9 V, ■, 10 C, 11 B, 12 E, ■, 13 A (L), 14 Q, 15 J, 16 H, ■

Row 2: 17 Q, 18 N, 19 L, ■, 20 C, 21 M, 22 N, ■, 23 Q, 24 N, 25 O, 26 T, ■, 27 T, 28 U, 29 D, ■, 30 A (E), 31 D, 32 C, 33 N, 34 L, 35 F

Row 3: ■, ■, 36 J, 37 A (E), 38 S, 39 G, 40 Q, 41 I, 42 C, 43 E, 44 H, 45 V, ■, 46 G, 47 M, 48 J, 49 L, 50 U, 51 P, 52 H, 53 Q, 54 D

Row 4: ■, 55 I, 56 N, 57 S, ■, 58 P, 59 N, 60 J, 61 H, 62 I, 63 E, ■, 64 H, 65 S, 66 V, 67 J, ■, 68 A (N), 69 H, 70 R, 71 J, 72 C, 73 L

Row 5: ■, 74 O, 75 R, 76 C, 77 G, 78 J, 79 Q, 80 H, 81 D, 82 V, ■, 83 D, 84 C, 85 L, 86 S, 87 A (S), ■, 88 J, 89 R, 90 T, 91 P, 92 S, 93 D

Row 6: 94 R, 95 G, 96 K, 97 J, 98 C, ■, 99 D, 100 S, 101 H, ■, 102 S, 103 T, 104 R, 105 M, ■, 106 W, 107 U, 108 A (L), ■, 109 G, 110 D, 111 F

Row 7: 112 M, 113 T, 114 N, 115 J, ■, 116 N, 117 J, 118 G, 119 Q, ■, 120 P, 121 N, 122 Q, 123 H, 124 J, 125 F, 126 S, ■, 127 G, 128 M, 129 I, 130 O

Row 8: 131 N, ■, 132 W, 133 L, 134 Q, 135 A (S), ■, 136 R, 137 F, ■, 138 I, 139 D, 140 Q, 141 F, 142 K, ■, 143 N, 144 U, 145 D, 146 A (W), 147 J, 148 W, 149 Q

Row 9: ■, 150 M, 151 C, 152 L, ■, 153 C, 154 E, 155 L, ■, 156 E, 157 W, 158 V, ■, 159 N, 160 R, 161 F, 162 U, 163 E, ■, 164 E, 165 H, 166 J, 167 S

Row 10: 168 E, 169 C, 170 N, ■, 171 B, 172 U, 173 P, 174 C, 175 Q, 176 L, 177 K, 178 V, ■, 179 J, 180 V, ■, 181 W, 182 L, 183 H, ■

Cues

Word list

N Negative outcome in Erikson's muscular-anal stage (three words)

___ ___ ___ ___ ___ ___ ___ ___
131 18 56 116 24   33 114 170

___ ___ [121] ___ ___
22 59 121 143 159

O Result of negative appraisals:_____ me self-concept

___ ___ [130]
74 25 130

P The infant's major source of pleasure and tension relief

___ [51] ___ ___ ___ ___
58 51 120 173 5 91

Q Sullivan's theories

___ ___ [122] ___ ___ ___ ___ ___ ___ ___ ___ ___
14 149 122 175 140 40 53 23 17 79 134 3 119

R Indicator of mental health/mental illness

___ ___ [160] ___ ___ ___ ___ ___
94 89 160 104 70 75 136 4

S _____ _____ development (two words)

[126] ___ ___ ___ ___ ___   ___ ___ ___
126 102 65 38 167 100   92 86 57

T Proponent of intrapsychic theory

___ ___ ___ [113] ___
27 90 103 113 26

U Area of libidinal pleasure between 18 and 36 months (two words)

___ ___ ___ ___   ___ ___ ___ [144]
7 162 172 107   50 28 1 144

V Coping device, of a sort

___ ___ ___ ___ ___ ___ [45]
82 66 180 178 9 158 45

W Wellness

___ ___ ___ ___ [132] ___
157 148 106 8 132 181

62

section III

the tools of psychiatric nursing

the self-awareness of the nurse

INTRODUCTION

"Whether the nurse can be a force for developing a truly therapeutic situation for the client depends on her ability to provide him with new and more positive experiences in living with other people. To accomplish this the nurse continuously strives to understand the client's behavior and the emotional needs expressed by that behavior. However, since it is the relationship between the nurse and the client that has the potential for becoming a therapeutic experience for the client, it is not sufficient for the nurse to understand only the client. In addition, she must develop self-awareness."*

Personal fears, anxieties, prejudices, biases, and hostilities, as well as more positive feelings such as joy and happiness, may interfere with the nurse's ability to focus on the client and the client's needs in an objective way. The nurse's perceptions of the client may be clouded by beliefs and affective responses. Unlike self-understanding, which requires a more in-depth self-analysis to arrive at a knowledge of why one feels and behaves as one does, self-awareness merely necessitates that one be in touch with one's feelings, attitudes, beliefs, and actions. Through self-awareness one recognizes and acknowledges one's responses, tries to identify their source, looks at the effect they have on behavior, and, if necessary, tries to modify them if they interfere with, rather then enhance, relationships with others and the therapeutic care of clients.

The purpose of this chapter is to promote self-awareness in the nurse and to demonstrate practical applications of nursing principles to the nursing care of clients.

*From Taylor, C.M.: Mereness' essentials of psychiatric nursing, ed. 12, St. Louis, 1986, The C.V. Mosby Co., Chapter 7.

OBJECTIVES	1. To reflect on personal responses as a step toward greater self-awareness.
	2. To support nursing activities with nursing principles.
	3. To identify goals of psychiatric nursing.
EXERCISES	**1** What do you feel about. . . ?
	a Listed below are 10 statements about mental illness, mentally ill persons, and their caretakers. Read each statement, decide whether you agree or disagree with it, and then place a check in the box in the appropriate column.

Statements	Agree	Disagree
1. Mentally ill persons are fragile and can be severely damaged by inexperienced student nurses.	☐	☐
2. Drastic measures are needed to control most mentally ill persons.	☐	☐
3. Mentally ill persons have less value than healthy persons because they are not productive society members.	☐	☐
4. Tax monies should not be spent on the care of the mentally ill because mental illness is hopeless.	☐	☐
5. Mentally ill persons are all aggressive and dangerous and should be locked up to protect society.	☐	☐
6. Persons working with the mentally ill for extensive periods will most likely become mentally ill themselves.	☐	☐
7. Mentally ill persons are too sick to be helped by student nurses.	☐	☐
8. Persons with histories of mental illness are unreliable and should be handled carefully.	☐	☐
9. Mentally ill persons are intellectually inferior to mentally healthy persons.	☐	☐
10. Persons working with the mentally ill do so because they too have severe emotional problems.	☐	☐

b All those statements are misconceptions of mental illness, the mentally ill, and the people who care for them. With how many did you agree?

c Share your feelings and beliefs with classmates and colleagues in a supervised classroom setting. The following questions are suggested to help focus the discussion:

1. Can you identify the source of your feelings? (Example, a past experience; something you have read, seen, or heard).
2. What effect would communicating any of these feelings or beliefs to an emotionally ill person have on your efforts to develop a nurse-client relationship?
3. What can you do to begin to overcome these feelings and beliefs now that you are aware of them?

2 Using the Johari Window as a model, identify your beliefs and feelings about psychiatric nursing, mentally ill persons, and mental illness that you have shared with others and therefore are known both to them as well as to you. List these in the *open window*. Also identify those feelings and beliefs that you have not shared with others and list them in the *private window*. The blind area contains beliefs and feelings of which you are unaware. They may be known to others and you may discover some of these if you are alert to verbal and nonverbal cues from others. Also, be alert to your responses to these cues. For example, if you find you respond defensively, you are probably protecting yourself from developing insights in this blind area. A limited amount of space is provided for you to list new learnings in the *blind window*. The closed area is less accessible. Ideally one strives to decrease the size of the blind and private areas, thereby increasing the size of the open area. Achieving this goal gives you more control over your own behavior and an increased understanding of others' responses to you.

Open	Blind
Private	Closed

3 Principles are rules or laws that evolve out of beliefs and experiences. They are useful in giving direction to nursing care in most if not all nursing situations. Listed below are 7 psychiatric nursing principles discussed in the text. Also listed are nursing activities that may be supported with these nursing principles. In the following exercise read each nursing activity and place the number of the nursing activity opposite the psychiatric nursing principle that best supports it. A principle may support several nursing activities. An example has been provided to help you get started.

Psychiatric nursing principles

a The nurse views the client as a holistic being with a multiplicity of interrelated and interdependent needs. _____

b The nurse focuses on the client's strengths and assets, not on his weaknesses and liabilities. __(1)_____

c The nurse accepts the client as a unique human being who has value and worth exactly as he is. _____

d The nurse has the potential for establishing a relationship with most, if not all clients. _____

e The nurse explores the client's behavior for the need it is designed to meet or the message it is communicating. ____

f The nurse views the client's behavior nonjudgmentally while assisting him to learn more effective adaptations. ____

g The quality of the interaction in which the nurse engages with the client is a major determinant of the degree to which the client will be able to alter his behavioral adaptations in the direction of more satisfying, satisfactory interpersonal relationships. _____

Nursing activities

1. Encourage the client to meet those needs he is able to meet for himself.
2. Listen to the client with undivided attention.
3. Seek out the client rather than wait for the client to take the initiative.
4. Observe the client for signs of physical illness.
5. Help the client evaluate the consequences of his behavior.
6. Provide the client with more positive experiences than he had experienced in the past.

7. Treat the client with respect even though his behavior is sometimes inappropriate.

8. Do not assume that the client's physical symptoms are merely manifestations of emotional stress.

9. Assist the client to unlearn old, ineffective adaptations without making value judgments about them.

10. Plan nursing care based on an understanding of the client's behavior and needs.

11. Expose the client to a warm, caring, nurse-client relationship in which his needs take priority.

12. Support the client's efforts to care for himself.

13. Assess the client in relation to his social system.

14. Give recognition and approval to the client for successful undertakings.

15. Respect the client's right to confidentiality by not talking about the client in nonprofessional situations.

16. Call the client by his correct name rather than dehumanizing him with references to "the psycho."

17. Establish communication with the client based on areas of similarity.

18. Help the client to modify behavior in more productive ways.

19. Encourage the client to make appropriate decisions, such as what to wear and what game to play.

20. Sets limits on the client's inappropriate behaviors without being judgmental of him as a person.

4 List 3 goals of psychiatric nursing.

1. _____

2. _____

3. _____

TEST ITEMS

DIRECTIONS: Select the *best* response. (Answers appear in the Appendix.)

1 A nurse's primary and *most* unique tool in working therapeutically with emotionally ill clients is his/her:

  a Personality makeup.   **c** Emotional reactions.

  b Theoretical knowledge.   **d** Communication skills.

2 The effective practice of psychiatric nursing requires that the nurse develop self-awareness. The purpose of this effort is to accomplish which one of the following?

  a Develop an understanding of why one behaves as one does.

  b Adopt beliefs and feelings conducive to giving therapeutic care.

  c Arrive at an in-depth knowledge of one's affective response.

  d Test and compare attitudes and beliefs with others.

3 Using the Johari Window as a model, the "window" that is know to one's self but is unknown to others is:

  a Private.   **c** Open.

  b Closed.   **d** Blind.

4 The treatment procedure of psychoanalysis is *most* helpful in exploring which one of the following quadrants of the Johari Window?

  a Private.   **c** Open.

  b Closed.   **d** Blind.

5 Principles are *best* defined as:

  a Opinions.   **c** Rules.

  b Beliefs.   **d** Emotions.

6 The psychiatric nurse who is alert to both the physical and emotional needs of clients is working from the philosophical framework that states:

  a Each individual has strengths and a potential for growth.

  b All behavior is purposeful and is designed to meet a need or to communicate a message.

  c Each individual is unique and has inherent value.

  d. A human being is a complex system of interrelated parts, the whole of which is greater than the sum of the parts.

7 The psychiatric nursing principle that states that the nurse views the client as a holistic being requires that nurses should be equipped with which of the following skills?

  a Interpersonal skills.

  b Knowledge of psychopathology.

  c Understanding of religious and cultural practices.

  d All of the above.

8 The psychiatric nursing principle that states that the nurse focuses on the client's strengths and assets, not on his weaknesses and liabilities, is basic to which one of the following treatment modalities?

a Psychotropic agents.   **c** Institutional care.

b Community mental   **d** Physical therapy.
  health movement.

9 Use of the psychiatric nursing principle that states that the nurse has potential for establishing a relationship with most, if not all, clients is *most* facilitated by the nurse and the client sharing which of the following?

a Emotional problems.   **c** Intellectual ability.

b Experiential background.   **d** None of the above.

10 The nurse's willingness and ability to focus on personal feelings in order to better understand the client's feelings is *most* specific to the development of which one of the following?

a Communication.   **c** Acceptance.

b Empathy.   **d** Observation.

11 The mentally ill person is most vulnerable to the nurse whose care is:

a Unskilled.   **c** Impersonal.

b Inexperienced.   **d** Inappropriate.

12 Which one of the following statements about mentally ill persons is a misconception?

a Mentally ill persons have been badly hurt in their early relationships with other people.

b Mentally ill persons have the potential to change and grow in a positive direction.

c Mentally ill persons are all aggressive and dangerous and society must be protected from them.

d Mentally ill persons are sensitive to the efforts of inexperienced, but concerned, nurses.

13 Which one of the following nursing activities is *best* supported by the psychiatric nursing principle that states that the nurse explores the client's behavior for the need it is designed to meet or the message it is communicating?

a The nurse applies a knowledge of psychodynamics to clients' behavior.

b The nurse treats clients with respect even if their behavior seems strange.

c The nurse helps clients change ineffective behavior patterns.

d The nurse sets limits on clients' inappropriate behavior in nonjudgmental ways.

14 Which one of the following nursing activities is *least* supported by the psychiatric nursing principle that states that the nurse accepts the client as a unique human being who has value and worth exactly as he is?

a The nurse addresses clients by their first names.

b The nurse sets limits on clients' inappropriate behaviors in nonjudgmental ways.

c The nurse uses therapeutic communication skills to help clients talk about themselves.

d The nurse allows clients to behave in any way they need to.

15 A major goal of psychiatric nursing is to:

a Protect the client from life's stresses and crises.

b Allow the client to recover at his own rate.

c Help the client learn the reasons for his illness.

d Expose the client to new, positive experiences.

effective communication

INTRODUCTION

"Communication refers to the reciprocal exchange of information, ideas, beliefs, feelings, and attitudes between two persons or among a group of persons. As such, it is a dynamic process requiring continual adaptations by those involved. Communication is considered to be effective when it accurately and clearly conveys the intended messages. The communication process is basic to all nursing practice and, when effective, greatly contributes to the development of all therapeutic relationships."*

In the past, communication played a relatively minor role in nursing education. Nurses' competency was measured in terms of how presentable and comfortable they made the patient, how technically skilled they were in giving physical care, and how efficiently they carried out medical orders. Communication with a patient was limited to seeking and giving information, to teaching very specific health-related matters, and to filling the awkward silences occurring in the performance of intimate physical care with casual conversation. Nurses who approached patients and sat with them to explore thoughts and encourage the expression of feelings were unique and often the target of criticism by colleagues. Effective communication was an activity delegated to psychiatric nurses. Nurses of today who continue to function within this narrow framework are working at a distinct disadvantage to both themselves and their clients. Nursing has moved from a task orientation to a client-centered focus. What the client thinks, believes, and feels has become increasingly important to the nurse and, as a result, it is necessary for all nurses to acquire knowledge and skill in communicating effectively with the client and the client's family.

Often it is not what is said, but rather *how* it is said that is most important in communicating effectively. In the interest of

*From Taylor, C.M.: Mereness' essentials of psychiatric nursing, ed. 12, St. Louis, 1986, The C.V. Mosby Co., Chapter 8.

learning, however, it becomes necessary to identify specific verbal skills such as reflecting, focusing, suggesting, and exploring. Many books have been written about this subject alone, and different authors use a variety of terms to label these skills. Interest in communication skills can serve a useful purpose in learning the multiplicity of ways one can respond in any situation. There is never just one correct response and one should not become so preoccupied with techniques and their labels that spontaneity, individuality, and purpose are lost. For example, it is helpful to know that there is a communication skill called clarification. The name, in this case, identifies the purpose of the approach. The actual use of clarification, however, should vary among nurses. How monotonous it would be for a client to be approached by several different nurses who all respond identically, using textbook examples. The personality of each nurse should be evident in effective communication to avoid sterotypic and stilted phrases. One of my students once said that she felt she had failed to communicate effectively with clients as long as she used "communication techniques." She went on to explain that when she discarded the "techniques" and responded purposefully but more naturally, using her own words, she found that clients were more responsive. She concluded that it was the use of communication skills that made her ineffective. However, after reviewing her conversations with her clients, she saw that she had not relinquished the skills but had merely discarded the excessive use of mechanical, automatic responses that did not reflect her personality. By listening carefully, by keeping purposes in mind, and then speaking in words with which she was more comfortable, she began to communicate more effectively with her clients. It was the artificiality of her initial attempts at communication that had interfered with her effectiveness, not the communication skills themselves. They had not been discarded, only adapted to the situation.

The emphasis in the text is not on technique but rather on developing and using communication effectively. The purpose of this chapter is to support this broad goal while recognizing the need of the beginning nurse to become familiar with a variety of different communication skills and to learn to identify them by name, to discuss their purposes, to evaluate their effectiveness, and to develop a personalized approach to their use.

OBJECTIVES

1. To differentiate between therapeutic and nontherapeutic, verbal and nonverbal approaches.
2. To identify the purposes of selected therapeutic communication skills.
3. To describe personalized examples of selected therapeutic communication skills.
4. To explain why or how selected verbal approaches interfere with effective communication.

EXERCISES

1 The text identifies several general types of nonverbal approaches, some therapeutic and some not. In the space provided in the grid below, describe two or three examples of nonverbal approaches that you consider to be therapeutic or nontherapeutic. An example has been filled in to help you get started.

Nonverbal approaches	Examples	
	Therapeutic	**Nontherapeutic**
1. Body posture	Leaning forward	Backing away
2. Tone of voice		
3. Facial expression		

75

2 In the following situations between nurses and clients a variety of different communication skills are illustrated. Each one has been italicized and numbered. Place the number of the examples in the space provided after each communication skill. A communication skill may be illustrated more than once; an example may illustrate more than one skill. The first one has been filled in to help you get started.

a Mr. Robinson and Mrs. Crowe

Communication skills

1. Clarifying   _____
2. Encouraging   _____
3. Focusing   _____
4. Giving information _____
5. Giving recognition _(a)_
6. Introducing neutral _____
   topic

7. Nonverbal   _____
   communications
8. Reflecting   _____
9. Refocusing   _____
10. Seeking information _____
11. Suggesting   _____
12. Understanding   _____

SITUATION

a.   **N** *"Good morning, Mrs. Crowe."*
      C "Good morning."

b.   **N** *"My name is Mr. Robinson. I am your student nurse today."*
      C "A male nurse? I'm not sure I want a man taking care of me."

c.   **N** *"You're not sure you want a male nurse giving you care?"*
      C "No. Have you had the same preparation as the other student nurses? The women, I mean."

d.   **N** *"Yes. I am a senior and will be graduating at the end of the term."* Silence. Mr. Robinson observes a frown on Mrs. Crowe's face.

e.   **N** *"You are frowing,"* and he continues:

f.   **N** *"Is it my being a student or a man that troubles you?"*
      C "Both."

g.   **N** *"Go on, Mrs. Crowe. Tell me what you are thinking."*
      C "Well, now that I think about it, I guess I'm just being a silly old woman." She laughs. "A male nurse is probably as good as a female nurse."

h.   **N** *Smiling and sitting down in a chair at the bedside,* Mr. Robinson says:

i.   **N** *"I think I am. But you're still not sure.".*
      C "I've never been taken care of by man before. I've been very lucky. In all my 72 years I've only been in the hospital four times. . ."

j.   **N** *"Yes. . . ."*

k.   **N** *Mr. Robinson leans forward in his chair and maintains eye contact with Mrs. Crowe.*
      C ". . .and that was when my last four children were born."

l.   **N**   *"Last four children?"*

m.   **N**   He continues, *"How many children do you have?"*

      C   "Ten. Six of them were born at home. I had a terrible fear of hospitals and avoided going to them. As I said, I was very lucky. I've been healthy all my life. Its just been the last few months that I haven't felt too well. This is the first time I've been in a hospital in a very long time and I've never been cared for by a man before and. . . ."

n.   **N**   *". . .you feel embarrassed about my giving you care?"*
Mrs. Crowe nods silently then asks, "Are you going to give me a bath?"

o.   **N**   *"Yes."*

      C   "I've been doing some of my bath for myself."

p.   **N**   *"Fine. There is no reason to change that."* He continues:

q.   **N**   *"I'll help you with as much as you need. You will be screened and draped, and I will not expose you unnecessarily."*

      C   "And then I'll get out of bed?"

r.   **N**   *"Yes. Perhaps you would like to sit in the solarium for a few minutes while I change your bed."*

      C   "That might be nice."

s.   **N**   *"I was just out there. It's a sunny day today and nice and cheerful with the sunshine streaming in. Did you know that there are only 29 days until spring is officially here?"*

      C   "No, I didn't. I've sort of lost track of time since coming to the hospital. I used to love spring and getting out in my garden to work the soil. I always had flowers and vegetables." Mrs. Crowe pauses, then asks, "You won't forget me out in the solarium? Yesterday the nurse left me there all morning and I grew so weary."

t.   **N**   *"That must have been hard on you. It sounds like you were not able to call the nurse."*

      C   "No, I couldn't. There was no one to help me."

u.   **N**   *"I will leave a call bell with you in case you wish to call me."*

      C   "Thank you. That's a relief. . . . What did you say your name was?"

v.   **N**   *"Robinson. Tom Robinson."*

      C   "I'm pleased to meet you, Mr. Robinson. I think we are going to get along just fine. I'm ready for you to start my care now."

w.   **N**   *"Fine. Now as I get things ready, tell me more about yourself."*

x.   **N**   He continued, *"You said you haven't been feeling well for several months."*

b Helen Jeffers and Willie Cole: In this situation note the occasional use of a nontherapeutic response and the nurse's efforts to evaluate the care, including the use of self-assessment and revision of care. The nontherapeutic approaches have been identified with an asterisk (*).

Verbal approaches

1. Clarifying _____
2. Disagreeing* _____
3. Encouraging _____
4. Exploring _____
5. Focusing _____
   (on client)
6. Giving advice* _____
7. Giving _____
   disapproval*

8. Giving _____
   information
9. Reflecting _____
10. Seeking _____
    information
11. Suggesting _____
12. Understanding _____
13. Using persuasion* _____
14. Using stereotypic _____
    labels*

SITUATION: A student nurse approached a newly admitted client and initiated contact:

a. **N** *"My name is Mrs. Helen Jeffers. I'm a student nurse on this unit."*
   C "So? Who cares?"

b. **N** *"What is your name?"*
   C "If you're so smart, you find out."

c. **N** *"You don't feel like telling me your name now?"*
   C "That's right. You've got the picture!"

d. **N** *"Why are you being so hostile?"*
   C "I'm not hostile. I just don't feel like rapping. I have important things on my mind."

e. **N** *"Oh?"*
   C "You don't believe me?"

f. **N** *"I believe it's hard for you to talk about yourself."*
   The client and student sat in silence. Finally, Mrs. Jeffers said:

g. **N** *"You really should open up and talk about yourself."*
   More silence and the student continued:

h. **N** *"I think you would feel better if you shared your thoughts with me."*
   The client did not respond and they continued to sit in silence. In a little while the client started to take furtive glances at the student who observed his behavior and acknowledged the client with an embarrassed smile. She had been thinking about the interaction and recognized that several of her responses had not been very helpful. She asked:

i. **N** *"Has anyone shown you around the ward and introduced you to the other clients?"*

C   "No. I don't need the red-carpet treatment. I'm not planning to stay here long."

j.   N   *"You think you will be leaving soon? What have you been told?"*

C   "Nothing. But I'm not sick, so there is no need for me to stay here in this looney bin. I'm just going to sort out my head then I'm signing myself out. You're married?"
The student nodded her head. The client continued; "You love the guy?"

k.   N   *"That's really not your concern. You shouldn't ask me personal questions about myself."*

C   "Its not OK for me to ask you questions, but I bet you got a million questions you're dying to ask me. You students are all alike. Always asking questions and then blabbing to your classmates."

l.   N   *"That's not so. I wouldn't break a confidence."*
Silence. Helen Jeffers reflected on her response and saw that she had again been defensive with this client. She was aware that she felt threatened by this attractive and aggressive young man.

m.   N   *"That was abrupt of me. You seem to have some questions you want to ask me. Perhaps I can answer some of them."* She continued.

n.   N   *"Yes, I am married. My husband and I have been married 3 years. And yes, I do love my husband. I am also a student nurse and I like what I am doing very much. We do talk together about our clients and share some things with staff so we can help you better."* She paused, then said:

o.   N   *"That bothers you?"*

C   "Naw. I guess not. You're just doing your job. But students sure do ask a lot of questions."

p.   N   *"Tell me something about yourself."*

C   "What do you want to know about me? What have I got to tell you that can possibly be interesting?"

q.   N   *"You shouldn't put yourself down like that."* After a short pause Mrs. Jeffers said:

r.   N   *"You could start by telling me your name."*

C   "My name is Willie Cole. . . and I'm all messed up."
After greeting the client by name and shaking his hand, Mrs. Jeffers responded:

s.   N   *"You're all messed up?"*
The client was silent, hesitating to continue.

t.   N   *"What do you mean when you say you're 'all messed up'?"*

C   "I'm gay. Know what that means?"

u.   N   *"Tell me what it means to you."*

C   "It means I dig other guys."

v.   N   *"Are you saying that you like men better than women?"*

C   "Yes. . . No. . . I don't know. I can't talk about it right now. What time is it? I'm hungry. Is it almost time for lunch?"
After giving Mr. Cole information regarding the day's schedule, Mrs. Jeffers said:

w.   **N** *"All right Mr. Cole. I can see it is difficult for you to talk about this now. Perhaps we can continue the conversation later."* The nurse added:

x.   **N** *"Come to the recreation room. There is a bingo game going on that you might enjoy participating in until lunchtime."*

3 Listed on p. 81 are selected verbal skills that can be used to promote effective communication between the nurse and the client. An example illustrating each skill and a statement of purpose has been provided. In this exercise, fill in the space provided in the grid with the purpose of each skill and a personalized example of each one.

Communication skill	Example	Purpose	Personalized example
1. Giving information	"My name is Carol Lofstedt. I am the author of this book."	Giving client specific data.	
2. Seeking information	"Tell me your name."		
3. Reflecting	Client: "I hate Jack. He's a bully, always picking on others." Nurse: "You hate Jack because you feel he's a bully?"		
4. Clarifying	"I don't understand. Are you saying Jack has been picking on you?"		
5. Focusing (on client)	"Tell me about yourself, Helene."		
6. Introducing a neutral topic	"I see you've been reading the paper. What's happening today that's interesting?"		
7. Encouraging conversational lead	"Go on Sheila. I'm listening.		
8. Suggesting	"Perhaps you'd feel better if we walked in the hallway for a little while.		
9. Giving recognition	"Hello Mr. Scott."		
10. Exploring	"And then what happened?"		
11. Refocusing	"Earlier you were telling me about your school experiences. Let's talk some more about that."		
12. Understanding	"You seem upset when you describe those early experiences. They must have been difficult times for you."		

4 Listed below are 8 verbal approaches that interfere with effective communication. In the space provided in the grid, evaluate each one, explaining how or why they are ineffective. An example has been provided to help you get started.

Nontherapeutic approaches and behavioral examples	Evaluation
1. Using stereotypical labels: 　N　"I know a con artist when I see one."	Labels mean different things to different people, but directed at the client, they dehumanize him and create emotional distance.
2. Focusing on self: 　N　"I love to cook. As a matter of fact yesterday I. . . and I. . ."	
3. Giving advice: 　N　"If I were you I would. . ."	
4. Giving disapproval: 　N　"That's wrong."	
5. Probing: 　N　"Why don't you ever talk about your mother?"	
6. Using persuasion: 　N　"You should really take a bath now."	
7. Disagreeing: 　N　"No, that's not so."	
8. Giving reassurance: 　N　"Don't worry. Everything will be all right."	

TEST ITEMS

DIRECTIONS: Select the *best* response. (Answers appear in the Appendix.)

1 Communication is *most* effective when verbal, nonverbal, and metacommunication are:

a Reciprocal.　　　　**c** Acceptable.

b Congruent.　　　　**d** Simultaneous.

2 Which one of the following developmental tasks must be negotiated to some degree before communication between two persons is generally effective?

a Trust.　　　　**c** Initiative.

b Autonomy.　　　　**d** Industry.

3 Which one of the following personality traits in the nurse would contribute *most* to the nurse's being able to communicate effectively with a nonverbal client?

  a Creativity.   **c** Intelligence.

  b Assertiveness.   **d** Patience.

4 In the initiation phase of the nurse-client interaction, which one of the following nursing approaches should generally be used *first?*

  a Introducing a neutral topic.

  b Focusing on the client's health.

  c Seeking factual information.

  d Introducing oneself to the client.

5 Which one of the following responses *best* illustrates the communication skill of focusing on the client?

  a "Tell me about yourself."   **c** "Hello Mrs. Brown."

  b "What is your name?"   **d** "Go on, I'm listening."

6 The primary reason the nurse introduces a neutral topic is to:

  a Explore a client's interests and hobbies.

  b Fill anxiety-producing silences.

  c Avoid focusing on stress-related topics.

  d Initiate a conversation with a new client.

7 Which one of the following goals does *not* characterize most nurse-client interactions?

  a To establish rapport between the nurse and client.

  b To encourage the client to express his thoughts.

  c To set the tone for subsequent conversations.

  d To reassure the client that he will improve.

8 The client asks the nurse, "What should I do? Should I call my husband?" The nurse says, "If I were you, I'd call him." This is an example of which one of the following nontherapeutic responses?

  a Using persuasion.   **c** Giving advice.

  b Focusing on self.   **d** Giving disapproval.

9 The client says to the nurse, "I'm so upset; I have so many problems and I don't know what to do." The nurse responds by asking; "Can you identify anything in particular that is upsetting you?" This is an example of:

  a Exploring.   **c** Clarifying.

  b Seeking information.   **d** Probing.

10 When the nurse asks clients intelligent, reality-oriented questions to help them discuss their thoughts and feelings in some depth, the communication skill being used is:

a Probing. **c** Exploring.

b Seeking information. **d** Reflecting.

11 Which of the following pairs of skills can be *either* effective or ineffective in promoting communication, depending on how they are used?

a Reassurance, silence. **c** Persuasion, surprise.

b Probing, suggesting. **d** Reflecting, advising.

12 The main reason that probing is considered nontherapeutic is because it:

a Dehumanizes the client and creates emotional distance.

b Encourages the client to talk about things before he is ready.

c Implies that the nurse knows better than the client what is best for him.

d Shows the client that the nurse does not understand what he is feeling.

13 A client asks the student nurse if he can go off the floor until lunchtime. Which one of the following responses by the nurse *best* illustrates *double-bind communication?*

a "I don't know. You will have to ask the head nurse."

b "I can't let you off the unit but I'll walk you to the door."

c "Do you think you really should leave the ward now?"

d "We're going to play some records. Come join us."

14 Special problems in communicating with the mentally ill include their:

a Previous experiences with incongruent communication.

b Adaptation of retreating from reality into psychoses.

c Repeated past exposures to double-bind communication.

d All of the above.

15 The client offers to tell the nurse a secret as long as she promises not to tell anyone. Which one of the following would be the *most* appropriate response for the nurse to make?

a "A secret? Go on, you can trust me."

b "I'd like to hear what you have to say but I may need to share it with the staff."

c "I don't think you should tell me. I'll have to tell the staff."

d "I'll listen to what you have to say, but I don't like secrets."

chapter 9

interpersonal interventions

INTRODUCTION

"Many mentally ill persons have a long history of having failed at establishing and maintaining satisfying interpersonal relationships. To the degree that the nurse's interactions with the client reflect acceptance of him and consistency in response to him, they will be therapeutic by providing experiences that are corrective of earlier, less helpful interpersonal experiences."* Of all the health professionals, nurses are in the unique position of having multiple opportunities to provide these corrective experiences, showing clients that all interpersonal relationships are not to be feared and avoided. These contacts may be brief interactions, as when the nurse greets the client by name, answers a question, or sits with a client for a short conversation. In these interactions the client and nurse generally know each other, but the nurse is not primarily responsible for the client's treatment The goals of such an interaction are supportive of the treatment goals of others who are working with the client in a closer relationship. These closer-type associations are nurse-client relationships in which there is a high degree of involvement and commitment, with the nurse and client working together over an extended period of time to meet the client's physical and emotional needs. Finally, the third type of interpersonal intervention is one that occurs in an emergency situation. The client and nurse may or may not know each other. The goal of this intervention is for the immediate resolution of a severe problem, such as setting limits with a client who is acting out, intervening in a suicide attempt, sitting and listening to a client who is crying and upset, or responding to a physical emergency such as a hypoglycemic reaction.

To some nurses such interpersonal interventions are the most challenging and rewarding part of nursing. Depending on an un-

*From Taylor, C.M.: Mereness' essentials of psychiatric nursing, ed. 12, St. Louis, 1986, The C.V. Mosby Co., Chapter 9.

derstanding of human behavior, a knowledge of psychiatric nursing principles, a sensitive use of personality, a skilled use of communication skills, an openness to reflect on one's feelings and attitudes, and a willingness to evaluate one's actions, the nurse can reach out to clients experiencing emotional pain and intervene therapeutically.

The purpose of this chapter is to emphasize the importance of all interpersonal interventions in nursing. Although the long-term nurse-client relationship is the most effective vehicle for providing corrective interpersonal experiences, the role of short-term interventions should not be minimized. Intervening in emergency situations and conducting brief interactions with clients with sensitivity, understanding, and caring communicates to the client a new appreciation of his worth as a human being.

OBJECTIVES

1. To differentiate among three types of interpersonal interventions.
2. To identify the characteristcs, goals, and nursing responsibilities associated with a nurse-client relationship.
3. To list the sequential steps in initiating a nurse-client relationship.
4. To identify physical and emotional problems suitable as a focus in the maintenance phase of the nurse-client relationship.
5. To evaluate accepting and nonaccepting, consistent and inconsistent, nursing responses.
6. To differentiate between social and therapeutic relationships.

EXERCISES

1 Differentiate among the three types of interpersonal interventions. Read the following list of 15 nursing actions and determine whether they are most appropriate to emergency interventions, nurse-client interactions, or nurse-client relationships. Place a check after each one in the box in the appropriate column. The first one has been entered to help you get started.

Nursing actions	Nurse-client interventions		
	Emergency	Interaction	Relationship
1. Arranges regular weekly sessions with a client.	☐	☐	☑
2. Introduces self to a client and invites him to play checkers.	☐	☐	☐
3. Waits prescribed time for client to keep appointment.	☐	☐	☐
4. Sits with new client who is crying in the dayroom.	☐	☐	☐
5. Greets a client who is known only superficially by the nurse.	☐	☐	☐
6. Reports newly admitted client's threat to escape.	☐	☐	☐
7. Responds with acceptance and consistency to testing behaviors.	☐	☐	☐
8. Intervenes in suicide attempt.	☐	☐	☐
9. Helps feed lunch to an unresponsive client.	☐	☐	☐
10. Identifies and works with client on specific problems.	☐	☐	☐
11. Prepares client for termination.	☐	☐	☐
12. Administers care to client experiencing a seizure.	☐	☐	☐
13. Helps client work through loss associated with termination.	☐	☐	☐
14. Administers routine medications to all clients on the unit.	☐	☐	☐
15. Helps client transfer positive aspects of the association to others.	☐	☐	☐

2 Read the following situation involving Annie Johnson and complete the exercises as directed.

SITUATION: Annie Johnson, a 49-year-old, unmarried, obese woman, has a long history of hospitalizations for mental illness. She is usually untidy and has a strong body odor. When angry or frustrated, she tends to soil herself. Miss Johnson avoids routine shower periods by hiding from the staff. She is prone to loud, angry outbursts in which she uses gross profanity. Sometimes she brandishes chairs, wastepaper baskets, and other available articles and threatens to throw them at others.

Miss Johnson eats at every opportunity. At mealtimes she grabs food from other clients sitting at her table. Whenever she gets the chance, she rummages through the trash cans, eating any scraps of food or garbage she can find and hiding other bits of rubbish on her person or at her bedside. When not eating, looking, or begging for food, Miss Johnson sits alone in the dayroom, sleeping, rocking, or openly masturbating. Other clients tend to avoid her because of her menacing behaviors and slovenly personal habits. Miss Johnson also tends to keep away from other clients and staff, approaching them only when she wants something.

Miss Oliver, a student nurse, is assigned to Miss Johnson's unit and chooses to work with the client for the duration of her psychiatric clinical rotation. Her objective is to develop a therapeutic nurse-client relationship with Miss Johnson.

a Miss Oliver recognizes that the nurse-client relationship usually proceeds through three developmental phases. In the grid below identify the characteristics, goals, and nursing responsiblities for the orientation, maintenance, and termination phases of the nurse-client relationship.

	Orientation	Maintenance	Termination
1. Characteristics			
2. Goals			
3. Nursing responsibilities			

b List in a logical sequence at least 4 approaches that Miss Oliver might use to initiate a nurse-client relationship with Miss Johnson.

1. _____
2. _____
3. _____
4. _____

c The goal of the maintenance or working phase of the nurse-client relationship is to identify and work with the client on specific physical and emotional problems. Referring to descriptive data presented in the situation, identify and list 5 problems that may be the focus of the working phase of the nurse-client relationship with Miss Johnson. Be sure to include one physical problem in your list.

1. _____
2. _____
3. _____
4. _____
5. _____

d Acceptance is often distorted to mean the right to feel, think, and behave without restraint. On the contrary, acceptance is not a license to behave without consideration for the rights of others. It neither condones nor approves, punishes nor condemns, but rather simply acknowledges that an individual has the right to be his own person and to respond in ways that reflect his state of being at a given time. Acceptance communicates an awareness that the person's expressions of self may not always be within the prescriptions of his society. The nurse as a professional, knowledgeable, helping, and caring person communicates the attitude and expectation that with support and guidance clients can modify their responses to function more acceptably with others without losing a basic sense of individuality.

Miss Oliver wants to communicate an attitude of acceptance to her client. Listed on p. 90 are 15 nursing approaches that Miss Oliver has used with Miss Johnson at various times in their relationship. Some are accepting and therapeutic, others are nonaccepting and nontherapeutic. Evaluate each approach as either accepting or nonaccepting, placing a check in the box in the appropriate column. The first one has been entered to help you get started.

Nursing approaches	Accepting	Nonaccepting
1. "Tell me what you are feeling."	☑	☐
2. "If you don't stop misbehaving I'm going to put you in seclusion."	☐	☐
3. "Put the chair down. You may hurt someone."	☐	☐
4. "I can't let you eat other people's food. Come, have a cup of coffee with me."	☐	☐
5. "I don't like you when you behave that way."	☐	☐
6. "You are out of control. You must go into seclusion until you regain control of yourself."	☐	☐
7. "I understand you are angry with me. I would prefer you tell me this, not swear at me."	☐	☐
8. "You should tell them when you are upset."	☐	☐
9. "That's a hostile thing to say."	☐	☐
10. "Come and work with clay instead of going through the garbage."	☐	☐
11. "If you can't control yourself better than that, I'm going to ask the nurse to give you an injection."	☐	☐
12. "Come to your room where you can masturbate in private."	☐	☐
13. "You need to change your clothing. I will help you."	☐	☐
14. "It's OK to talk about your anger, but I can't let you hit others."	☐	☐
15. "You want to be left alone? All right. I'll come back later to see you."	☐	☐

e Consistency is an approach that has two dimensions: doing what one promises to do and doing the same thing each time. Consistency is a significant component in the development of trust and the reduction of anxiety. Through the first aspect of consistency—commitments made and kept—the client discovers experientially that the nurse is someone who can be relied on to follow through on commitments and, consequently, is someone who can be trusted. The second aspect of consistency—the following of a routine, predictable pattern of behavior and the conveying of the same attitudes time after time—takes the unexpected out of a situation. It is often the unexpected that creates an element of uncertainty and contributes to the development of anxiety, especially in insecure persons. To the individual who has a dysfunctional life-style and who may be prone to or experiencing severe anxiety, the following of a predictable routine and the communication of a consistent attitude provide a degree of security that encourages more effective functioning.

Miss Oliver collaborated with the staff to plan a consistent approach to the care of Miss Johnson. In the following situation are 15 nursing approaches that have been italicized and numbered. Read the situation and evaluate these approaches. Using the grid provided list the approaches as either *consistent* (and *therapeutic*) or *inconsistent* (and *nontherapeutic*). Revise the nontherapeutic approaches by making them consistent. The first two have been completed to help you get started.

SITUATION: Miss Oliver *(1) spent 2 hours with Miss Johnson every Tuesday and Friday morning.* When she first started working with her, the client would sit from 5 to 10 minutes with the student nurse, then would walk away and sit by herself. *(2) Usually the student remained in her chair and waited 10 to 15 minutes for Miss Johnson to return. (3) If the client did not return, Miss Oliver would generally seek her out and offer to sit with her. (4) When approaching the client, Miss Oliver called her by name, sometimes calling her "Annie," but most of the time addressing her more formally as "Miss Johnson."* Miss Oliver worked hard to meet her client's needs. *(5) When she arrived for her visits, the student nurse would first observe the client's general appearance and then help with her hygiene. When this was completed, Miss Oliver would take Miss Johnson off the ward to the hospital cafeteria for a cup of coffee.* It was during these periods that the client began to talk more freely with the student nurse about herself, her family, her feelings, and her problems. Although some of the things Miss Johnson said were upsetting, *(6) the student always maintained an interested, accepting, and understanding manner.* These weekly visits to the cafeteria also gave Miss Oliver an opportunity to help Miss Johnson control her impulse to grab other people's food. *(7) Each time it occurred, Miss Oliver would hold Miss Johnson's hands, point out that her behavior was disturbing to others, and firmly tell her she could not come to the cafeteria if she could not control herself.* The measures were effective, and Miss Johnson gradually gave up this behavior. *(8) Miss Oliver could also be very matter-of-fact and firm with the client whenever she found Miss Johnson rummaging in the garbage. She discovered that Miss Johnson enjoyed working with clay and was easily distracted with this activity.* However, when Miss Johnson would swear and shake her fist in a menacing way, Miss Oliver felt helpless. *(9) Sometimes the student nurse tried to control the client verbally, telling her to stop. But most of the time she would leave the room and ask the staff for help.* Although threatened by her aggressive behavior, Miss Oliver was embarrassed by Miss Johnson's sexual activities and *(10) usually looked away and ignored Miss Johnson when she was masturbating.* With help from her instructor, Miss Oliver learned to respond more therapeutically whenever her client masturbated in public. *(11) As the relationship approached termination, Miss Oliver introduced the topic at each visit and reminded Miss Johnson of the time they had left.* She also brought a calendar and oriented the client by pointing out relevant dates. Miss Oliver was experiencing some feelings of guilt for leaving the client. *(12) As a result, she did not always focus on the client's feelings of anger and loss when they were expressed.* When the client began to soil herself again, *(13) Miss Oliver tried to be patient and understanding, but her feelings of frustration and helplessness at seeing the client regress interfered and she was increasingly impatient and abrupt with Miss Johnson.* As the date of termination grew nearer, Miss Johnson's earlier testing behaviors also returned. She would leave in the middle of the conversation and hide from Miss Oliver, waiting to see if she would go look for her. *(14) Miss Oliver responded in different ways. Sometimes she sought out Miss Johnson and sometimes she waited to see if the client would return on her own.* Miss Oliver's instructor worked closely with her, help-

Therapeutic-consistent approaches	Nontherapeutic-inconsistent approaches	Revision of nontherapeutic approaches
(1)	(2)	The student nurse remained in her chair and waited 10 to 15 minutes for the client to return

ing the student nurse reflect on her feelings and the roles they were playing in her responses to the client. As Miss Oliver dealt with her own feelings, she was again able to respond more therapeutically to her client. *(15) In response to the client's repeated requests for her to visit after the clinical experience was over, Miss Oliver firmly and kindly said she could not, and told the client that she would never forget her.*

3 Listed below are 10 characteristics of either *social* or *therapeutic* relationships. Differentiate between each one by placing a check in the box in the appropriate column. The first one has been filled in to help you get started.

Characteristics	Social	Therapeutic
1. The activities are goal-directed, aimed at meeting the client's needs.	☐	☑
2. The relationship develops spontaneously, without a conscious plan.	☐	☐
3. The nature of the relationship is being objectively reflected upon.	☐	☐
4. The relationship is ended in a way that encourages further relationships.	☐	☐
5. The needs of both persons involved in the relationship have equal priority.	☐	☐
6. Guidance is sought in assessing the developmental phases of the relationship.	☐	☐
7. The goal of the relationship is usually for mutal pleasure.	☐	☐
8. Activities are planned around meeting specific physical and emotional needs.	☐	☐
9. Both parties involved share mutual concern regarding reciprocal approval.	☐	☐
10. The meeting of social needs is the primary focus of the relationship.	☐	☐

TEST ITEMS

DIRECTIONS: Select the *best* response. (Answers appear in the Appendix.)

1 The major overall objective in intervening interpersonally with clients is to:
  a Provide clients with a variety of social interactions.
  b Expose clients to experiences corrective of earlier relationships.
  c Help clients learn to trust other people again.
  d Show clients that they are unique human beings.

2 Which one of the following factors has been the *most* helpful in making clients receptive to interpersonal treatment modalities?
  a Somatic therapies.   **c** Psychosurgery.
  b Psychotropic drugs.   **d** Hospitalization.

3 Consistency is to predictable as nonjudgmental is to:
  a Accountable.   **c** Subjective.
  b Discriminatory.   **d** Acceptance.

4 A nonjudgmental attitude is reflected in a nurse who:

  a Avoids setting limits on socially unacceptable behaviors.

  b Adopts an impersonal attitude toward the client's behavior.

  c Gives approval to the client for his behavior.

  d Recognizes the client's behavior as an adaptation to stress.

5 Maintaining the same basic attitude toward the client exemplifies:

  a Acceptance.   **c** Consistency.

  b Objectivity.   **d** Understanding.

6 Interpersonal interventions can *best* be differentiated by the degree of involvement and the goals of the intervention. Which one of the following statements best reflects *emergency intervention?*

  a There need not be any involvement between the nurse and the client and the goal resolution is immediate.

  b The nurse and the client may have some degree of involvement and the nurse assumes a supportive role in helping others work with the client.

  c The nurse and the client know each other and the goals of the association are long-term.

  d There is a high degree of involvement between the nurse and the client, and the goals are aimed at providing positive interpersonal experiences.

7 A client has been on the ward for 3 weeks. He rebuffs all attempts to help him relate to others. Mr. Fine, a student nurse, always makes an effort to seek out the client at some time during the day, even though he is consistently rejected. Which one of the following *best* describes the level of interaction between this client and the student?

  a Emergency intervention.

  b Orientation phase of the nurse-client relationship.

  c Maintenance phase of the nurse-client relationship.

  d Nurse-client interaction.

8 During the orientation phase of the nurse-client relationship, *all but which one* of the following would be appropriate nursing activities?

  a Visiting the client at different times each week until a suitable meeting time is found.

  b Limiting the amount of time spent together to that which was mutually agreed upon.

   c Responding with acceptance and consistency to testing and manipulative behaviors.

   d Reflecting on feelings of frustration associated with a slow rate of progress.

9 A behavior that generally signals that the getting-acquainted phase of the nurse-client relationship has ended is when the client:

   a Seeks out the nurse.

   b Agrees to meet regularly with the nurse.

   c Decreases the testing behaviors.

   d Asks about the end of the relationship.

10 A major goal of the maintenance phase of the nurse-client relationship is to:

   a Help the client transfer positive aspects of the relationship to others.

   b Give the client insights into the nature of the illness.

   c Prepare the client for the end of the relationship.

   d Encourage the client to share feelings, thoughts, and problems.

11 In response to termination the client asks the student nurse to continue the visits after the relationship has ended. Which one of the following responses by the student would be *most* therapeutic?

   a "I'd really like to visit you but my instructor won't let me."

   b "No, I can't visit. I'm afraid it wouldn't be proper."

   c "We've had a good relationship, haven't we? It's hard to end it."

   d "I don't know. Perhaps I could come visit sometime."

12 Some people have a difficult time dealing with the feelings associated with termination. When they do not accept the reality that the end of the relationship is inevitable, they are probably using the ego defense mechanisms of repression and:

   a Denial.   **c** Suppression.

   b Projection.   **d** Isolation.

13 Other people may respond to a loss by manifesting symptoms that had been relinquished. In such a situation which one of the following ego defenses is being used to handle stress?

   a Reaction-formation.   **c** Introjection.

   b Displacement.   **d** Regression.

14 In handling their personal responses to termination, nurses need to do which one of the following?

   a Delay talking about termination until their feelings of loss have subsided.

   b Use the process of self-awareness to assess their responses to termination.

   c Continue the relationship until the feelings associated with termination are resolved.

   d Maintain an objective, impersonal attitude toward termination.

15 A social relationship differs from a therapeutic one in that in a *social relationship* the:

   a Needs of both parties involved must be met satisfactorily for the association to continue.

   b Goal of the association is to meet the physical and the emotional needs of both parties.

   c Association always progresses through several predictable developmental phases.

   d Nature of the relationship is always reflected upon in an objective way.

chapter 10

psychotropic agents

INTRODUCTION

INTRODUCTION

The use of psychotropic agents in the care of the emotionally ill is a relatively recent phenomenon. Although other physical treatments have been used since the dawn of history, they were often primitive and barbaric. Based on the belief that persons lost their reasoning abilities because of severe trauma, it was thought that rationality could be restored through the experience of another equally disturbing event. Measures such as flogging, starving, ducking people in ice-cold water, and throwing them into pits filled with snakes were used in an effort to shock mentally ill persons back into reality. In other words, what would normally shock a mentally healthy person into insanity was thought to shock the mentally ill person back into reality.

Then, in the 1950s, chlorpromazine was introduced into the United States and used on a research basis in the treatment of mentally ill persons. Since that time many chemical agents have been discovered and used in treatment. The widespread use of these psychotropic agents has revolutionized the care of the mentally ill. "Because of them, other treatment modalities, such as psychotherapy and the various group therapies, have been made available to large numbers of individuals. Although the psychotropic drugs do not cure mental illness, they do normalize behavior. Thus many people are able, for the first time, to participate therapeutically with others in a variety of group activities."*

In addition, the use of these medications has had significant impact on the role of the nurse. Just as these psychotropic agents have helped make emotionally ill persons more amenable to other treatment measures, so too have they increased the import of the nurse-client relationship and made it essential for the nurse to be able to relate therapeutically and communicate effectively with clients. Although the technical role of the nurse has

*From Taylor, C.M.: Mereness' essentials of psychiatric nursing, ed. 12, St. Louis, 1986, The C.V. Mosby Co., Chapter 10.

always been important, the introduction of psychotropic medications into psychiatric treatment settings has expanded the roles of nurses working in such settings to include the preparation and administration of such agents. Nurses working with drugs need a sound knowledge base from which to carry out these functions: drug classification, action, range of daily dosage, route of administration, contraindications, precautions, drug idiosyncrasies, side effects, adverse effects, and nursing implications. The purpose of this chapter is to help build such a knowledge base through the review of the four major classifications of psychotropic agents used to alter disturbed behavioral patterns in mentally ill clients and the identification of nursing actions specific to the use of these agents.

OBJECTIVES

1. To build a knowledge base about antipsychotic agents, antianxiety agents, antidepressants, and lithium carbonate.
2. To identify general and specific nursing measures used in the administration of psychotropic agents.

EXERCISES

1 Learning about medications requires self-discipline, incentive to learn, repetition, and several good source books on medications. In addition to your psychiatric text, you will want to refer to a reputable pharmacology book and, perhaps, the current *Physicians' Desk Reference,* which is generally available on most hospital units as well as in college libraries. If you have already established a useful pattern for learning about medications in other nursing courses, it is hoped you will incorporate your system into the study and learning of psychotropic agents. If you have not, you may find the following exercises useful in helping you develop such a system. It is based on the collection of data on "drug cards." You can develop your own format or use the one suggested here. You can use any size cards convenient for you, but they should be uniform in size to file for future reference. If you own or have access to a personal computer with a printer, you can set up your "cards" on the computer, enter and store your data, and make a hard copy to take to the clinical area for reference. Later, as you gather additional data or are assigned to other clients receiving the same medications, you can update your drug cards without having to recopy all the material previously entered.

   Psychotropic medications are grouped into four major categories: antipsychotic agents, antianxiety agents, antidepressants, and lithium carbonate. Antidepressants can be further subdivided into two categories: tricyclic antidepressants and monoamine oxidase inhibitors, commonly referred to as MAOs. Complete the following exercises, each of which is based on a client situation and one of these categories of drugs.

   a SITUATION: Henrietta Hurley was brought to the psychiatric emergency room by the local police. She had been found wandering in the streets, partly disrobed, talking to herself, giggling inappropriately, and obviously confused. Her identity was tentatively established from identification cards in her purse which she held tightly to her. She was admitted to the psychiatric service for observation and was given a complete physical examination. Except for several recent bruises, abrasions, and low blood pressure, she was found to be in good health. Thioridazine, 100 mg t.i.d., was ordered for Ms. Hurley.

1. Fill in the data on the drug card.

(Side one)

Generic name: Thioridazine
Trade name: Mellaril

Classification:
Other drugs in this classification:

Action:

Range of daily dosage/route of administration:

Date/client initials/dosage:

Contraindications/precautions:

Drug idiosyncrasies:

(Side two)

Side effects and nursing implications for each:

Adverse effects and nursing implications for each:

Miscellaneous nursing implications:

Source of data:

2. Ms. Hurley failed to respond to the thioridazine as expected. The medication was discontinued and another antipsychotic agent was ordered. In the table provided list the names and dosages of five other antipsychotic medications that could be ordered for the client.

	Generic name	Trade name	Range of daily oral dosage in milligrams
a.			
b.			
c.			
d.			
e.			

b SITUATION: Cindy Kavannaugh is the lead singer in a country-western band. Her work necessitates travel, most of which is done by bus or train. Occasionally, however, the band must cover long distances rapidly and air travel is required. This is very stressful for Cindy, who is very anxious about flying. To help her cope with her anxiety, Cindy takes a prescribed antianxiety medication.

1. In the table provided list the generic names and dosages of 5 antianxiety medications that would help reduce Cindy's anxiety.

	Generic name	Trade name	Range of daily oral dosage in milligrams
a.			
b.			
c.			
d.			
e.			

2. Select one of the antianxiety medications you identified in Exercise b-1 and complete the following drug card.

(Side one)

Generic name:
Trade name:

Classification:
Other drugs in this classification:

Action:

Range of daily dosage/route of administration:

Date/client initials/dosage:

Contraindications/precautions:

Drug idiosyncrasies:

(Side two)

Side effects and nursing implications for each:

Adverse effects and nursing implications for each:

Miscellaneous nursing implications:

Source of data:

c SITUATION: Flora Shimken, a 58-year-old woman, was brought to the Community Mental Health Center by her daughter. Mrs. Shimken complained of feelings of hopelessness, expressed suicidal thoughts, and exhibited classic signs of depression. She cried easily during the interview and wrung her hands in obvious anguish. Her daughter described how her mother had been finding it increasingly difficult to function in the home. Mrs. Shimken was given a complete physical and was found to be in good health. In addition to a program of group therapy and activities at the center, desipramine, 50 mg t.i.d., was ordered for Mrs. Shimken.

1. Fill in the data on the drug card.

(Side one)

Generic name: Desipramine
Trade name(s): Pertofrane, Norpramin

Classification:
Other drugs in this classification:

Action:

Range of daily dosage/route of administration:

Date/client initials/dosage:

Contraindications/precautions:

Drug idiosyncrasies:

Side effects and nursing implications for each:

Adverse effects and nursing implications for each:

Miscellaneous nursing implications:

Source of data:

2. Four weeks after Mrs. Shimken was started on desipramine, there had been little change in her general condition. She continued to be depressed, suffered from insomnia and anorexia, and, in addition, had taken an overdose of her daughter's sleeping tablets. Although she denied she had tried to kill herself, insisting she had taken the sleeping pills to help her sleep, her doctor felt she was a real suicide risk and had her hospitalized. In addition, he placed Mrs. Shimken on suicidal precautions and discontinued the desipramine preparatory to ordering tranylcypromine 3 weeks hence. Fill in the data on the drug card.

(Side one)

Generic name: Tranylcypromine
Trade name(s): Parnate

Classification:
Other drugs in this classification:

Action:

Range of daily dosage/route of administration:

Date/client initials/dosage:

Contraindications/precautions:

Drug idiosyncrasies:

(Side two)

Side effects and nursing implications for each:

Adverse effects and nursing implications for each:

Miscellaneous nursing implications:

Source of data:

105

d SITUATION: Tony Wilder has a long history of a bipolar, manic-type disorder that has been controlled with lithium carbonate. His daily dosage is regulated by monthly blood tests of the serum lithium levels. He is currently receiving 300 mg t.i.d. to maintain a therapeutic serum level of 0.6 to 1.0 mEq/L (milliequivalents per liter).

1. Fill in the data on the drug card.

(Side one)

Generic name: Lithium carbonate
Trade name(s): Eskalith, Lithane

Classification:
Other drugs in this classification:

Action:

Range of daily dosage/route of administration:

Date/client initials/dosage:

Contraindications/precautions:

Drug idiosyncrasies:

(Side two)

Side effects and nursing implications for each:

Adverse effects and nursing implications for each:

Miscellaneous nursing implications:

Source of data:

2. Despite its effectiveness, recent studies indicate that lithium therapy may produce adverse effects in the body even without toxic warning symptoms. Identify three organs of the body that may be so affected.

a. _____

b. _____

c. _____

2 The nurse assumes a major role in the preparation and administration of medications.

a The following exercise lists 20 side and adverse effects associated with the administration of psychotropic agents and 14 nursing actions that should be carried out in response to these effects. In the space provided after each side or adverse effect enter the letter designating the most appropriate nursing action. A nursing action may be used more than once; side/adverse effect may require more than one nursing action. The first nursing action has been entered to help you get started.

Side and adverse effects

1. Agranulocytosis __(1)__
2. Akathisia _____
3. Constipation _____
4. Diarrhea, vomiting _____
5. Drug dependency _____
6. Dry mouth _____
7. Dystonia _____
8. Hypertensive crisis _____
9. Jaundice _____
10. Leukopenia _____
11. Nausea, fine tremor, thirst _____
12. Ocular changes _____
13. Paradoxical reaction ___
14. Paralytic ileus _____
15. Photosensitivity _____
16. Postural hypotension ___
17. Pseudoparkinsonism ___
18. Sedation _____
19. Tardive dyskinesia _____
20. Urinary hesitance/ retention _____

Nursing actions

    a. Notify physician and withhold medication.

    b. Notify physician for medical examination prior to withholding drug.

    c. Take client's blood pressure before starting drug and ambulate gradually at any sign of dizziness or light-headedness.

    d. Report complaints of blurred vision or squinting to physician and provide periodic eye examinations.

    e. Avoid foods containing tyramine and excessive caffeine; avoid drugs containing ephedrine and epinephrine.

    f. Use for short periods; withdraw drug slowly in long-term use.

    g. Offer fluids, sugarless chewing gum, or hard candy.

    h. Protect from rays of the sun by keeping client in shade, having client wear hat and long sleeves.

    i. Notify physician and administer antiparkinsonism drugs such as Artane or Cogentin as ordered.

    j. Warn client not to engage in activities such as driving that require mental acuity.

    k. Monitor drug levels through regular blood work.

    l. Check out and report any symptoms of colds or sore throat and see that white blood counts are carried out periodically.

    m. Provide fluids, balanced diet with roughage; use laxatives as necessary.

    n. Provide balanced diet, normal salt intake, 2500 to 3000 ml fluids daily.

b List 5 general nursing measures used in the administration of medications to the mentally ill:

1. _____
2. _____
3. _____
4. _____
5. _____

DIRECTIONS: Select the *best* response. (Answers appear in the Appendix.)

1 In general, psychotropic agents may be described *most* accurately as having which one of the following actions?
   a Curing mental illness.
   b Alleviating depression.
   c Normalizing behavior.
   d Reducing anxiety.

2 Which one of the following symptoms reflects endocrine changes that sometimes occur with the use of antipsychotic drugs?
   a Dry mouth.
   b Weight gain.
   c Constipation.
   d Hypotension.

3 In response to orthostatic hypotension, the nurse can be *most* helpful to the client by taking which one of the following actions?
   a Staying with the client until the hypotensive episode passes.
   b Teaching the client to dangle his legs briefly before standing.
   c Encouraging the client to walk slowly.
   d Checking the client's blood pressure at regular intervals.

4 The development of extrapyramidal reactions can be prevented/treated through the use of which one of the following medications?
   a Artane (trihexyphenidyl).
   b Aventyl (nortriptyline).
   c Haldol (haloperidol).
   d Serax (oxazepam).

5 Akathisia is identifiable by which one of the following symptoms?
   a Masklike facies.   c Restlessness.
   b Carpopedal spasm.   d Lethargy.

6 The nurse might suspect that a client on Thorazine (chlorpromazine) was developing agranulocytosis if the client complained of:
   a Blurred vision.   c Tremor.
   b Sore throat.   d Dizziness.

7 Valium (diazepam) is not commonly used in the treatment of schizophrenia primarily because it:

   a Cannot be given in sufficient amounts to be effective.

   b Does not have an antipsychotic action.

   c Has the potential for creating physical and emotional dependence.

   d Produces an undesirable sedative action.

8 Miltown and Equanil are both trade names for which one of the following generic drugs?

   a Diazepam.   **c** Flurazepam.

   b Chlordiazepoxide.   **d** Meprobamate.

9 If a client on an antianxiety medication develops a paradoxical response, the nurse should take which one of the following actions *immediately?*

   a Withhold the drug and notify the physician.

   b Administer an antiallergic medication.

   c Put the client to bed in a dark room.

   d Institute dietary restrictions.

10 Which one of the following antidepressants is classified as a MAO inhibitor?

   a Tofranil (imipramine).   **c** Sinequan (doxepin).

   b Elavil (amitriptyline).   **d** Niamid (nialamide).

11 *All but which one* of the following side or adverse effects is common to both MAOs and tricyclics?

   a Dry mouth.

   b Urinary retention.

   c Hypertensive crisis.

   d Postural hypotension.

12 Which of the following lunch menus would be preferred for a person taking Marplan (isocarboxazid)?

   a Cheese omelet, apple pie, black coffee.

   b Spaghetti and meatballs, chocolate pudding, milk.

   c Hamburger on a bun, french fries, diet soda.

   d Chopped chicken liver on rye bread, toss salad, tea.

13 Lithium toxicity can *best* be prevented by monitoring which one of the following?

   a Urine for excretion of the drug.

   b Blood for elevated white count.

   c Blood pressure for signs of hypertension.

   d Blood for drug levels.

14 Symptoms of lithium toxicity include which one of the following?

   a Ocular changes.   **c** Pseudoparkinsonism.

   b Abdominal cramps.   **d** Confusion.

15 Which one of the following nursing actions is *most* specific to the administration of medications to mentally ill clients?

   a Observing clients for signs of drug toxicity.

   b Keeping the medication tray inaccessible to clients.

   c Orienting clients to the action of the medications.

   d Monitoring clients' physiological response to drugs.

the therapeutic environment

INTRODUCTION

"It is generally believed that the environment in which the mentally ill person is treated is a major factor in enhancing or impeding the therapeutic effects of other treatment modalities. It is further believed by some that the environment itself has therapeutic potential."* Consequently, the trend in recent years has been to treat mentally ill persons in their communities, maintaining them either in their homes or in settings with a homelike atmosphere and at the same time, providing them with medications, group activities, and opportunities for socialization. However, community-based care is not suitable for all clients. Some persons require hospitalization for varying lengths of time.

To be therapeutic, a hospital environment must meet certain short-term goals (including helping a person develop a sense of worth and improving a person's ability to trust and relate) and, finally, a long-term goal (to promote a person's return to the community at large as a more effectively functioning member of society). For these goals to be realized, the environment in which the individual is cared for needs to be therapeutic.

The environment may be described as having two distinct, yet interrelated parts, that is, the physical environment and the emotional or interpersonal environment. The physical environment includes such elements as the size and temperature of the area and the light, sound, and furnishings in the area. The emotional or interpersonal environment, on the other hand, refers to the emotional tone set by the staff, the nature of interpersonal relationships between staff and clients, the degree of limit setting, and the manipulation of elements in the physical environment to promote security and relatedness among the residents.

The nurse assumes a major role in influencing the therapeutic potential of the hospital environment. Although nurses do not generally paint hospital walls, they can be influential in color se-

*From Taylor, C.M.: Mereness' essentials of psychiatric nursing, ed. 12, St. Louis, 1986, The C.V. Mosby Co., Chapter 11.

lection. Similarly, the nurse can do much to enhance the physical climate through the appropriate use of light, the regulation of heat, promotion of adequate ventilation, the appropriate use of music, art, books, games, magazines, calendars, clocks, and bulletin boards listing schedules, therapy groups, client privileges, etc. However, the nurse's greatest impact is probably on the emotional or interpersonal climate. A nurse who is sensitive, caring, and responsive to the needs of clients sets a tone for a therapeutic emotional climate and serves as a role model for other staff members. Rules and regulations also influence the emotional climate. It is important that rules give sufficient structure to provide a sense of security without rigidity and inflexibility that might interfere with opportunities for decision-making. Nurses need to be aware that many clients' dysfunctional behaviors interfere with relatedness, and the staff should be available to interact with clients and to promote socialization. Nurses need to manipulate elements in the physical environment in ways conducive to relatedness, such as moving chairs lined up in rows into position for face-to-face interactions. Watching television, for example, can be a very effective and socially acceptable way for clients to withdraw and avoid relating and, to that extent, may be seen as an element in the physical environment that has a negative effect on the emotional climate. However, a staff-led group discussion following a television viewing can promote interaction and enhance the emotional climate.

Recognizing the importance of the physical and emotional climate, the challenge to nurses and other health care workers in psychiatric inpatient settings is to promote the therapeutic potential of the hospital environment for those persons requiring hospitalization. The purpose of this chapter is to assess the hospital environment and to reflect on the therapeutic potential of the physical and emotional climate.

1. To differentiate between the physical environment and the emotional environment.
2. To evaluate elements in the physical and emotional environment as either therapeutic or nontherapeutic.
3. To revise nontherapeutic elements in the environment.
4. To manipulate elements in the physical environment in a way that enhances the therapeutic potential of the emotional environment.
5. To list the major goals of a therapeutic community.

1 In the following situation 20 physical and emotional elements in the hospital environment have been italicized and numbered. Complete the following exercises in the space provided.

   a Identify whether or not the element described best illustrates the physical or emotional environments by placing a check in the box in the appropriate column.

   b Evaluate whether or not the element described is either therapeutic or nontherapeutic and revise all nontherapeutic elements by briefly describing how each element could be altered to make it more therapeutic. An example has been provided to help you get started.

	Environmental elements		
Situation	**Physical**	**Emotional**	**Evaluation/ revision**

The student nurses arrived for their first clinical day on a psychiatric ward. Instructor and students proceeded down ① *the long drab corridor, devoid of any pictures or other decorations.* ② *There were several two and three bedrooms opening off the hall, each equipped with individual lockers, bedside tables, and colorful drapes on the windows and matching spreads on the beds. The rooms appeared clean.* ③ *Otherwise the rooms were barren.* There were no personal belongings in evidence. At the end of the corridor were two large rooms. ④ *One was a dormitory with 20 beds, 10 beds lined up on each wall. The beds were close together and there were no separating tables between them.* The other large room, the "dayroom", appeared to be a combination sitting and activity room. ⑤ *A Ping-Pong table stood in the center of the room; an old upright piano stood against one wall. Several small tables were placed around the room. A television set was turned on and seemed to be a focal point of interest as several people were seated in chairs facing it.* ⑥ *Most of the other people in the room seemed unaware of what was going on, staring into space and not talking to each other. Several people seemed to be sleeping.* At the appearance of the student group, several clients greeted them and invited them to sit down. One client asked a student to play Ping-Pong. ⑦ *The students moved around the room and oriented the clients as to who they were and what they were doing there.* A number of people who had seemed particularly withdrawn and uninvolved initially grew more alert and responsive as the students interacted with them. ⑧ *Most of the clients seemed to be dressed in their own clothes rather than hospital garb.* After the brief interaction, the group promised to return in a little while and then continued their tour of the ward. ⑨ *The students were particularly surprised to see the laundry room, equipped with a washer and a drier.* ⑩ *A client was doing his laundry with the help of a male staff member. The staff member communicated genuine interest and concern in the client he was helping.* ⑪ *All the other members of the staff seemed to be involved in a meeting in the nurses' station. Although the staff could observe most areas from the glassed-in nurses' station, the students noted that there was almost no one out on the ward interacting with clients.* ⑫ *One client knocked on the station door and asked for a cigarette.* He was reminded that cigarettes had been given out after the administration of medications and that they would be given out again after the next meal. Following the tour of the ward, ⑬ *the students returned to the dayroom as they had promised and spent the balance of their clinical day visiting with different people.* ⑭ *At the end of the experience the group bid everyone good-bye and told them when they would be returning.* ⑮ *As the students left the area, two staff members entered the day room and called five or six persons by name to come for art therapy.* In their postclinical conference the students reviewed their experiences, shared their feelings, and described several other observations they had made about the environment including: ⑯*although there were several tables in the room, the only available chairs were too low to use the tables effectively;* ⑰ *the bathroom smelled of urine, the sinks were dirty, and several of the toilet stalls lacked doors;* ⑱ *the dining room was a large area equipped with long tables seating 20 to 22 persons; it seemed to be serving several wards;* ⑲ *staff were responsive and seemed pleased to have students on the ward;* ⑳ *an outdated schedule of events was taped to one wall.* The balance of the student discussion focused on the effect these physical and emotional elements had on the therapeutic nature of the environment as well as the students' role in enhancing the therapeutic potential of both the physical and emotional climates.

Environmental elements checkboxes:

Item	Physical	Emotional
①	☑	☐
②	☐	☐
③	☐	☐
④	☐	☐
⑤	☐	☐
⑥	☐	☐
⑦	☐	☐
⑧	☐	☐
⑨	☐	☐
⑩	☐	☐
⑪	☐	☐
⑫	☐	☐
⑬	☐	☐
⑭	☐	☐
⑮	☐	☐
⑯	☐	☐
⑰	☐	☐
⑱	☐	☐
⑲	☐	☐
⑳	☐	☐

Evaluation/revision:

① Nontherapeutic: use cheerful color on walls; display art work.

2 Study the following layout of the "dayroom," focusing on the physical elements in the environment. Then in the space below describe how 6 physical elements could be utilized to enhance the emotional climate.

1. _____

_____

2. _____

_____

3. _____

_____

4. _____

_____

5. _____

_____

6. _____

3 List at least 5 major goals of a therapeutic community.

1. _____

2. _____

3. _____

4. _____

5. _____

DIRECTIONS: Select the *best* response. (Answers appear in the Appendix.)

1 Historically, which one of the following factors was *most* influential in terminating the moral treatment approach to psychiatric care?

  a Increased numbers of immigrants to the United States following the Civil War.

  b Decreased public concern with morality after the Victorian Era.

  c Economic decline during the Depression in the United States.

  d Readjustment problems experienced by U.S. servicemen after World War II.

2 Dr. Maxwell Jones' book entitled *Social Psychiatry* emphasized which one of the following treatment modalities?

  a Psychotropic medications. **c** Custodial care.

  b Individual psychotherapy. **d** Group living.

3 A therapeutic environment is characterized as one that:

  a Meets all of a client's physical and emotional needs.

  b Requires that a client participate in decision-making.

  c Provides a client with optimum safety from injury.

  d All of the above.

4 Which one of the following is the *most* important environmental factor in helping clients achieve improved emotional health?

  a Availability of activities. **c** Interpersonal climate.

  b Presence of nursing staff. **d** Physical layout.

5 Which of the following examples of limit-setting is the *least* appropriate?

  a Expecting that all clients attend their program of activities each day.

  b Restricting sexual activities between all clients.

  c Requiring that all clients be bathed and dressed and attend breakfast.

  d Restricting smoking for all clients after one client is found to have matches illegally.

6 Which of the following is conducive to a therapeutic environment?

  a Provisions for privacy.

  b Availability of planned activities.

c Opportunities for social interaction.

d All of the above.

7 The primary reason for encouraging clients to wear their own clothing rather than hospital garb is to:

a Reduce the economic strain on the hospital.

b Provide opportunities for problem solving.

c Individualize the care of clients.

d Brighten the environment with cheerful colors.

8 The therapeutic community is an attempt to introduce democracy into the hospital setting. Which one of the following approaches taken by the staff *best* reflects this philosophy?

a Meeting the client's needs for him.

b Encouraging clients to help plan their care.

c Continuing to make important decisions for clients.

d Setting up ward policies to regulate client behavior.

9 The network of communication in a therapeutic community primarily refers to which one of the following?

a Use of therapeutic communication skills in a nurse-client relationship.

b Open channels of communication between all staff and clients on the unit.

c Respect for chain of hierarchical communication between ward staff and hospital administrators.

d Sharing of feelings and experiences at weekly community meetings.

10 The nurse needs to take an active, responsible role on units subscribing to the concept of the therapeutic community primarily because:

a Nurses are uniquely qualified to meet clients' physical and emotional needs.

b With the discarding of many rules, care needs to be more individualized.

c Clients turn more to nurses in an environment that expects their participation.

d Other staff members are usually resistant and neglect their responsibilities.

11 The emotional environment is to supportive efforts to explore new patterns of behavior in relating as the physical environment is to:

    a Individualized care.   **c** Socialization.

    b Decision-making.   **d** Ward layout.

12 Which one of the following *fails* to reflect full utilization of elements in the physical environment to enhance the emotional climate?

    a Stocking the ward bookcase with reading materials and games.

    b Encouraging a sing along around the ward piano.

    c Referring to the clock when orienting clients to scheduled activities.

    d Moving chairs in a circle for a group discussion.

chapter 12

the nursing process

"Although the terms used to describe the nursing process vary, the process is always an adaptation of the problem-solving technique and involves the phases of assessing, diagnosing, planning, implementing, and evaluating."*

In the assessment phase the nurse collects pertinent information about the client, referring to family and friends of the client, the client's current and previous medical records, other health care workers, and relevant textbooks. In addition, the nurse utilizes observation and interviewing skills to identify recurring themes in the data. These recurring themes are basic to the next step in the nursing process, the diagnostic phase. In this phase the nurse makes a statement that should accomplish two things. First, the statement needs to define the theme reflected through the client's behavioral adaptation. Second, the statement should give a tentative explanation of the stressor affecting the client's adaptation. The nursing diagnosis is a necessary preliminary to the next phase of the nursing process, the planning phase. In the planning phase the nurse develops a course of nursing action. A nursing goal or objective is stated, the rationale for the goal is identified, nursing actions through which the goal will be accomplished are outlined, and the anticipated results, or outcome criteria, are described. Implementation is the fourth phase of the nursing process. In this phase the nurse carries out the nursing actions set forth in the plan. Finally, the fifth phase of the nursing process is evaluation. Although identified as the final phase, the steps involved in evaluation are often carried out simultaneously with other phases of the nursing process. In evaluation the nurse refers to the anticipated results described in the planning phase and notes how closely the actual results of care match the anticipated results. Generally, the closer the match, the more effective is the care. Also in the phase of evaluation are the steps of revi-

*From Taylor, C.M.: Mereness' essentials of psychiatric nursing, ed. 12, St. Louis, 1986, The C.V. Mosby Co., Chapter 12.

sion of care and self-assessment. Having critically appraised the care as either effective or ineffective, the nurse is now in a position to identify the actions taken that should be continued and the ones that should be revised. Similarly, in self-assessment the nurse reflects on feelings, beliefs, and attitudes and, sometimes with the help of peers, supervisors, or colleagues, alters responses that appear not to have been helpful.

In conclusion the nursing process is an essential tool used to provide a logical and sequential approach to the identification of client needs, the development of goal-directed activities, the implementation of a course of action, and the critical appraisal of the effectiveness of care. The purpose of this chapter is to apply the steps of the nursing process to the care of persons with emotional problems.

OBJECTIVES

1. To list the goals of each of the five phases of the nursing process and a nursing action that exemplifies each goal.
2. To utilize selected phases of the nursing process in hypothetical client situations.
3. To identify the roles of the nurse as reflected through nursing actions.

1 In the grid below list the goals or purposes of each of the 5 phases of the nursing process and give an example of a nursing action to illustrate each one. The first one has been filled in to help you get started.

Phases of the nursing process	Purpose (goals)	Examples of nursing action
1. Assessment	a. To collect data	Use observation skills, involving all the senses, to note client's behavior.
	b.	
	c.	
2. Diagnostic	d.	
3. Planning	e.	
4. Implementation	f.	
5. Evaluation	g.	
	h.	
	i.	

2 Apply the steps of the nursing process to the following situation:

SITUATION: An elderly white woman was admitted to the hospital for observation after an accident in which she was struck by a car while crossing the street against the light. At the time of admission she was awake but did not know her name or the names of any family or friends. She could not recall her address, the date, or the name of the city she was in. Her speech was slurred. Her clothing was disheveled, smelling strongly of urine. Her hair was matted and sour smelling, and her body was crusted with dirt and feces. There was evidence of old bruises. Her skin was scaly and dry to the touch. Through a Medic Alert band she was wearing on her wrist, the woman's identity was determined.

The client is a 78-year-old woman named Jennie Brown. It was learned that she had a history of hypertension and had been hospitalized the previous year with a cerebrovascular accident. At the time of her discharge from the hospital she was being maintained on anticoagulant therapy. Miss Brown's previous medical records were obtained.

The history revealed that Miss Brown is a retired schoolteacher who lives alone in a single room at a boardinghouse. Her family consists of a married younger sister who lives in another city. She has not seen her sister in many years.

Miss Brown's neighbors were contacted by hospital personnel. They seemed genuinely concerned about her condition and expressed feelings of helplessness about how to assist her. They revealed that in the past 6 months she had seemed confused. They also described how she spent more and more time alone and had been leaving the boardinghouse for days at a time without telling anyone her whereabouts. On several occasions when she failed to return, the police had been notified and were instrumental in returning her home. The local police validated these reports. They also added that Miss Brown was usually found wandering in the streets, sleeping in alleys with stray dogs, and eating out of garbage cans.

a List 5 sources of assessment data in this situation.

1. _____

2. _____

3. _____

4. _____

5. _____

b A tool used by the nurse in assessment is observation. It is a skill by which the nurse takes in information about the client, using multiple senses. Listed below are 10 observations made regarding Miss Brown's general condition at the time of the current admission and the senses used to gather the data. Categorize each observation in terms of the senses used to gather the data by checking the boxes in the appropriate columns. The first one has been filled in to help you get started.

Observations	Senses			
	Seeing	Hearing	Smelling	Touching
1. Elderly white woman.	☑	☐	☐	☐
2. "My name? My name? I don't remember."	☐	☐	☐	☐
3. Disheveled clothing.	☐	☐	☐	☐
4. Skin dry and scaly.	☐	☐	☐	☐
5. Odor of urine.	☐	☐	☐	☐
6. "I don't know where I live."	☐	☐	☐	☐
7. Old bruises on the body.	☐	☐	☐	☐
8. Matted and tangled hair.	☐	☐	☐	☐
9. Slurred speech.	☐	☐	☐	☐
10. Sour-smelling hair.	☐	☐	☐	☐

c As Miss Brown began to recuperate, the nurse was able to interview her. List in the space below 4 goals of an interview.

1. _____

2. _____

3. _____

4. _____

d Interviews are generally structured, and the nurse used direct questions when interviewing Miss Brown. Listed below are 10 approaches that need revision. Using the spaces provided, revise each one into a direct question that could be appropriately used in Miss Brown's interview. The first one has been filled in to help you get started.

Approach	Revision
1. "Where would you like to begin?"	"What do you remember about your accident?"
2. "You are frowning."	
3. "You say you have a pain?"	
4. "Tell me about your usual diet."	
5. "I understand you have a daughter."	
6. "Tell me about your sleeping patterns."	
7. "You seem upset."	
8. "I notice you have some bruises on your arms."	
9. "I met some of your neighbors. They seem very helpful."	
10. "Have you any feelings about returning to the boardinghouse?"	

e In caring for Miss Brown the nurse used a variety of nursing actions and nursing roles. Listed on p. 127 are 15 nursing actions and 7 nursing roles. Categorize each action in terms of the nursing roles involved in carrying it out by checking the boxes in the appropriate columns. Keep in mind that more than one role may be involved in a nursing action. The first one has been entered to help you get started. (See Chapter 2 for a review of nursing roles.)

Nursing actions	Nursing roles						
	Technical role	Creator of therapeutic environment	Socializing agent	Teacher	Mother surrogate	Nurse therapist	Counselor
1. Communicates acceptance, honesty, and sincerity.	☐	☑	☐	☐	☐	☐	☐
2. Promotes interaction between Miss Brown and others.	☐	☐	☐	☐	☐	☐	☐
3. Listens to Miss Brown in a positive, empathic way.	☐	☐	☐	☐	☐	☐	☐
4. Sets limits when Miss Brown tries to get out of bed alone.	☐	☐	☐	☐	☐	☐	☐
5. Performs follow-up physical assessment with client.	☐	☐	☐	☐	☐	☐	☐
6. Administers vitamins and antihypertensive medications to Miss Brown.	☐	☐	☐	☐	☐	☐	☐
7. Encourages Miss Brown to think through her problems.	☐	☐	☐	☐	☐	☐	☐
8. Conveys realistic reassurance by staying with Miss Brown when she is upset.	☐	☐	☐	☐	☐	☐	☐
9. Introduces Miss Brown to another client.	☐	☐	☐	☐	☐	☐	☐
10. Records observations and care given in client's chart.	☐	☐	☐	☐	☐	☐	☐
11. Allows client to keep some personal belongings brought in by neighbors.	☐	☐	☐	☐	☐	☐	☐
12. Feeds and bathes Miss Brown when she is confused.	☐	☐	☐	☐	☐	☐	☐
13. Demonstrates socially acceptable behaviors to client.	☐	☐	☐	☐	☐	☐	☐
14. Helps Miss Brown dress appropriately.	☐	☐	☐	☐	☐	☐	☐
15. Works collaboratively with health team in planning, implementing, and evaluating Miss Brown's care.	☐	☐	☐	☐	☐	☐	☐

3 Using the descriptive data that has been gathered through the assessment phase of the nursing process, state an appropriate nursing diagnosis and develop a plan for nursing intervention by identifying a nursing goal, rationale relevant to the goal, several nursing actions, and anticipated results for each of the following situations.

    a SITUATION: The student nurse approached the male patient sitting alone in the corner of the dayroom. She had learned from staff that his name was "Joe." She had been discouraged from seeking him out, having been told, "He won't talk to you. Don't waste your efforts on him. He's been here 2 weeks and hasn't said a word in all that time." In spite of these comments, the student greeted Joe by name and sat down beside him. She introduced herself and waited in silence for him to respond. He said nothing, but after a few minutes he raised his eyes and cast side glances at the student.

Nursing diagnosis:

Nursing goal	Rationale	Nursing actions	Anticipated results

b SITUATION: A student nurse expressed interest in a young black woman called Billie Sue. The client could be observed walking in the hallway, talking to other clients in a loud, booming voice. At times she paused, posed in karate fashion, and made menacing gestures at other people. The instructor shared some information from Billie Sue's chart with the student. Billie Sue had been an abused child, and in the first 6 years of her life, she had been in and out of hospitals for medical/surgical treatments of burns, fractures, and concussions, all allegedly occurring from "accidents." When she was 6-years-old, she was placed in the first of a series of foster homes. She never stayed long in any one place because she bullied and fought with the other children in the homes. She was large for her age, strong, and loud, and was generally avoided by others. At the age of 10 she killed another child with a baseball bat and was subsequently placed in a residential treatment center. When she reached adult status, she was transferred to an adult psychiatric center. On her chart she was further described as "explosive and potentially dangerous to others."

Nursing diagnosis:

Nursing goal	Rationale	Nursing actions	Anticipated results

DIRECTIONS: Select the *best* response. (Answers appear in the Appendix.)

1 The need for an organized, efficient approach to client care became *most* apparent as a result of the:
   a Nursing shortage before, during, and after World War II.
   b Development of nursing specialties in the twentieth century.
   c Inadequate state of nursing education prior to World War I.
   d Increasing number of dependent nursing functions in the nineteenth century.

2 Which of the following resulted from the development of the nursing care plan?
   a Standardized care among nurses.
   b Facilitated communication between nurses.
   c Rendered nursing care more effective.
   d All of the above.

3 In the assessment phase of the nursing process which one of the following sources of data is generally *most* significant?
   a Client.   c Client's family.
   b Medical records.   d Relevant textbooks.

4 When the nurse is to conduct an interview for the purpose of gathering specific information, which one of the following takes priority?
   a Identifying specific goals to be accomplished in the interview.
   b Orienting the client as to the purpose of the interview.
   c Providing a comfortable setting in which to conduct the interview.
   d Determining the client's perception of his problems.

5 *All but which one* of the following activities are involved in the assessment phase of the nursing process?
   a Observing behavior.
   b Carrying out nursing care.
   c Analyzing data.
   d Validating observations.

6 Which one of the following examples *best* illustrates a direct approach used in interviewing a client?
   a "Were you a healthy child?"
   b "Can you tell me about yourself?"

    c "What has happened to upset you?"

    d "You have a pain in your side?"

7 Which one of the following is the *best* statement of a nursing diagnosis?

    a The client is experiencing anxiety due to increased insecurity.

    b The client needs to be free from overwhelming amounts of anxiety.

    c The client's anxiety is related to interpersonal transmission and contagion.

    d The client's anxiety is caused by unconscious intrapsychic conflicts.

8 A nursing diagnosis should do *all but which one* of the following?

    a Define a theme of the client's adaptation.

    b Explain the stressor eliciting the client's adaptation.

    c Synthesize all available assessment data.

    d Identify the definitive cause of the client's adaptation.

9 The planning phase of the nursing process includes statements concerning:

    a Nursing diagnosis, nursing objectives, outcome criteria, and observational data.

    b Nursing goals, rationale, projected nursing actions, and anticipated results.

    c Nursing objectives, explanations for nursing diagnosis, outcome criteria, and critical appraisal.

    d Nursing goals, rationale, anticipated results, and analytical speculations.

10 Which one of the following immediately *proceeds* the phase of implementation?

    a Planning phase.

    b Evaluation phase.

    c Assessment phase.

    d Diagnostic phase.

11 Which one of the following is the *best* example of an outcome criteria? Within 6 weeks the client will be:

    a Discharged symptom free.

    b Experiencing an increase in self-esteem.

    c Assuming increased responsibility for his own grooming.

    d More aware of the underlying reasons for his behavior.

12 In the implementation phase of the nursing process the nurse *most* specifically:

   a Observes the client for anticipated results of care.

   b Functions in a variety of nursing roles.

   c Evaluates his or her own responses to the client.

   d Utilizes thoughtful interviewing techniques.

13 Nurses reflect on their own feelings, beliefs, attitudes, and behavioral responses to clients *primarily* during:

   a Assessment.   **c** Intervention.

   b Planning.   **d** Evaluation.

14 Although a discrete phase in the nursing process, which one of the following phases must also overlap with *all the other phases* if it is to be fully effective?

   a Assessment.   **c** Implementation.

   b Planning.   **d** Evaluation.

15 In the evaluation phase of the nursing process which one of the following steps generally occurs *last?*

   a Reviewing assessment data and the nursing diagnosis.

   b Studying the nursing care outlined in the nursing plan.

   c Comparing anticipated results of care with actual results of care.

   d Revising or continuing the plan of care as necessary.

section III word games

1 Crosshatch

DIRECTIONS: Fit the words listed below into the proper boxes. The words read left to right or top to bottom, one letter per box. NURSING has been entered to give you a starting point. (Solution appears in the Appendix.)

4 letters
CARE
DATA
FEAR
HOPE
MAOS
PLAY
ROLE

5 letters
CHART
DRUGS
EDEMA
GOALS
NURSE
PLANS
QUIDE
TOOLS

6 letters
ACTION
AMOUNT
ASSESS
ATAXIA
CLICHE
CLIENT
COPING
DOSAGE
EFFECT
ELAVIL
GROWTH
JOHARI
NARDIL
PHASES
RELATE
THEMES

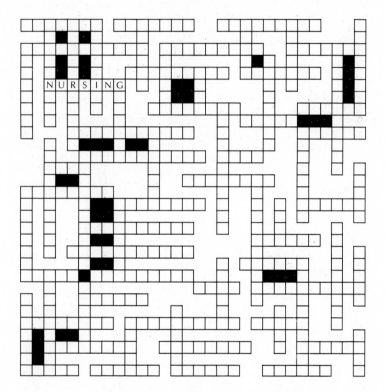

7 letters
BELIEFS
GENERIC
MARPLAN
√ NURSING
OPTIMUM
PURPOSE
SILENCE
TEACHER
TESTING

8 letters
AKINESIA
BEHAVIOR
DYSTONIA
FEELINGS
FOCUSING
JAUNDICE
MELLARIL
PLANNING
REVISION
SURPRISE
SYMPTOMS
TARACTAN
TOFRANIL

9 letters
ALLEVIATE
ATTITUDES
COUNSELOR
INTERVIEW
LAG PERIOD
LISTENING
RATIONALE

10 letters
ACCEPTANCE
OBJECTIVES
PERSUASION
PHILOSOPHY
PRINCIPLES
REFLECTION

11 letters
DISAPPROVAL
EXPLORATION
INFORMATION
MAINTENANCE
OBSERVATION
ORIENTATION
PSYCHIATRIC
TERMINATION

2 Fill-in: Nursing process

DIRECTIONS: Using the definitions provided, fill in the blanks in the word list with selected content related to the nursing process. (Solution appears in the Appendix.)

Definitions	Word list
A Third phase of the nursing process	_ _ _ <u>N</u> _ _ _ _
B Critical assessment of care	_ _ _ _ <u>U</u> _ _ _ _ _
C Skill used to gather data	_ _ _ _ <u>R</u> _ _ _ _ _ _
D Phase of data collection	_ _ _ _ <u>S</u> _ _ _ _
E Check out perceptions with others	_ _ _ <u>I</u> _ _ _ _
F Major source of assessment data	_ _ _ _ <u>N</u> _
G Nursing objectives	<u>G</u> _ _ _ _
H Nursing diagnosis	_ _ <u>P</u> _ _ _ _ _ _ _
I Implementation	_ _ _ _ <u>R</u> _ _ _ _ _ _ _
J Nursing activities	_ _ _ _ <u>O</u> _ _
K Client's hospital record	<u>C</u> _ _ _ _
L Component of nursing diagnosis	_ _ _ _ <u>E</u>
M Final step in evaluation	_ _ _ _ <u>S</u> _ _ _
N Outcome criteria	_ _ <u>S</u> _ _ _ _

3 Quote-a-crostic

DIRECTIONS: Using cues on the left, fill in the words in the list on the right. Transfer each letter in the word list to the corresponding numbered square in the puzzle grid. Shaded squares in the grid represent the end of a word. Work back and forth between grid and word list until both are completed. (Note the letters and consecutive numbers that have been entered in the grid to help in location of words.) The completed grid will be a quotation relevant to Section III of the text. The source of the quote and its author are spelled out in the boxed-in letters in the word list. One word in the list has been filled in to help you get started. (Solution appears in the Appendix.)

Cues

A Type of communication

B Drug dosage (two words)

C Drug _____

D Explored through self-awareness

E Nursing function: instruct

Word list

A: — — [11] — — — — — —
29 48 11 95 82 100 121 113 43

B: — — —   — — — [126] — —
107 70 56   20 37 7 126 91 118

C: — — — [109] — — —
8 89 98 109 67 112 80

D: — — — — — — [119]
130 61 97 10 73 108 119

E: — [31] — — —
86 31 13 84 53

1 F		2 F	3 R	4 N	5 G E		6 O	7 B		8 C	9 P	10 D
11 A	12 K		13 E	14 F	15 L	16 M	17 G T		18 O	19 N	20 B	21 J
	22 F	23 L	24 I	25 P		26 F	27 R		28 M	29 A		30 J
31 E	32 L	33 F	34 P	35 G E	36 M		37 B	38 H	39 L	40 M	41 N	
42 K		43 A	44 P	45 F	46 M		47 L	48 A		49 R	50 O	51 I
52 P	53 E		54 M	55 K	56 B	57 P	58 F		59 L	60 J	61 D	62 G S
	63 K	64 L	65 R		66 O	67 C	68 Q	69 H	70 B		71 H	72 J
73 D		74 R	75 I	76 Q		77 H	78 G H	79 J	80 C		81 O	82 A
83 J	84 E	85 K		86 E	87 N		88 M	89 C	90 P	91 B	92 I	93 K
		94 O	95 A	96 L		97 D	98 C	99 K	100 A	101 H	102 G E	103 O
	104 H		105 F	106 H	107 B		108 D	109 C	110 Q	111 F		112 C
113 A	114 M	115 K	116 F	117 O	118 B	119 D		120 K	121 A	122 F	123 H	124 P
	125 O	126 B	127 J	128 M	129 F		130 D	131 N	132 R	133 I	134 H	135 F

Cues	Word list

Cues

F Technique used in the nursing process (two words)

G To suffer violent internal excitement

H Expression of unconscious emotional conflicts through behavior (two words)

I Psychotropic _____

J Objective and insightful awareness of feelings of another

K Side effect of antipsychotic agents

L Nurse-client relationship (three words)

M (See Cue D)

N Nonverbal act of aggression

O Type of client treated with antipsychotic agents

P Point of view that sees the individual as more than a mere aggregate of parts

Q Tool used to communicate with a child

R Johari _____

Word list

F: ___ 33 | ___ 58 | ___ 122 | ___ 14 | 2 | ___ 116 | ___ 111
___ 135 | ___ 26 | ___ 105 | ___ 45 | 1 | ___ 129 | 22

G: S 62 | E 35 | E 102 | T 17 | H 78 | E 5

H: ___ 104 | ___ 69 | ___ 71 | ___ 38 | ___ 101 | 134 | ___ 106 | ___ 123 | 77

I: ___ 75 | 92 | ___ 24 | ___ 133 | ___ 51

J: ___ 79 | ___ 127 | ___ 30 | ___ 83 | ___ 21 | ___ 72 | 60

K: ___ 99 | ___ 12 | ___ 120 | ___ 85 | ___ 55 | ___ 115 | ___ 93 | ___ 42 | 63

L: ___ 15 | 64 | ___ 59 | - | ___ 47 | ___ 32 | - | ___ 23 | ___ 39 | 96

M: ___ 128 | ___ 114 | ___ 54 | ___ 28 | ___ 88 | ___ 16 | 40 | ___ 46 | ___ 36

N: ___ 41 | ___ 19 | ___ 87 | ___ 4 | 131

O: ___ 66 | ___ 94 | ___ 6 | ___ 125 | ___ 103 | 81 | ___ 50 | ___ 18 | ___ 117

P: ___ 9 | ___ 44 | ___ 34 | ___ 90 | 25 | 124 | ___ 57 | ___ 52

Q: ___ 68 | 110 | ___ 76

R: ___ 49 | ___ 132 | 27 | ___ 65 | 3 | ___ 74

section IV

consumers of psychiatric nursing

chapter 13

adults with thought disturbances

INTRODUCTION

Adults with thought disturbances are generally given the medical diagnosis of schizophrenia. "Schizophrenia is classified as a functional psychosis. This term is used to describe those mental illnesses in which the person's perception of reality is severely distorted due to factors other than demonstrable organic disease or intellectual deficit. . . . The symptoms of schizophrenia are all-pervasive, affecting all aspects of the individual's existence."* Difficulties with communicating and relating, expressing feelings, problem solving, and, most specifically, perceiving reality, are commonly seen in the person experiencing a thought disturbance and diagnosed as schizophrenic.

The textbook acknowledges that genetic and biochemical factors may indeed contribute to the development of this severe form of mental illness. However, the text's major emphasis is on the development of thought disturbances in adults associated with highly unsatisfactory and anxiety-laden interpersonal relationships early in life, coupled with difficulties experienced in mastering the developmental tasks.

In review the interpersonal theory of psychiatry proposes that persons with thought disturbances have predominantly bad-me/not-me self-concepts resulting from combinations of negative reflected appraisals, excessive anxiety, and unmet needs. Patterns of interaction between an individual and his or her significant other in the early years of the individual's development were often characterized by double-bind communication. In double-bind communication two contradictory messages are relayed simultaneously by the significant other, contributing to anxiety and confusion in the individual. Repetitive experiences of this type with other significant persons throughout the formative years interfere with the development of a healthy self-concept and reenforce the early learning that relating is painful and best avoided.

*From Taylor, C.M.: Mereness' essentials of psychiatric nursing, ed. 12, St. Louis, 1986, The C.V. Mosby Co., Chapter 13.

The cultural theory of development states that an individual proceeds through eight periods of life. Associated with each period is a culturally determined task that is identified as a challenge to be met and mastered. According to the cultural theory, a person with a thought disturbance experiences traumas in infancy that interfere with the successful mastery of the first developmental task of trust. Inconsistently met needs, unpredictability, covert and overt expressions of indifference, and lack of love from parenting figures contribute to the negative outcome of mistrust and lay the foundation for nontrusting relationships with others in subsequent years. In addition, because each age builds on earlier ages, difficulty mastering trust in infancy interferes with the mastery of subsequent tasks in later stages of life if the individual continues to be exposed to negative life experiences.

Both the interpersonal and cultural theories stress that persons with thought disturbances have experienced personality disruption during infancy. Because these individuals are essentially dependent at this time, they are most vulnerable and lack the tools with which to deal effectively with painful and anxiety-producing situations. If these anxiety-producing situations continue to predominate during the developmental years, personality development will be further impaired. Subsequent stressors in adolescence and adulthood can be overwhelming and precipitate a profound psychotic response in the form of a thought disturbance as the individual tries to cope ineffectively with the situation.

The purpose of this chapter is to provide the student with an opportunity to apply these two theoretical frameworks and the steps of the nursing process to the care of adults with thought disturbances.

OBJECTIVES

1. To categorize behaviors exhibited by adults with thought disturbances according to the five subtypes of schizophrenia.
2. To analyze behaviors using interpersonal and cultural theories.
3. To apply selected steps of the nursing process to clinical situations.

EXERCISES

1 People with thought disturbances are given a medical diagnosis of schizophrenia. In addition, they are further classified according to subtypes, depending on the predominant behavioral patterns exhibited. The following exercise lists 10 behaviors commonly observed in schizophrenic persons and the 5 subtypes of schizophrenia. Read and categorize each behavior, placing a check in the box in the appropriate column. The first one has been entered to help you get started.

Behaviors	Subtypes of schizophrenia				
	Disorganized	Catatonic	Paranoid	Chronic undiff.	Residual
1. Soiling self (regression).	☑	☐	☐	☐	☐
2. Maintaining motionless state.	☐	☐	☐	☐	☐
3. Responding with bursts of overactivity.	☐	☐	☐	☐	☐
4. Accusing others falsely.	☐	☐	☐	☐	☐
5. Exhibiting flat, blunt affect.	☐	☐	☐	☐	☐
6. Isolating self from others, but no overt psychotic signs.	☐	☐	☐	☐	☐
7. Masturbating openly.	☐	☐	☐	☐	☐
8. Expressing grandiose delusions.	☐	☐	☐	☐	☐
9. Projecting fears and suspicions onto others.	☐	☐	☐	☐	☐
10. Giggling inappropriately.	☐	☐	☐	☐	☐

2 Read the following situation and then complete the exercises as directed.

a In this situation the nurse, using assessment skills, noted that many of the client's behaviors reflect problems with developmental tasks. Refer to the 12 italicized and numbered behaviors in the situation and indicate in the following grid which developmental tasks or negative outcomes of developmental tasks they reflect. Some behaviors may reflect more than one task or outcome. One behavior has been filled in to help you get started. Although you could merely write in the number of the behavior in the space provided, it is recommended that you write out the behavior as in the example.

SITUATION: Penny Porter, a 25-year-old white, single woman, was brought to the admitting office by her mother. Mrs. Porter expressed frustration over her daughter's recent behavior, saying, *(1) "Last month Penny stopped going to her job and*

141

sat at home talking to herself. She wouldn't talk to me." Penny's mother continued, "And, as if that wasn't enough, *(2) she has gotten so suspicious. She says that I hate her and am trying to poison her. She refuses to eat with me. The only time she goes out is to buy herself some food, which she eats immediately. She won't share anything with me.* I'm an old lady. I don't deserve to be treated this way." Mrs. Porter sat back in her chair and glared angrily at her daughter who appeared not to notice anything that had been said. Further information elicited in the interview was that Mr. Porter had walked out on his wife and daughter when Penny was an infant. Penny was raised in a series of foster homes while her mother went out to work. *(3) Penny had no friends in school. She prefered solitary activities such as reading and watching television to interacting socially with her peers. (4) Mrs. Porter recalled that Penny had to wear faded and mended clothing belonging to other children in the foster homes, and she was embarrassed to go to school where she felt "different" from the other children.* When Penny graduated from high school, she returned to her mother's house and worked at a variety of unskilled jobs. However, because of her uncommunicative and aloof manner, she never stayed in any job very long. *(5) After being terminated in a job, she would come home crying, saying how bad she was for not being better able to help her mother. She would punish herself by standing in a corner for long hours, just as she had been punished as a child.*

Penny Porter was admitted to the psychiatric service for observation and treatment. In the unit *(6) she sat alone, talking to herself. She usually sat facing the door, and her eyes followed all who entered. If approached from the rear, she would whirl around snarling, "Don't you sneak up on me!" (7) She took no responsibility for her personal hygiene and appeared disheveled unless staff intervened. When encouraged to choose what she would wear, she became anxious and unable to make a decision. (8) Initially she refused to follow any suggestions and often did the opposite of what was expected of her. (9) Later she would find a remote area, sit on the floor, close her eyes, and chant in a loud voice devoid of feeling, "Dear God, dear God. Forgive her for her sins. She is so bad. Punish her, God. Send her to Hell. Forgive her, God, dear God, dear*

142

God." (10) In addition to referring to herself as "she" and "her," there were times when Penny would not respond to her name, saying, "Penny? Who is Penny? Call me 'Nobody.' " (11) Penny was given clay to mold but had a hard time concentrating on even the simplest craft activity, such as making an ashtray out of clay. She never completed anything she started. Even with encouragement she expressed feelings of inadequacy saying, "Oh, I could never do that. It would never be good enough to suit Mother." (12) At meals she continued to experience episodes of suspiciousness, accusing staff of trying to poison her "just like my mother."

Developmental tasks/ Negative outcomes	Discussion
1. Trust/mistrust	
2. Autonomy/shame and doubt	
3. Initiative/guilt	
4. Industry/inferiority	
5. Identity/role confusion	
6. Intimacy/isolation	(1) Staying at home and isolating herself from fellow workers and her mother; talking to herself rather than to others.

b Using Sullivan's interpersonal theory, briefly speculate on the nature of Penny Porter's relationships with others. Begin with Penny's first significant other, her mother, and trace her relationships with others up to the onset of her psychotic symptoms. (Where possible, use available data such as the father's leaving home when she was an infant. Speculate on the effect this had on Penny and her mother and Penny's subsequent relationships with men.)

c Although it is generally preferable that assessment data in the form of observational material be described in detail, it is also necessary for the nurse to be aware of the commonly used psychiatric terminologies applicable to behaviors exhibited by persons with thought disturbances. Listed below are 12 behaviors observed at different times in Penny Porter and 12 psychiatric terms that can be attached to these behaviors. Read each behavior and write the most correct term in the space provided. A term may be used only once. The first term has been filled in to help you get started.

Terminology

a. AUTISM
b. DERAILMENT
c. FLAT AFFECT
d. HALLUCINATION

e. INAPPROPRIATE AFFECT
f. MUTISM
g. NEGATIVISM
h. PERSECUTORY DELUSION

i. PSYCHOMOTOR RETARDATION
j. REGRESSION
k. SOMATIC DELUSION
l. WITHDRAWAL

Behaviors	Terminology
1. Sitting alone and avoiding all interpersonal contacts.	l. Withdrawal
2. Communicating in hard-to-follow sentences, jumping from one unrelated topic to another.	
3. Expressing an unfounded belief that people are trying to poison her.	
4. Talking out loud when no one else is present.	
5. Reverting back to infantile behaviors such as untidiness and soiling herself.	
6. Failing to communicate feelings either in her speech or her facial expression.	
7. Appearing deep in her own private thoughts and not sharing them with others.	
8. Expressing a belief that her body is rotting away in spite of the lack of physical symptoms.	
9. Growing increasingly inactive, standing or sitting immobile for hours at a time.	
10. Refusing to act on suggestions, often responding in a manner opposite to that expected.	
11. Laughing for no apparent reason.	
12. Becoming increasingly nonverbal, not speaking for weeks at a time.	

d Having observed the client, assessed her behaviors, and speculated on the predisposing factors contributing to her development of a thought disturbance, develop a plan of care for Penny Porter. A nursing diagnosis and 2 nursing goals have been filled in to help focus you on specific areas requiring nursing intervention. Complete the exercise by providing rationale, several appropriate goal-directed nursing activities, and anticipated results of care for each nursing goal.

Nursing diagnosis: Disturbance in personal identity and self-concept related to negative interpersonal experiences.

Nursing goal	Rationale	Nursing actions	Anticipated results
1. To help client develop a more appropriate identity and self-concept.			
2. To assist the client to assume more responsibility for meeting her hygiene needs.			

3 Read the following situation and develop a nursing care plan for the client. A nursing diagnosis and 3 nursing goals have been filled in to help you focus on specific areas requiring nursing intervention. Complete the grid by providing rationale, several appropriate goal-directed nursing actions, and anticipated results for each goal.

SITUATION: Paddy Worthkowski, a 42-year-old man, lived alone in a single room, sharing kitchen and bathroom facilities with his neighbors. He worked at the local post office, where increased automation was forcing him into jobs requiring more decision making. This caused him great anxiety. Another source of stress centered on his having to share the toilet and kitchen facilities at his place of residence. He grew increasingly preoccupied with the need for privacy. He began to experience delusions that the toilet was inhabited by reptiles that were trying to devour his genitals. He also believed the kitchen and all his food was contaminated with radioactive materials. He openly expressed the suspicion that everyone was "out to get him," and he began to withdraw. He stopped going to work, avoided his neighbors, and would not come out of his room even to use the kitchen and bathroom. His neighbors complained to the landlord that the area outside his door smelled badly. He barricaded the entrance to his room with furniture and arranged empty pie tins on the floor in front of his door to create a noisy obstacle in the event anyone gained entry. He was hospitalized.

Nursing diagnosis: Self-care and relationship deficit related to lack of trust and perceptual impairment.

Nursing goals	Rationale	Nursing actions	Anticipated results
1. To provide a nurse-client relationship.			
2. To assist the client to assume some responsibility for meeting his hygiene needs.			
3. To provide the client with adequate nutrition.			

DIRECTIONS: Select the *best* response. (Answers appear in the Appendix.)

1 The term *schizophrenia* was first used by:
   a Eugene Bleuler.   c Emil Kraepelin.
   b Jean Charcot.   d Manfred Sakel.

2 The DSM-III published in 1980 was the first diagnostic manual to do which one of the following?
   a Define the many varieties of mental disorders.
   b Analyze the behaviors in mentally ill persons.
   c Assess mentally ill persons holistically.
   d Classify mental disorders systematically.

3 A functional psychosis is one in which the person's perception of reality is severely distorted relative to:
   a Demonstrable organic brain disease.
   b Intellectual deficit and dysfunction.
   c Severe physical and psychological trauma.
   d Persistently high levels of anxiety in early life.

4 Schizophrenia may be categorized into one of several subtypes. Individuals who exhibit some inappropriate, but not psychotic, behaviors would be classified according to which one of the following subtypes?
   a Residual.   c Catatonic.
   b Undifferentiated.   d Paranoid.

5 A person with a diagnosis of schizophrenia, disorganized subtype, would generally exhibit which of the following behaviors?
   a Explosive bursts of overactivity and expressions of confused thinking.
   b Loss of animation and a tendency to remain in the same position for long periods.
   c Aggressive acts and false accusations directed at others.
   d Hallucinatory behaviors and open masturbation in front of others.

6 A positive prognosis for a person with a thought disturbance is *primarily* based on which one of the following factors?
   a Client's diagnosis and subtype.
   b Client's willingness to take medications.
   c Client's available resources.
   d Client's prepsychotic personality.

7 Massive interpersonal anxiety and conflictual feedback from

significant others during infancy and early childhood *primarily* contributes to which one of the following?

   a Fear and the "fight or flight" response.
   b Development of the not-me self-concept.
   c Use of coping measures.
   d Feelings of worthlessness.

8 *All but which one* of the following behaviors is associated with withdrawal?

   a Auditory hallucinations.   **c** Flat affect.
   b Depressed feelings.   **d** Autistic thinking.

9 The main reason the nurse calls a new client "Mr. Smith" rather than use his first name of "John" is *primarily* to:

   a Acknowledge the fact that he and the nurse are still strangers.
   b Indicate to the client early in their association that their relationship is a professional one.
   c Provide the client with an opportunity to develop feelings of trust in the nurse.
   d Communicate a sense of respect and the feeling that the client is a worthwhile person.

10 When a client expresses delusional ideas, the nurse can be *most* effective by:

   a Pointing out to the client why his ideas are untrue.
   b Explaining away the client's delusions.
   c Listening to the client's beliefs without comment.
   d Encouraging the client to explain his delusions.

11 Which one of the following activities would be *most* suitable for a very aloof and suspicious client?

   a Playing Ping-Pong with the nurse.
   b Joining other clients for a card game.
   c Working in the ward dining room.
   d Attending a dance with clients from different wards.

12 Which one of the following physical problems is commonly seen in clients exhibiting psychomotor retardation?

   a Obesity.   **c** Edema.
   b Hypotension.   **d** Diabetes.

13 Which one of the following nursing goals would be *most* specific to the nursing diagnosis that states: "Self-care deficit in bathing, dressing, grooming, and toileting related to perceptual impairment?"

a To help increase the client's feelings of self-esteem.

b To diminish the client's auditory hallucinations.

c To assist the client to assume responsibility for hygiene needs.

d To provide the client with adequate nutritional intake.

14 Positive reflected appraisals are *most* specifically utilized with a client who:

a Manifests regressive behaviors.

b Takes more pride in his appearance.

c Manifests fewer signs of hallucinations.

d Calls the nurse by name.

15 When the client's behaviors fail to reflect the anticipated results after a given period of time, the nurse should do which one of the following *first?*

a Set more realistic outcome criteria.

b Identify and work on another nursing goal.

c Transfer the care of the client to another nurse.

d Check on the client's current medication dosage.

chapter 14

adults with mood disturbances

INTRODUCTION Whereas schizophrenia is essentially a disturbance of thought reflected in affect and behavior as well as thinking, mood disturbances are primarily disorders of affect reflected in thought and action as well as feelings. Almost everyone can identify with affective experiences, having felt sadness and depression as well as joy and happiness at some time in their lives. Depression can occur in varying degrees from mild to severe, from normal to pathologically incapacitating. Joy, too, can be within normal limits but can also occur in excess and interfere with functioning.

Like thought disorders, mood disturbances are also believed to have their origins in the early developmental years. Unlike schizophrenics, who never experienced a warm and loving relationship in infancy, it is generally agreed that persons with mood disorders experienced a loving, caring, and trusting relationship during infancy. Then, sometime in late infancy or early childhood, the individual experienced a cessation of this love. The loss of love at that early time in life may have been real or it may have been fantasized. A real loss, such as of a parent through death or separation, or an imagined or perceived loss, such as might have been the interpretation placed on a parent's shift in attention to a new sibling or the disapproval associated with toilet training, raised feelings of doubt in the individual, mixed feelings of love and hate (ambivalence) about the lost love object, and guilt stemming from the belief that the individual was somehow responsible for the loss of love. The feelings of anger and guilt were introjected, or turned inward, and the feelings of love were expressed openly. The individual curbed the expression of negative feelings in an unconscious effort to regain the lost love.

Losses, real or imagined, experienced years later by the adult evoke feelings associated with the original loss. Some adults adapt to these losses with depression, underactivity, and suicide; other adults respond with elation, overactivity, and aggression expressed outwardly; still other adults respond with a cyclical combination of depressive and manic episodes. A functional psychosis that reflects a manic-depressive response to loss is called a mixed bipolar affective disorder.

"Mood disturbances severely interfere with the quality of life enjoyed by the affected person and his family. In addition, depression increases the risk of death by suicide. Nurses in all settings have a responsibility to recognize and appropriately intervene in situations where the individual is experiencing a mood disturbance."* The purpose of this chapter is to review theoretical concepts basic to an understanding of mood disorders and to apply the phases of the nursing process to the care of adults with mood disturbances.

OBJECTIVES

1. To categorize the various losses experienced in depression.
2. To differentiate between normal grief and depression.
3. To review therapeutic communication skills used in terminating a nurse-client relationship with a depressed person.
4. To apply selected phases of the nursing process to the care of hypothetical clients with mood disturbances.

EXERCISES

1 Psychodynamically the underlying phenomenon in the development of all depressions is essentially the same thing—loss. Associated with all losses is the loss of self-esteem. Loss can take many forms. The most obvious loss is the loss of a loved one through death, precipitating a depression known as mourning and grief. Other events can also be perceived as losses and bring on a depressive response.

Listed on p. 155 are 10 events and 8 types of losses. Categorize each event in terms of the loss experienced by checking the boxes in the appropriate columns. Keep in mind that more than one loss may be associated with an event. The first one has been filled in to help you get started.

*From Taylor, C.M.: Mereness' essentials of psychiatric nursing, ed. 12, St. Louis, 1986, The C.V. Mosby Co., Chapter 14.

Event	Losses							
	Self-esteem	Love object	Independence	Freedom	Physical integrity	Youth	Autonomy	Material possessions
1. Laura experienced a depression that lasted several weeks after her first baby was born.	☑	☐	☑	☑	☑	☑	☑	☐
2. Vinnie was falsely convicted of a crime, became despondent, and attempted suicide in his cell.	☐	☐	☐	☐	☐	☐	☐	☐
3. Mr. Warren felt depressed when he was forced to retire prematurely because of physical disabilities.	☐	☐	☐	☐	☐	☐	☐	☐
4. Georgia became sad and cried at length on the eve of her marriage to Oscar.	☐	☐	☐	☐	☐	☐	☐	☐
5. Susan has blue spells every year on her birthday.	☐	☐	☐	☐	☐	☐	☐	☐
6. David feels fine as long as he is working but gets irritable and morose on days off and on vacations.	☐	☐	☐	☐	☐	☐	☐	☐
7. Clint became depressed when his crop was lost during a severe drought.	☐	☐	☐	☐	☐	☐	☐	☐
8. Mark became depressed when his boss of many years died suddenly and he was promoted to his position.	☐	☐	☐	☐	☐	☐	☐	☐
9. Mr. Keller's depression developed insidiously after a prostatectomy and impotency problems.	☐	☐	☐	☐	☐	☐	☐	☐
10. Tino became depressed when his house burned down and his family died despite all his efforts to save them.	☐	☐	☐	☐	☐	☐	☐	☐

2 List four differences between normal grief and depression.

Normal grief responses

a _____

b _____

c _____

d _____

Depression

a _____

b _____

c _____

d _____

3 Read the following situation involving an interaction between a nurse and a client who had been admitted to the hospital following a suicide attempt, and complete the exercises as directed.

a In the interaction the nurse uses at least 10 different therapeutic communication skills to help the client work through her feelings associated with an impending termination of the relationship. Each example of a skill has been italicized and numbered. Place the numbers of the examples in the spaces provided after each communication skill. A communication skill may be illustrated more than once; an example may illustrate more than one skill. The first one has been filled in to help you get started.

Communication skills

a. Clarifying ⎯⎯⎯⎯⎯	f. Giving recognition __(1.)__
b. Encouraging ⎯⎯⎯⎯	g. Reflecting ⎯⎯⎯⎯⎯
c. Exploring ⎯⎯⎯⎯⎯	h. Refocusing ⎯⎯⎯⎯
d. Focusing ⎯⎯⎯⎯⎯	i. Suggesting ⎯⎯⎯⎯
e. Giving information ⎯⎯	j. Understanding ⎯⎯⎯

SITUATION: The nurse has developed a nurse-client relationship based on trust. At the onset the nurse identified several client-centered goals, including helping the client to develop a more realistic self-concept, to express her feelings in less self-destructive ways, to relate to others more comfortably, and to plan for her return to the community. However, before all these goals could be realized, the nurse applied for a leave of absence so that she could return to school. In meeting with Karen the nurse told her client of her plans as the first step in terminating the nurse-client relationship. This is their second interaction focusing on termination.

1. **N** *"Hello Karen."*
   (Silence.)

2. **N** *"You are very quiet today. Is there anything you would like to talk about?"*
   (Silence.)

3. **N** *"Perhaps we could talk some more about my leaving."*
   C Angrily, "I don't want to talk about it. What good is talking going to do?"

4. **N** *"You sound angry."*
   C "Of course I'm angry. Why shouldn't I be?"

5. **N** *"You feel I am deserting you?"*
   C "Well, aren't you? You're like all the rest."

6. **N** *"All the rest?"*
   (Silence.)

7. **N** *"Go on Karen. Tell me what you are feeling."*
   (Silence.)

8. **N** *"Perhaps it would help to talk about it."*
   C Crying, "I'm sorry. I shouldn't take it out on you. I've brought this on myself."

9. **N** *"I don't understand. What do you mean? How have you brought this on yourself?"*
   C "Getting involved. I should never have gotten involved with you."
   (Silence.)

10. **N** *"You have reason to be disappointed and to feel angry. Just when we were getting somewhere, I leave you."*

    C "It's not fair."

11. **N** *"I guess it does seem that way."*
    (Pause.)

12. **N** *"Earlier you said, 'You're like all the rest.' What did you mean by that?"*

    C "I don't know if I can. It's hard. I don't like to think about it, let alone talk about it. Most of the time I don't, but when you told me you were going away, all the old feelings came rushing back."

13. **N** *"These are painful feelings?"*

    C "I don't like to get involved with anyone. When they go away, I get a panicky feeling."

14. **N** *"Is that what you are feeling now?"*

    C "Yes. I thought it would be different with you, you being a nurse and all. I guess I figured since it was your job, I was safe, that I could always count on you, at least until it was time for me to leave the hospital."

15. **N** *"You thought I would always be there when you needed me and I let you down?"*

    C "Yes. Just like my mother. I counted on her and she went away too."

16. **N** *"What happened?"*
    (Silence.)
    "When I was a little girl we used to have good times together. She took me to the park and I fed the ducks. She'd buy me a balloon and I'd ride on the merry-go-round. I thought she loved me."

17. **N** *"And then?"*

    C "She killed herself."

18. **N** *"Oh. You've never mentioned this before. This must be difficult for you to talk about."*

    C "Yes and no. It's hard, but it's a relief to share this with you. Sometimes, even now, I think it must have been my fault. If I had been a better daughter she wouldn't have done it."

19. **N** *"You've been feeling responsible all these years? That's a tough feeling to live with."*

    C "Sometimes it's more than I can bear. I feel so responsible."

20. **N** *"Like before, when you were feeling it was your fault that I'm leaving?"*

    C "I was feeling that if I was a better person you would stay."

21. **N** *"And now? What are you feeling now?"*

    C "Numb. I'm going to miss you. But it isn't my fault, is it? You said you're going back to school? I thought that was just an excuse to get away from me."

22. **N** *"When people feel bad about themselves, it's hard for them not to think everything is their fault."*
    (Silence.)

23. **N** *"It's not your fault. I've always wanted to go back to school to get my degree, and now I have my chance."*
    (Pause.)

24. **N** *"I'm going to miss you too, Karen. You're pretty special to me."* (Silence.)

   C "I feel drained."

25. **N** *"We have been sharing a lot of feelings. That's hard work."* (Pause.)

   C "Will we talk some more before you go?"

26. **N** *"Yes, of course. We will continue meeting until the end of the month."*

   C "Tell me again when you start school."

27. **N** *"In about 3 weeks."* (Pause.)

28. **N** *"Would you like to talk any more now?"*

   C "No. I think not. I'm all talked out."

29. **N** *"Perhaps we have done enough for now. Come, let's go play a game of Ping-Pong. It might do us both good."*

   C (Laughing) "I'll beat you."

30. **N** *(Laughing) "I'm sure you will. I've not won a game yet. You are the best player on the unit."*

b Using your understanding of the dynamics of depression, briefly explain why it is essential for Karen to have ample opportunity to work through termination with her nurse.

c Listed in the grid on p. 159 are 3 nursing goals specific to termination. In the space provided give the rationale and at least one nursing action that the nurse might use with Karen in the remaining 3 weeks to facilitate each of the goals. A nursing diagnostic statement has been filled in to help you get started.

Nursing diagnosis: Anticipatory grieving related to perceived potential loss of significant other.

Nursing goals	Rationale	Nursing actions
1. To express feelings associated with the anticipated loss.		
2. To review what has been learned through the relationship.		
3. To transfer positive aspects of the professional relationship to another person or persons.		

4 Listed below are 10 nursing diagnostic statements that can be applied to the care of persons with a medical diagnosis of bipolar affective disorder, manic type. Read and complete each one. Each statement should vary somewhat and should reflect your theoretical knowledge about persons who exhibit manic behaviors. The first one has been completed to help you get started.

a Self-care deficient in terms of feeding, bathing, dressing/grooming, and toileting related to _overactivity and an inability to maintain sustained attention._

b Sarcastic and profane language related to _____

c Susceptibility to physical injury related to _____

d Anxiety and hyperactivity related to _____

e Impaired verbal communication related to _____

f Potential for violence directed at others related to _____

g Ineffective individual coping related to _____
_____

h Alteration in health maintenance related to _____
_____

i Social isolation related to _____
_____

j Inappropriate attire related to _____
_____

5 Using the descriptive data gathered through the assessment phase of the nursing process, develop a plan for nursing intervention. Identify a nursing goal, rationale, nursing actions, and anticipated results for the following situation. The nursing diagnosis has been filled in to help you get started.

SITUATION: Frankie Foster, known as "Fast Fingers" Foster to his friends, is a competent jazz composer-musician who plays several musical instruments. Except for occasional episodes of hyperactivity and elation requiring brief periods of hospitalization, Mr. Foster has led a productive life, supporting himself as a pianist at local night spots. On the unit he is generally well liked, friendly, and outgoing and willingly plays the ward piano for the other clients, although his attention span is relatively short. The behaviors that tend to isolate him from others are his profane and vulgar speech patterns and his occasional sexual aggressiveness. It is not unusual to find him going into the women's dormitory at night.

Nursing diagnosis: Profane and vulgar language and sexually aggressive behaviors related to lack of adequate ego control.

Nursing goal	Rationale	Nursing actions	Anticipated results

160

DIRECTIONS: Select the *best* response. (Answers appear in the Appendix.)

1 The cyclic nature of mood disorders was first recognized by:

a Kraepelin.
c Hippocrates.
b Bleuler.
d Cerletti.

2 Which one of the following behaviors is more characteristic of a person with a thought disorder than a mood disorder?

a Manifests euphoric mood.
b Complains of constant fatigue.
c Exhibits boundless energy.
d Smiles or laughs inappropriately.

3 Bereavement is a reaction to which one of the following?

a Real loss of a highly valued object.
b Symbolic loss of an intangible object.
c Anticipated loss of a fantasied love object.
d Imagined loss of a tangible object.

4 One of the phases of normal grief is called:

a Denial.
c Termination.
b Restitution.
d Depression.

5 The defense mechanism operating in depression when angry feelings are repressed is *primarily:*

a Reaction formation.
c Introjection.
b Rationalization.
d Isolation.

6 The superego in depression is *best* described as:

a Laissez-faire.
c Punitive.
b Idealistic.
d Hostile.

7 When a depressed person experiences psychomotor retardation, he exhibits which one of the following?

a Severe anxiety.
c Marked agitation.
b Feelings of worthlessness.
d Lack of energy.

8 Which one of the following is a fallacy about suicide?

a People who talk about suicide are thinking about it.
b Introducing the topic of suicide to a depressed person will precipitate a suicide attempt.
c Suicide attempts are usually preceded by some warning.
d Almost every person who makes a suicide attempt is suffering from depression.

9 Which one of the following nursing approaches would be *most* helpful and realistic to use with depressed clients?

a Presenting a cheerful, energetic manner to clients.

b Expecting clients to take initiative in self-care.

c Providing clients with opportunities for decision making.

d Establishing a simple daily schedule of activities for clients.

10 One of the common temporary side effects of electroconvulsive therapy occurring after five or six treatments is:

a Postural hypotension.　　**c** Muscle weakness.

b Urinary incontinence.　　**d** Memory loss.

11 Which one of the following nursing diagnoses is *least* appropriate for a person exhibiting manic behaviors?

a Sarcastic and profane language related to lack of ego controls.

b Anxiety and hyperactivity related to change in socioeconomic status.

c Dysfunctional grieving related to actual or perceived object loss.

d Ineffective individual coping related to situational crisis.

12 In response to the overactive, elated individual's vulgar speech and seductive behavior, the nurse can be *most* helpful:

a Responding to the client with understanding and acceptance.

b Pointing out to the client that the behaviors are bad.

c Telling the client he will be punished if he does not behave.

d Avoiding the client until he can control his behavior.

13 Which one of the following activities would be the *least* appropriate outlet for the manic individual's excess energy?

a Team sports.　　**c** Writing.

b Ping-Pong.　　**d** Drawing.

14 Listed below are four luncheon menus. Which one should be *both* nutritious and appropriate to serve to a hyperactive individual?

a Spaghetti and meatballs, salad, banana.

b Beef and vegetable stew, bread, vanilla pudding.

c Broiled chicken leg, ear of corn, apple.

d Fried fish sticks, stewed tomatoes, chocolate cake.

15 The hyperactive client is receiving lithium carbonate daily. Which one of the following nursing measures is *most* indicated?

  a Arranging a regular schedule of blood work.
  b Checking vital signs four times a day.
  c Limiting fluid intake to 1000 ml per day.
  d Taking blood pressure before administering medication.

adults with anxiety disturbances

INTRODUCTION

Anxiety is an energy force that promotes activity and productivity on the one hand and interferes with functioning on the other. In thought disorders anxiety restricts logical thinking, reality perception, and relatedness with others. In mood disorders anxiety seems to propel individuals into flurries of disorganized activity or reduces them to energyless states of inertia. These individuals are all psychotic.

This chapter focuses on nonpsychotic individuals who strive to control anxiety through the use of repetitive patterns of behavior (rituals), physical symptoms with no organic bases (conversions), and fears out of proportion to the stimuli (phobias). Prior to 1980 and the revised classification of psychiatric disorders, these individuals were labeled neurotic.

These adults with anxiety disturbances differ from persons with disturbances in thought and mood in that they have a greater degree of ego strength. This is reflected in behavior: they are in touch with reality and possess varying degrees of insight that they are not experiencing life to its fullest. They engage in problem solving with some success and are generally able to seek help and relief from their increasingly incapacitating symptoms. They utilize repression in combination with other ego defenses to keep unconscious conflicts out of awareness. Their memories are usually intact and their judgment fairly sound except when anxiety reaches extreme proportions.

"Because individuals suffering from anxiety disturbances are in touch with reality and often recognize the inappropriateness of their behavior, many nurses have difficulty accepting them as persons in need of health care. To achieve a more understanding attitude toward these individuals, it is important to develop some knowledge about the emotional conflicts with which they struggle and the ways in which they use symptoms to cope with the anxiety that stems from these conflicts."* The purpose of this

---

*From Taylor, C.M.: Mereness' essentials of psychiatric nursing, ed. 12, St. Louis, 1986, The C.V. Mosby Co., Chapter 15.

chapter is to promote greater understanding of adults with anxiety disturbances and to apply phases of the nursing process to their care.

OBJECTIVES

1. To identify ego defense mechanisms used by adults with anxiety disturbances.
2. To differentiate between the primary and secondary gains of these anxiety-based disorders.
3. To describe nursing actions that discourage secondary gains.
4. To apply selected phases of the nursing process to the care of clients experiencing anxiety disturbances.

EXERCISES

1 The use of defenses in characteristic patterns reflects the nature of anxiety disturbances. For example, in the somatoform disorder of conversion the defenses of conversion and symbolism are used consistently. In fact, the use of conversion is exclusive to this disorder. In phobic and obsessive-compulsive disorders the mechanisms utilized are displacement and preoccupation as well as symbolism. In phobias the preoccupation is with the object of fear that is avoided in order to control anxiety; in compulsions the preoccupation, or obsession, is a thought that keeps recurring. In addition, undoing is operating when the individual compulsively carries out repetitive acts to try to blot out the troubling thought as well as magically erase or "undo" the unconscious conflict, anxiety, and guilt that underlie these behaviors. All of these defenses are, of course, working with the ego defense of repression, trying to keep the unconscious conflicts out of awareness.

Listed on p. 166 are 10 examples of behaviors associated with selected defenses. Read each one and identify which defenses are operating by placing a check in the box in the appropriate column. The first one has been filled in to help you get started.

	Defenses					
Behavioral responses	Displacement	Symbolism	Conversion	Preoccupation	Undoing	Repression
1. Edwardo was obsessed with the belief that he was dying of a brain tumor although multiple physical examinations and laboratory tests did not support his fears.	☑	☑	☐	☑	☑	☑
2. Roger's father, a military man, hoped that his son would also follow a military career. After graduation from high school Roger enlisted in the infantry but was unable to report for duty because of sudden, unexplained paralysis in his legs. No organic reason could be found for his symptoms.	☐	☐	☐	☐	☐	☐
3. One day Mike was mistakenly locked in a closet for 10 hours while playing in an abandoned building. He was 7 years old. As an adult he had no recall of the incident but continued to experience severe anxiety when alone in windowless areas such as elevators, closets, or enclosed stairwells.	☐	☐	☐	☐	☐	☐
4. Helen's freedom of movement was severely restricted because of recurring thoughts that she had neglected to turn off the water in the sink before leaving the house. She acknowledged that her fears were groundless, but she could not resist the urge to return home to check out her concerns.	☐	☐	☐	☐	☐	☐
5. When Thelma was 6 years old she was physically threatened by her mother for masturbating. Thelma never masturbated again and never mentioned the incident to anyone. Years later when she engaged in heavy petting with a boyfriend, she experienced a severe anxiety attack. The next day she awoke with an unexplained paralysis of both hands. She felt little concern over the incapacitating symptoms.	☐	☐	☐	☐	☐	☐
6. Watson became panicky when faced with air travel. This had not been a problem until his job required extensive travel. For days before a trip Watson could think about nothing else. In therapy he revealed that his father had died in a plane crash when he was 6 years old and he had felt guilty about it for years.	☐	☐	☐	☐	☐	☐
7. Everything about Katie was meticulous: her appearance, her home, and her work. Every night after work she carried out elaborate cleaning procedures before eating dinner. She would take the telephone off the hook so she would not be disturbed. Any interference caused her great stress, and she was forced to start her ritual over from the beginning.	☐	☐	☐	☐	☐	☐
8. Fran had a morbid fear of the dark. A childhood fear, she had apparently "outgrown" it. However, shortly after she married, the old thoughts recurred, and she insisted that all the lights be left on in the apartment. The marriage was now in peril because she would not sleep without a bright light in the bedroom and her husband had moved out into the living room.	☐	☐	☐	☐	☐	☐
9. Lucy still lived at home with her parents. It was a close-knit but undemonstrative family. She rarely was kissed by her parents and had never seen them embrace. One day she came home from work early and found her parents in the act of sexual intercourse. She experienced a confusing mixture of horror and sexual stimulation. The next morning she awakened and could not see.	☐	☐	☐	☐	☐	☐
10. Tina was very concerned with her weight. She weighed and measured all her food before eating it, after making meticulous calculations of caloric values. She also weighed herself before and after every meal and kept elaborate records of her intake. Any distractions that interfered with her completing her rituals caused Tina great anxiety.	☐	☐	☐	☐	☐	☐

2 The individual with an anxiety disturbance has no insight into why a particular symptom develops or what purpose is served by the symptom. The fact that an unconscious conflict is being kept out of awareness by the combined use of repression and other defenses is unknown to the client. What is experienced is the control of anxiety. This relief from anxiety is the purpose of developing the symptoms and is called the *primary gain* of the illness. In addition to the primary gain, the client on occasion may experience a *secondary gain* from the illness. Secondary gains occur when the client experiences attention, sympathy, material benefits, special consideration, and control over others and, in effect, seems to be rewarded for being ill. Although some secondary gains are to be expected and perhaps are even desirable, the nurse needs to be aware of their dangers. An understanding that primary gains control anxiety is the theoretical basis for allowing a client to retain his patterns of behavior and to relinquish them at his own pace. Similarly, an understanding that a client may consciously or unconsciously retain these same patterns of behavior because of their secondary gains is the theoretical basis for using nursing activities that do not unduly reenforce these gains and interfere with the client's recovery. (Chapter 16 of the text elaborates further on primary and secondary gains in adults with psychophysiological disturbances.)

a Listed below are 10 behavioral examples that reflect either primary (I°) or secondary (II°) gains. Differentiate between each one by placing a check in the box in the appropriate column. The first one has been filled in to help you get started.

Behavioral examples	Gains	
	I°	II°
1. Carl did not mind staying home when he was sick because he could watch baseball games on TV.	☐	☑
2. Harry collected disability insurance after he injured his hand on the assembly line at work.	☐	☐
3. Martha felt more secure if she followed an exact routine every day.	☐	☐
4. Susan anticipates having her mother make her favorite chicken soup whenever she is ill.	☐	☐
5. Webster's friends rallied to his side when they learned he was terminally ill.	☐	☐
6. Dolly feels safer at home where she can avoid open spaces, which she morbidly fears.	☐	☐
7. Rose's ritualistic cleaning behaviors fill her with feelings of security associated with neatness and order.	☐	☐
8. Rose's emphasis on neatness and order has earned her the respect and admiration of her friends.	☐	☐
9. Al feels more secure when he can make detailed lists of his planned daily activities.	☐	☐
10. Warren's anxiety is reduced dramatically if he can carry out his repetitive hand-washing activities.	☐	☐

b Persons who are blind, deaf, or paralyzed for no organic reason are prone to secondary gains from their illnesses. Family, friends, and staff can unwittingly reinforce these gains and prolong a person's illness. Keeping this in mind, list 6 nursing measures that could be taken to avoid reinforcing secondary gains. For example, a general nonaction response might be to avoid being overly sympathetic with these clients. Now, go on to state what attitude or manner would be more appropriate to use, as well as other nursing actions that discourage secondary gains.

1. _____

2. _____

3. _____

4. _____

5. _____

6. _____

3 Read the following situation and complete the exercise as indicated.

SITUATION: Carl Coates was brought into the emergency room with multiple fractures following an automobile accident. When he learned he was to be admitted to the hospital, he showed less concern about his injuries than he did about the fact that he would have to be hospitalized. He went on to shyly reveal that he had a morbid fear of the dark and was greatly relieved when he was told by the emergency room nurse that he could keep a small light on in his room. Following treatment for his injuries he was transferred to the orthopedic unit where, on the basis of the assessment data, a staff nurse developed a tentative plan of care for Mr. Coates. The two problems identified were (1) impaired physical mobility related to multiple fractures and (2) phobic fear of the dark (achluophobia, nyctophobia, scotophobia).

The plan of care developed relative to his fear of the dark was:

Nursing goal	Rationale	Nursing action	Anticipated results
To help client give up his fear of the dark.	The client's fear is both embarrassing and incapacitating, interfering with functioning.	Leave a light on in the client's room. Each night reduce the amount of available light until the room is in darkness. When client talks about his fears, reassure him that there is nothing to be afraid of. Give client logical and reasonable explanations why his fears are irrational. Tell him about "insight" therapy and advise him to seek it.	Within 2 weeks the client will: No longer show overt signs or symptoms of anxiety when in the dark. No longer verbalize fear of being in the dark.

At the team conference the plans were reviewed. It was agreed that the client's priority problem was the physical one. The staff's response to Mr. Coates' nyctophobia was mixed. Several persons felt that his fear was an attention-getting device and that he should not be given special attention or privileges because of it. Further, others felt that "he could snap out of it if he wanted to." Finally, after much discussion, it was agreed that some measures needed to be identified to help the client with his fear of the dark, but that it was neither realistic nor appropriate to expect him to give up his fears at this time. As a member of the team, revise the original plan of care in the space provided. The revised nursing goal has been entered to help you get started.

Nursing goal	Rationale	Nursing action	Anticipated results
To prevent anxiety and fear associated with the client's fear of the dark.			

TEST ITEMS

DIRECTIONS: Select the *best* response. (Answers appear in the Appendix.)

1 Another term for obsession is:
   a Compulsion.   **c** Preoccupation.
   b Ritual.   **d** Fear.

2 The ego defense mechanism *unique* to obsessive-compulsive disorders is:
   a Displacement.   **c** Repression.
   b Conversion.   **d** Undoing.

3 Persons with conversion disorders manifest which one of the following?
   a Indifference to their symptoms.
   b Anger at being incapacitated.

    c Multiple physical problems.

    d Very high levels of anxiety.

4 Which one of the following nursing diagnostic statements is *most* applicable to an adult with anxiety disturbances?

    a Ritualistic acts related to overwhelming unconscious conflicts.

    b Blindness related to organic changes in the retina.

    c Compulsive behavior related to perceptual impairment.

    d Fear related to threat to biological integrity.

5 The person who must control anxiety with elaborate repetitive rituals will experience the greatest security if the nurse does which one of the following?

    a Distracts him with other activities.

    b Encourages him to talk about the purpose of his rituals.

    c Allows him to carry out his rituals.

    d Limits the time he spends in ritualistic activities.

6 The *most* effective long-term treatment of anxiety disorders is:

    a Behavior modification.   **c** Desensitization.

    b Antianxiety agents.   **d** Psychotherapy.

7 Supportive psychotherapy is to coping with problems as insight psychotherapy is to:

    a Uncovering unconscious material.

    b Dealing with current stressors.

    c Reducing extremes of anxiety.

    d Repressing painful experiences.

8 Problems of the individual characterized by obsessive-compulsive behavior are said to have originated during which of the following periods in life?

    a Infancy.   **c** Later childhood.

    b Early childhood.   **d** Preadolescence.

9 The day after a very traumatic emotional experience, Sue developed paralysis of her arm. Which one of the following actions takes *priority?*

    a Encouraging Sue to talk about her feelings.

    b Referring Sue for a psychiatric consultation.

    c Checking out that Sue's paralysis has no organic basis.

    d Pointing out to Sue she could move her arm if she tried.

10 Jason is admitted to a surgical service for hernia repair. On the admission interview he tells the nurse that he is morbidly afraid of the dark. Which one of the following responses by the nurse would be the *most* helpful to the client?

   a "How long have you been afraid of the dark?"

   b "Would you feel more comfortable if a light is kept on in your room?"

   c "Afraid of the dark? It's OK. You don't need to be afraid here."

   d "That must be very inconvenient sometimes."

11 A person with an anxiety disturbance may experience primary and/or secondary gains from their illness. Which one of the following behavioral examples *best* reflects primary gains?

   a Laura feels anxious when she has to make decisions.

   b Al feels more secure making lists of his planned daily activities.

   c Tessie received disability insurance after being injured at work.

   d Jack has a morbid fear of airplanes.

12 In order to *avoid* reenforcing the development of secondary gains in a hospitalized client, the nurse should do which one of the following?

   a Maintain a sympathetic manner toward the client at all times.

   b Encourage the client to talk about the details of his illness every day.

   c Emphasize the positive aspects of the illness, such as getting an unexpected "holiday."

   d Encourage the client to assist in as much of his care as possible.

chapter 16

adults with psychophysiological disturbances

INTRODUCTION

"The phenomenon referred to as somatization is a process whereby an individual's feelings, emotional needs, or conflicts are manifested physiologically. When the need, feeling, or conflict is on a conscious level the somatization process occurs as an adaptation to the stress of the emotion. When the emotion is an unconscious level somatization also serves the function of defending the individual against conscious awareness of the nature of the emotion. In either instance, the process of somatization supports the widely accepted belief that the functions and reactions of the mind and body are inextricably related."* It can be safely stated that everyone has at some time been affected with physical symptoms in response to emotional experiences. Pallor and perspiration in response to fear, blushing and stuttering induced by embarrassment, headaches and muscle stiffness brought on by tension, nausea and vomiting precipitated by anxiety, palpitations and insomnia evoked by nervous anticipation, and vegetative symptoms such as constipation and anorexia associated with depression are all examples of symptomatic expressions demonstrating the close relationship between the mind (and emotions) and the body.

In some instances the physiological response heightens awareness of the emotional experience. Such is the situation with love, pleasurable anticipation, and mild anxiety. The response can be stimulating and at times exciting. In other instances, such as with increasing fear and anxiety, the physiological response serves to mobilize the individual into action, to take flight or perhaps to stand and fight in a threatening situation. In cases in which the physical symptoms are observable to others, they serve as modes of nonverbal communication to the astute observer.

*From Taylor, C.M.: Mereness' essentials of psychiatric nursing, ed. 12, St. Louis, 1986, The C.V. Mosby Co., Chapter 16.

If these somatic responses to emotional situations are sustained and produce measurable changes in the body's organs, the individual is said to have a psychophysiological disturbance. Although there is still some resistance to the belief that the functions and reactions of the mind and body are closely intertwined, most people acknowledge that a few disorders may have such a relationship. Peptic ulcers, bronchial asthma, and eczema fall into this category. The notion that a relationship exists between the physical symptoms of other conditions such as essential hypertension, ulcerative colitis, and rheumatoid arthritis and the underlying emotional factors contributing to their onset still evokes disbelief. The idea that a mind-body relationship exists with still other conditions such as tuberculosis, coronary heart disease, and cancer is met with outspoken skepticism.

Despite these different responses, there is growing evidence to support the belief that all physical illnesses are inextricably bound up with an indivdual's emotional state and personality structure. The purpose of this chapter is to increase understanding of psychophysiological disturbances and to apply selected phases of the nursing process to the care of adults with these disorders.

OBJECTIVES

1. To identify the emotional component in everyday figures of speech related to parts of the body.
2. To differentiate among conversion, hypochondriasis, malingering, and somatization.
3. To apply selected phases of the nursing process to the care of clients experiencing psychophysiological disturbances.

EXERCISES

1 The relationship between mind and body is often expressed in everyday conversation. The English language is filled with idiomatic expressions that symbolically use a body part to reflect feelings. The expression, "She turned a deaf ear to his plea," is an example of "body language" in which indifference is clearly being expressed. The list of 10 idioms on p. 175 is a sampling of emotion expressed verbally through reference to a body part. Read each one and in the adjoining space identify the feeling message that is being conveyed. The first one has been filled in to help you get started. In addition, fill in lines 11 to 15 with other "body language" idiomatic expressions with which you are familiar.

Idiomatic expression	Feeling message
1. "My stomach was in my throat."	Fear, anxiety
2. "He's got a heart of stone."	
3. "She makes my skin crawl."	
4. "He was up in arms when he heard the news."	
5. "Keep a stiff upper lip."	
6. "He fell head over heels for her."	
7. "You give me a pain in the butt."	
8. "He's a hard-nosed individual."	
9. "You're a sight for sore eyes."	
10. "She gave him the cold shoulder."	
11.	
12.	
13.	
14.	
15.	

2 There are four phenomenon that are often confused: somatization, conversion, hypochondriasis, and malingering. Somatization is a process by which anxiety is expressed through physical symptoms that have an organic basis and in which physiological changes can be demonstrated in the involved organ. Conversion is a process by which anxiety is controlled through physical symptoms that have no organic basis and in which there is no demonstrable change in the body part. Hypochondriasis is a state of mind in which the individual experiences a heightened awareness of, and a preoccupation with, bodily functions in spite of the fact that there are no demonstrable physical symptoms or physiological changes in the organs involved. Malingering is a purposeful, conscious feigning of illness or injury in the absence of any physical problem in order to derive secondary gains, such as monetary rewards. In the following exercise read each of the 10 behavioral manifestations listed and differentiate among somatization, conversion, hypochondriasis, and malingering by placing a check in the box in the appropriate column. The first one has been filled in to help you get started.

Behavioral manifestations	Somatization	Conversion	Hypochondriasis	Malingering
1. Morgan pretended to have a cold and fever so he could stay home to watch the World Series.	☐	☐	☐	☑
2. Linda experiences severe migraine headaches when under stress.	☐	☐	☐	☐
3. Hannah goes from one physician to another seeking reassurance that she does not have cancer even though no pathology has been identified.	☐	☐	☐	☐
4. Jack feigned symptoms of whiplash following a car accident in hopes of collecting disability insurance.	☐	☐	☐	☐
5. Barbara developed an unexplained paralysis of her right hand after she beat her son.	☐	☐	☐	☐
6. Marco's stomach ulcer flares up before he has to lecture, and he takes antacids for temporary relief.	☐	☐	☐	☐
7. Flora's mother died from cardiovascular disease. Ever since then Flora has been obsessed with her heart and blood pressure. She has bought a blood pressure apparatus and checks her blood pressure six or seven times a day.	☐	☐	☐	☐
8. Dale is allergic to dogs and develops upper respiratory–like symptoms when in close contact with them.	☐	☐	☐	☐
9. Lena developed sudden and unexplained blindness after witnessing her parents making love.	☐	☐	☐	☐
10. Tim faked physical symptoms in order to avoid an undesirable work assignment.	☐	☐	☐	☐

3 In the assessment phase of the nursing process the nurse collects, validates, and analyzes data. In the following exercise utilize these steps of assessment and describe the physical and emotional factors contributing to the onset of symptoms in adults with psychophysiological disturbances. The first one has been entered to help you get started.

Psychophysiological disturbances	Physical factors	Emotional factors
1. Ulcerative colitis	Gastrointestinal disorder in which the blood supply to the bowel is reduced, leading to ischemia and the formation of ulcers in the walls of the bowel.	Prior to the onset of symptoms the individual experiences ambivalent feelings toward the mother and conflict over dependency needs. Obsessive-compulsive features are used to control others. Anger and rage are internalized and expressed symbolically through physical symptoms.
2. Peptic ulcer		
3. Essential hypertension		
4. Bronchial asthma		
5. Rheumatoid arthritis		

4 A major principle of psychiatric nursing that has particular relevance in caring for adults with psychophysiological disturbances is the "holistic principle." This principle states that the nurse views the client as a holistic being with a multiplicity of interrelated and interdependent needs. In the following exercise write a nursing diagnosis for each one of the disorders listed below. Each diagnostic statement should reflect use of this holistic principle and an understanding of the mind-body relationship that exists in each disorder. One nursing diagnosis has been filled in to help you get started.

a Peptic ulcer: Gastric hypermotility, increased gastric secretions, and epigastric pain related to unconscious dependency-independency conflicts.

b Ulcerative colitis: _____

_____

c Essential hypertension: _____

_____

d Bronchial asthma: _____

_____

e Rheumatoid arthritis: _____

_____

5 Using the following nursing diagnosis for an adult with a peptic ulcer, develop a plan of care in which both physical and emotional needs are met. Three nursing goals have been entered in the plan to help you get started.

Nursing diagnosis: Gastric hypermotility, increased gastric secretions, and epigastric pain related to unconscious dependency-independency conflicts.

Nursing goals	Rationale	Nursing actions	Anticipated results
1. To restore physiological homeokinesis.			
2. To meet client's dependency needs.			
3. To encourage expression of feelings.			

TEST ITEMS

DIRECTIONS: Select the *best* response. (Answers appear in the Appendix.)

1 Psychophysiological disturbances are characterized by *all but which one* of the following?
  a Organic change in one body system.
  b Innervation by the central nervous system.
  c Underlying unconscious emotional conflicts.
  d Presence of anxiety over symptoms.

2 Which one of the following theories *best* explains the "fight or flight" response in psychophysiological disorders?
  a Repressed conflict theory.
  c Symbolism theory.
  b Personality-type theory.
  d Organ weakness theory.

3 The primary gain associated with developing physical symptoms in response to stress is to:

a Accept dependency.   **c** Experience attention.

b Suppress anger.   **d** Decrease anxiety.

4 Minimizing secondary gains after the acute stage of illness can *best* be accomplished by which one of the following nursing actions?

a Encouraging the client to assume responsibility for some aspects of care.

b Assuming a consistently sympathetic manner with the client.

c Anticipating the client's needs for the duration of hospitalization.

d Emphasizing the positive aspects of the illness, such as giving the client a needed rest.

5 The personality of an individual prone to peptic ulcers is described as strong, self-sufficient, hardworking, and unemotional. Some theorists believe that these characteristics reflect a reaction formation to an unconscious conflict with:

a Trust.   **c** Dependency.

b Guilt.   **d** Love.

6 Which one of the following nursing goals takes *priority* for a client admitted to the hospital with a bleeding peptic ulcer?

a Restoring physiological homeokinesis.

b Meeting client's dependency needs.

c Encouraging the expression of feelings.

d Decreasing the client's anxiety.

7 The asthmatic wheeze is often described as a "cry for the mother." This interpretation reflects belief in the theory of:

a Repressed conflicts.   **c** Symbolism.

b Personality type.   **d** Organ weakness.

8 Which one of the following psychophysiological disturbances involves the integumentary system?

a Skin rashes.   **c** Asthma.

b Rheumatoid arthritis.   **d** Gastritis.

9 The statement "Keep a stiff upper lip" uses "body language" to express which one of the following emotions?

a Anger.   **c** Courage.

b Stubbornness.   **d** Indifference.

10 Tim confided to his best friend that he was going to feign an injury to avoid assignment to an undesirable job. This is an example of which one of the following?

   a Conversion.   **c** Somatization.

   b Hypochondriasis.   **d** Malingering.

11 All of the following terms characterize psychiatric nursing principles that have relevance to the care of adults with psychophysiological disturbances. Which one is *most* specific to the body-mind relationship in somatization?

   a Acceptance.   **c** Adaptation.

   b Holism.   **d** Understanding.

12 Which one of the following rationale statements is the *best* and most *specific* for the nursing goal of encouraging adults with psychophysiological disturbances to express feelings?

   a Externalization rather than internalization of feelings can aid in the prevention of physical symptoms in clients.

   b Explanations of diagnostic and treatment measures can contribute to feelings of control in clients.

   c Opportunities to meet their own needs can overcome clients' feelings of inadequacy.

   d Anticipation of needs can prevent the development of guilt feelings in clients.

chapter 17

adults with
substance dependence

INTRODUCTION

"Very few human behaviors have as far-reaching consequences as do those of the substance-dependent individual. In addition to affecting his own physical, emotional, and social well-being, the behavior of the substance-dependent individual affects the well-being of his family and that of the society at large."* The problem of substance dependence is probably one of our greatest health problems, and the nurse encounters individuals with this problem in a wide variety of settings. With the exception of detoxification and rehabilitation centers where nurses are directly involved on a consistent basis with the care of substance-dependent adults, many nurses may unwittingly be caring for individuals whose presenting problems are something else. In industry, absenteeism and injuries may be related to drug or alcohol use. Similarly individuals may be brought into general hospitals for physical problems related to drug or alcohol withdrawal, for accidental or intentional overdose, and for injuries sustained in automobile accidents as well as in domestic or other violent encounters while under the influence of an addicting agent. In schools increasing numbers of children and adolescents are being seen for poor performance and decreased productivity associated with substance dependence.

Adults with a substance-dependence problem often evoke negative feelings in others based on personal experiences, stereotypes, and misconceptions. Several years ago a therapist who was supportive and therapeutic with most clients was heard exploding in frustration and anger at the manipulations of an alcoholic client. She subsequently acknowledged that she could not tolerate alcoholics and that her negative feelings made it virtually impossible for her to respond therapeutically to persons who abused

*From Taylor, C.M.: Mereness' essentials of psychiatric nursing, ed. 12, St. Louis, 1986, The C.V. Mosby Co., Chapter 17.

alcohol. At the time a student nurse who had identified himself as a reformed alcoholic and a member of Alcoholics Anonymous requested to work with the client and the staff. The client experienced acceptance and understanding from the student and in a relatively brief period of time was accepted and supported by members of the staff. The staff developed a greater understanding of the problems and needs of alcoholic clients in general and this client in particular. Eventually the client was transferred to a facility supported by Alcoholics Anonymous that was more specifically designed to meet his needs. The first step in this positive outcome was to identify negative feelings about alcohol use and alcohol users and then to evaluate their effect on therapeutic intervention.

The purpose of this chapter is to focus on the nurse's self-awareness in relation to feelings and attitudes engendered by individuals dependent on alcohol and drugs, to promote an increased understanding of these dysfunctional responses, and to apply selected phases of the nursing process to the care of adults with substance dependence.

OBJECTIVES

1. To reflect on one's responses to substance-dependent adults as a step toward greater self-awareness.
2. To apply selected phases of the nursing process to the care of clients with substance dependence.
3. To evaluate selected treatment measures used in the care of substance-dependent persons.

1 What are your beliefs and attitudes toward the drinking of alcoholic beverages and the taking of drugs and toward individuals who engage in such activities?

  a Read each of the following 10 attitudinal statements and indicate whether you agree or disagree with it, placing a check in the box in the appropriate column.

Attitudes	Agree	Disagree
1. Parents who drink and use drugs should hide the fact from their children.	☐	☐
2. Drinking two or three cocktails before dinner is an appropriate way to relax.	☐	☐
3. People who rely on drugs are weak-willed individuals.	☐	☐
4. Everyone should have a medicine cabinet well stocked with pills to meet any emergency.	☐	☐
5. Alcohol makes you sexy.	☐	☐
6. All drug addicts are criminals and should be punished.	☐	☐
7. It is appropriate to take sleeping pills whenever you cannot sleep.	☐	☐
8. Alcohol is a stimulant and helps pep you up.	☐	☐
9. All alcoholics are ineffectual human beings who should be pitied.	☐	☐
10. People who use alcohol or drugs in response to stress are morally inferior to other people.	☐	☐

  b All of the above statements reflect beliefs and attitudes toward persons who use alcohol and drugs to varying degrees. With how many did you agree? What other beliefs or attitudes do you have that are not included on ths list?

  c Share your responses with classmates and colleagues in a supervised classroom setting. The following questions are suggested to help focus the discussion.

    1. What were the attitudes in your family toward the use of alcohol and drugs?

    2. What cultural or religious factors may influence your attitudes toward substance use?

    3. What experiences have you had with persons who have used alcohol or drugs to excess?

    4. If your attitudes are essentially negative and nonaccepting, how would you feel about caring for a person with a substance-dependency problem?

    5. How would you be able to control your feelings so as not to respond judgmentally while giving nursing care to these individuals?

2 The following list of 7 nursing diagnoses are applicable to adults with substance dependence. Using your knowledge of behaviors, symptoms, themes, dynamics, etc., make a brief statement about how or why each diagnosis applies. The first one has been filled in to help you get started.

a Acute state of confusion related to excessive use of alcohol: At a level of 0.10% alcohol in the blood, motor and speech activity is impaired. With increasing intake of alcohol, additional deterioration of functioning is seen, including confusion and disorientation.

b Alteration in sensory perceptions related to altered sensory reception, transmission, and/or integration:

c Social isolation related to unacceptable social behaviors:

d Deficient self-care (hygiene) related to perceptual and cognitive impairment from substance abuse:

e Violence potential directed at self or others related to ineffective ego functions (judgment, impulse control):

f Anxiety related to inaccessibility of alcohol and/or drugs on which individual is dependent:

g Chronic state of confusion related to prolonged use of alcohol:

3 Read the following situation and complete the exercises as directed.

    a Using the data provided, develop a nursing care plan for two problems manifested by the alcohol-dependent client in the situation. Diagnostic statements have been identified to help you get started. (See Taylor, Chapter 17.)

    SITUATION: When Mr. White, a widower with four children, was discovered in a semiconscious state by his friends in Alcoholics Anonymous, he was taken to a general hospital and admitted to a unit maintained by Alcoholics Anonymous. Physical examination at the time of Mr. White's admission revealed many old and new bruises apparently sustained from falls while under the influence of alcohol. He was malnourished and dehydrated. He was also disoriented in terms of time, place, and person. Mr. White was placed in a single room where the atmosphere was quiet and the lighting subdued. He was assigned to a nurse who would assume major responsibility for his care for the duration of his hospital stay. Intravenous fluids were started, and he was also to receive clear fluids and a normal diet when he was alert enough to take nourishment orally. An anticonvulsant medication and B vitamins, specifically thiamine and niacin, were administered. Side rails were used on his bed. Vital signs were taken, and he was found to have an elevated temperature. Cooling measures were instituted. When Mr. White regained consciousness, he expressed a wide range of emotions: concern for his children, embarrassment at finding himself on an alcoholic unit, despair over his inability to manage his life better, and fear for the future. The nurse spent time with him and listened to his feelings. She told him about the arrangements that had been made for his children and arranged for them to visit him. Mr. White's friends from Alcoholics Anonymous visited daily for the 2 weeks that he was in the hospital. They, too, listened to his feelings and problems and identified ways that the organization and its members could assist him, including helping him find a job and reestablishing himself with his children.

Nursing diagnosis	Nursing goals	Rationale	Nursing actions	Anticipated results
1. Acute state of confusion related to excessive use of alcohol.				
2. Alteration in health maintenance related to poor health habits associated with excessive alcohol use.				

b Evaluate the effectiveness of Alcoholics Anonymous by listing below 3 factors that have contributed to its success in the treatment of alcohol-dependent persons.

1. _____

2. _____

3. _____

4 Bobby Blake admitted himself into a drug treatment center in an effort to stop a long-standing drug habit that had begun in high school with the use of marijuana. At the time of his admission Bobby was in poor physical health. He had spent all available money to sustain his addiction and was undernourished. He had infected needle sites and many dental caries from neglecting his teeth. He spoke angrily about his parents and school officials, blaming them for his use of drugs and criticizing them for not being more alert to his drug use. At the time of admission Bobby had not used any drugs for over 24 hours and was experiencing withdrawal symptoms.

a As a part of assessment, describe the symptoms of withdrawal that might be observed in Bobby Blake at the time of his admission.

b Identify 2 nursing diagnoses that would apply to Bobby Blake at the time of admission. One diagnostic statement should focus on his physical problems and the other should focus on an emotional problem.

1. Physical diagnostic statement:

2. Emotional diagnostic statement:

c Bobby Blake was considered a candidate for methadone. At a staff meeting this treatment method was evaluated. List below at least 3 advantages and 3 disadvantages of methadone treatment. One advantage has been filled in to help you get started.

Advantages	Disadvantages
1. More humane withdrawal.	1.
2.	2.
3.	3.
4.	

TEST ITEMS

DIRECTIONS: Select the *best* response. (Answers appear in the Appendix.)

1 Physical dependence on a substance such as heroin is evident when the substance is unavailable and the individual:

  a Experiences extremely high levels of anxiety.

  b Continues to crave the substance.

  c Exhibits symptoms of withdrawal.

  d Expresses anger at unavailability of the substance.

2 The term *tolerance* used in relation to substance dependence refers to which one of the following?

  a Individual's need for increased amounts of alcohol or drugs in order to achieve the desired effect.

  b Family's acceptance or indifference to a member's drug or alcohol-dependency problem.

  c Government's failure to act responsibly in controlling availability of alcohol and drugs.

  d Individual's compulsive use of alcohol or drugs to achieve a sense of well-being.

3 Which on of the following nursing diagnostic statements is *most* specific to an adult with psychological dependence on alcohol or drugs?

  a Convulsions related to inaccessibility of addictive substance.

  b Hallucinations related to disrupted sensory perceptions from substance use.

c Confusion related to prolonged and excessive use of alcohol or drugs.

d Anxiety related to inaccessibility of substance on which an individual is dependent.

4 Some people describe alcohol as a "superego solvent," meaning that it removes the barriers to behavior normally provided by the superego. Which one of the following statements *best* reflects this phenomenon?

a Alcohol encourages the expression of id impulses.

b Alcohol releases an individual's learned inhibitions.

c Alcohol interferes with judgment and impulse control.

d Alcohol clouds an individual's memory for recent events.

5 *All but which one* of the following medications is indicated for a person experiencing an acute reaction to withdrawal from alcohol?

a Sedatives. **c** Vitamins.

b Anticonvulsants. **d** Antabuse.

6 In caring for an adult experiencing delirium tremens the nurse observes the client picking nervously at his sheets and complaining of the roaches in his bed. The nurse can respond most helpfully by saying:

a "I'll put the light on and they will go away."

b "It must be frightening to experience that. I'll stay with you."

c "That's terrible. I'll go call the exterminator right now."

d "Close your eyes and you won't be able to see them."

7 Methadone as a treatment for drug dependency is controversial mainly because it:

a Is just as expensive as heroin.

b Interferes with the individual's motivation to change.

c Is a synthetic opiate substance.

d Maintains the individual's dependence on another drug.

8 A nursing activity that is carried out prior to administering methadone to a person addicted to heroin is:

a Checking the dietary intake.

b Collecting a urine specimen.

c Drawing blood.

d Taking vital signs.

9 In which one of the following drug dependencies is it *absolutely essential* that the substance be withdrawn gradually?

   a Cocaine.   **c** LSD.

   b Heroin.   **d** Phenobarbital.

10 Which one of the following agents is *not* a central nervous system depressant?

   a Alcohol.   **c** Cocaine.

   b Barbiturates.   **d** Opiates.

11 Which one of the following defenses interferes the *most* with a person recognizing and accepting drug addiction as a problem?

   a Denial.   **c** Suppression.

   b Preoccupation.   **d** Regresson.

12 The nurse's goal is to help the adult with a substance-abuse problem develop alternative coping methods to deal with the stresses of life. Which one of the following nursing actions is *most* specific to this nursing objective?

   a Communicating a caring but firm attitude.

   b Giving negative appraisals for breaks in abstinence.

   c Encouraging participation in expressive activities.

   d Using therapeutic communication skills in interactions.

chapter 18

adults whose behavior is antisocial

INTRODUCTION

"Antisocial behaviors are somewhat unique in that their very existence is viewed as an assault on the fundamental values of society. This does not mean that the individual, his family, and immediate associates do not suffer as a result of his behavior; rather the nature of the individual's behavior is such that it threatens the community at large by opposing the social order, even though few people may be directly involved. Examples of such behaviors are antisocial acts and sexual deviations."*

Adults whose behaviors are antisocial are most often maligned and misunderstood by the general public. In addition, professional and nonprofessional caretakers alike sometimes fail to recognize that adults whose behaviors are antisocial are human beings with unique problems requiring accepting, respectful, and considerate treatment. Based on limited experiences, hearsay, and fear, negative feelings and stereotypical generalizations are an integral part of nontherapeutic responses and need to be recognized and dealt with in order to provide a therapeutic interpersonal environment in which to treat these individuals.

The purpose of this chapter is to focus on the nurse's self-awareness in relation to feelings and attitudes toward adults whose behaviors are sexually and socially disruptive, to promote an increased understanding of these individuals, and to apply selected phases of the nursing process to the care of antisocial clients.

OBJECTIVES

1. To reflect on one's responses to adults whose behaviors are sexually and socially disruptive as a step toward greater self-awareness and therapeutic effectiveness.
2. To identify characteristics of a therapeutic approach to adults who exhibit sexually deviant behaviors.

*From Taylor, C.M.: Mereness' essentials of psychiatric nursing, ed. 12, St. Louis, 1986, The C.V. Mosby Co., Chapter 18.

192

3. To analyze ego functioning in the antisocial individual.

4. To apply selected phases of the nursing process to the care of adults whose behavior is antisocial.

EXERCISES

1 In order to create a therapeutic interpersonal environment in which to treat adults whose behaviors are sexually and/or socially disruptive, nurses and other health care workers need to be aware of any negative attitudes they have toward such individuals.

a Listed below are 10 attitudinal statements about such individuals. Read each statement, decide whether you agree or disagree with it, and then place a check in the box in the appropriate column.

Attitudes	Agree	Disagree
1. People who practice antisocial acts should be imprisoned to protect society.	☐	☐
2. Sexual deviants could control their sexual impulses if they wanted to.	☐	☐
3. Antisocial individuals are hopeless and it is a waste of time to treat them.	☐	☐
4. People who engage in sexual acts offensive to society should not work with children.	☐	☐
5. Antisocial individuals should not be housed with the mentally ill who cannot protect themselves.	☐	☐
6. All homosexuals are sick and should be classified as such.	☐	☐
7. Experiencing pleasure through sexually deviant acts is sinful.	☐	☐
8. If you trust a "con artist," you deserve to be hurt by them.	☐	☐
9. Antisocial persons are all criminals and deserve punishment.	☐	☐
10. People who practice sexually offensive acts should be castrated.	☐	☐

b All of those statements are subjective responses to socially dysfunctional behaviors that can interfere with effective nursing activities. With how many did you agree?

c Share your feelings and beliefs with classmates and colleagues in a supervised classroom setting. The following questions are suggested to help focus the discussion:

1. Can you identify the source of your feelings? (Example, a past experience, something you have read, seen, or heard.)

2. What effect would communicating any of these feelings or beliefs to a person whose behavior is sexually or socially disruptive have on your efforts to develop a nurse-client relationship?

3. What can you do to begin to overcome these feelings and beliefs now that you are more aware of them?

2 Persons who request help to change their sexual orientations and to control their sexual activities are sometimes hospitalized to provide a supervised and structured environment in which their aggressive and sexual drives can be rechanneled into a schedule of daily activities. List below 5 additional characteristics of the therapeutic approach to these individuals.

1. _____
2. _____
3. _____
4. _____
5. _____

3 Nursing diagnosis: Inadequate impulse control related to inadequate or inappropriate ego development.

This nursing diagnosis formed the basis of a nursing care plan for a 32-year-old man who was admitted to the psychiatric service with a diagnosis (DSM-III) of adult antisocial behavior. It was based on assessment data and an analysis of his behaviors as they reflected ego functioning. Although his ego does function effectively to a limited degreee, such as reflected by a good memory and high intelligence, it generally is ineffective.

a Listed below are 12 behaviors reflecting ineffective ego functioning. A behavior may reflect more than one ego function. Read each behavior and place a check in the box or boxes in the appropriate ego function column(s). The first one has been completed to help you get started.

Behaviors	Ego functions			
	Use of cognitive abilities	Relating with others	Insight, judgment	Control of impulses
1. Uses his charm to "con" others.	☑	☑	☐	☐
2. Drinks heavily then drives his car.	☐	☐	☐	☐
3. Writes checks he cannot cover.	☐	☐	☐	☐
4. Loses his temper easily and acts out violently.	☐	☐	☐	☐
5. Denies that he has any emotional problems.	☐	☐	☐	☐
6. Fabricates (lies) to cover his misdeeds.	☐	☐	☐	☐
7. Blames others for his "misfortunes."	☐	☐	☐	☐
8. Manipulates others for profit.	☐	☐	☐	☐
9. Justifies stealing and cheating with rationalizations.	☐	☐	☐	☐
10. Spends money irresponsibly.	☐	☐	☐	☐
11. Acts out impulsively with no concern for consequences.	☐	☐	☐	☐
12. Maintains few loyalties.	☐	☐	☐	☐

b Develop a nursing care plan for the client. A nursing goal has been provided to help you get started.

Nursing goal	Rationale	Nursing actions	Anticipated results
To support the client's ego functioning.			

TEST ITEMS

DIRECTIONS: Select the *best* response. (Answers appear in the Appendix).

1 The pedophile's choice of a sex object is primarily based on:
  a Feelings of tenderness toward children.
  b Fears of incestuous impulses.
  c Preference for a passive sexual role.
  d Difficulty relating with adults.

2 An individual who finds sexual satisfaction by dressing in the clothing of the opposite sex is a(n):
  a Homosexual.   **c** Transvestite.
  b Exhibitionist.   **d** Voyeur.

3 The *most* effective approach to prevention of sexual deviance in children is:
  a Consistent and tactful approach to sex education in the schools.
  b Positive parent-child relationships in a healthy family setting.
  c Early detection and treatment of conflictual sexual identification.
  d Redirection of aggressive and sexual impulses into appropriate channels.

4 Which one of the following factors is *most* critical to successful treatment of a person with sexually deviant behavior?

  a Avoidance of legal involvements.

  b Money available for treatment.

  c Motivation to change.

  d Fear of disclosure.

5 Clients who are hospitalized for antisocial acts can benefit *most* from which one of the following environments?

  a Structured.   **c** Permissive.

  b Stimulating.   **d** Punitive.

6 Which one of the following *most* characterizes the adult who engages in antisocial acts?

  a Anticipatory anxiety.   **c** Criminal behavior.

  b Charismatic personality.   **d** Sexual acting-out.

7 A person who consciously fabricates stories to impress others and to get out of compromising situations is:

  a Rationalizing.   **c** Projecting.

  b Cheating.   **d** Lying.

8 Which part of the personality dominates the behaviors of persons with antisocial behaviors?

  a Id.   **c** Conscience.

  b Ego.   **d** Ego ideal.

9 Which one of the following nursing diagnoses is *least* applicable to the antisocial individual? Social isolation related to:

  a Unaccepted social behavior.

  b Inability to engage in satisfying personal relationships.

  c Unaccepted social values.

  d Deficiency in intelligence.

10 In response to a client's manipulative acts the nurse should provide:

  a Reasonable punishment.   **c** Friendly manner.

  b Permissive atmosphere.   **d** Consistent limits.

196

populations at risk

adolescents

INTRODUCTION

"Today's adolescent confronts this critical developmental period during a time of great stress generated by the highly complex postindustrial society in which he lives. The stresses of contemporary Western culture may contribute to the distress, alienation, loneliness, and despair that at times characterize the adolescent experience."* Adolescents who are unable to deal with the multiplicity of tasks of the era and who are overwhelmed with the impending responsibilities of adulthood may seek to escape these challenges through self-destructive behaviors, including suicide and drug and alcohol abuse. Or they may seek refuge in psychotic, somatic, and anxiety disorders commonly manifested in adults. Finally, dysfunctional behaviors such as truancy, juvenile delinquency, sexual promiscuity, and aggressiveness may reflect adolescents' problems with the emotions of fear, anxiety, and despair, and rather than talk about these feelings, they act them out instead.

The purpose of this chapter is to apply phases of the nursing process to this population at risk: adolescents.

OBJECTIVES

1. To apply selected phases of the nursing process to the care of adolescents whose behaviors are dysfunctional.
2. To reflect on one's responses to emotionally disturbed adolescents as a step toward greater self-awareness.

EXERCISES

1 Read the following mini-situations and write an appropriate nursing diagnosis for each one. The first one has been filled in to help you get started.

*From Taylor, C.M.: Mereness' essentials of psychiatric nursing, ed. 12, St. Louis, 1986, The C.V. Mosby Co., Chapter 19.

Mini-situations	Nursing diagnosis
1. Jeremy exhibited many behavioral problems in childhood—truancy, fire-setting, and shoplifting. At age 15 he raped his sister because "voices" told him to do it. He was hospitalized on a psychiatric service for observation. There was question, however, as to whether he was really psychotic or was claiming hallucinations to cover his inability to control his impulsive acts.	Aggressive behaviors directed at others related to poor impulse control.
2. Sarah's family traveled a good deal while Sarah was growing up. Consequently, she formed few friendships. When she was 16, her father died, and she and her mother settled down with her grandparents. Sarah attended high school and became involved with a peer group that was experimenting with drugs partly out of rebellion against authority and partly as a means to finding their identities. Sarah experienced a "bad trip" on LSD and was hospitalized because of severe anxiety, agitation, and violence directed toward herself and others.	
3. Alice has bulimia. She was admitted to the medical service and intravenous therapy was ordered to correct a severe electrolyte imbalance. Until last year, Alice engaged in secret binge and purge episodes. She was aware that her preoccupation with food and dieting and the episodic binges followed by self-induced vomiting were not normal, and she concealed her activities from her family and friends. However, the repeated and unexplained disappearance of large quantities of food in the household made her family suspicious, and when Alice had to be hospitalized for dehydration and electrolyte imbalance, her behavior patterns and preoccupations were revealed.	
4. There had been several successful and near-successful suicides at Mike's school. In the aftermath of the anger and grief over these tragic events, parent, teacher, and student groups mobilized their efforts to learn about suicide and how to prevent it. Therefore, when Mike was denied admission to the college of his choice and subsequently offered his car to his best friend and a treasured record collection to his brother, his family, friends, and teachers were sensitive to his depression and suicidal ideation and arranged for him to receive professional help.	
5. Wayne had always been a neat child. When the other children engaged in artwork, sports, or other activities that might get him dirty, he hung back and would not participate. His mother was assured it was a phase that he would outgrow. Instead of outgrowing it, Wayne's preoccupation with cleanliness, order, dirt, and pollution increased. He was taken for professional help when his obsessions and ritualistic cleaning activities interfered with his school attendance.	
6. Cheryl refused to go to school and stayed in bed with the covers pulled up over her head. She was nonverbal. She used the bathroom but refused to eat her meals with the family. Food left on a tray in her room disappeared and her mother assumed she was eating. After a month, Cheryl was admitted for treatment to an adolescent unit in the state hospital.	

2 Using the following nursing diagnosis for an adolescent client with anorexia nervosa, develop a plan of care in which short- and long-term goals and physical and emotional needs are met. Two nursing goals have been entered in the plan to help you get started.

Nursing diagnosis: Extreme weight loss related to fear of fat and distorted body image.

Nursing goals	Rationale	Nursing actions	Anticipated results
1. Short term: Restoration of normal nutritional status.			
2. Long term: Promotion of feelings of self-esteem and self-worth.			

3 Self-awareness is an integral part of all phases of the nursing process. Beginning with assessment, when initial contact with a client is made, and ending with evaluation, when you look at the outcomes of your care, you need to focus on your feelings about working with a young person. Although true for all nurses, self-awareness may have particular relevance for young nurses who may be close in age to their clients and for older nurses who may have children similar in age to the clients with whom they are working. The purpose of this exercise is to help all nurses recognize the need for self-assessment. The following list of topics is suggested for discussion, sharing of feelings, elaboration of personal experiences, and role-playing in a supervised group setting with colleagues and peers. You may be able to add other topics for discussion as you begin to work with adolescent clients who are emotionally disturbed. The success of this exercise is dependent on the members' willingness to share their feelings in the group and on peers' ability to respond with respect to the feelings being shared.

a The client is manipulating one staff member against another to try and get special privileges to watch TV. You discover that the client has succeeded in manipulating you to give him these privileges and you feel angry toward him.

b The client has a history of bulimia with episodes of binge feeding and purging. You come from a background where food was often scarce, and you feel that this client's behavior is wasteful and sinful.

c The client is a young, good-looking man who you find attractive. He invites you on a date and you feel in conflict.

d The client is a young, seductive woman who you find attractive. She has aroused your sexual feelings and you feel guilty.

e The client is an anorexic adolescent girl who is emaciated. Her physical appearance is repulsive to you, and you are finding it difficult to accept her and respond in a caring way.

f The client is a young adolescent who uses heroin to excess. You have recently been robbed by a drug addict and feel angry toward this client even though he was not involved in your losses.

g The client is a young adolescent who reminds you of your own children and evokes a variety of feelings (love, anger, guilt, etc.) that are interfering with your objectivity.

h The client is an adolescent who has made several unsuccessful suicide attempts. He comes from a family that is well-off financially and has had many opportunities denied a close friend or family member you know who succeeded in taking his own life. You are finding it difficult to respond in an understanding and accepting way to this young man.

i The client is an unwed mother who is debating whether or not to have an abortion. She has decided that she will not keep the baby should she carry it to term. Your religious and ethical values are making it difficult for you to respond therapeutically to this client.

j The client is depressed. You too have been feeling depressed and associating with this client intensifies your feelings. You find yourself identifying with this client and this is making it difficult for you to respond objectively.

TEST ITEMS

DIRECTIONS: Select the *best* response. (Answers appear in the Appendix).

1 Which one of the following theorists did the *least* work with adolescents?
  a Harry Stack Sullivan. **c** Erik Erikson.
  b Sigmund Freud. **d** Anna Freud.

2 *All but which one* of the following is characteristic of the adolescent era?
  a Acceleration of physical growth.
  b Maintenance of childish ties with the family.
  c Negotiation of the task of identity.
  d Renegotiation of childhood relationships.

3 Which one of the following emotional disturbances is experienced by adolescents?
  a Psychotic disorders. **c** Eating disorders.
  b Substance abuse. **d** All of the above.

4 Which one of the following factors is the *most* influential in promoting emotional health in the adolescent?
  a Successful negotiation of the developmental stages.
  b Close peer-group affiliations.
  c Community interest in the adolescent.
  d Safe and secure environment.

5 Which one of the following factors contributes *most* to difficulty recognizing emotional disturbances in adolescents?
  a Normal rebellion against authority figures in adolescents.
  b Failure of severe emotional problems to emerge until adulthood.
  c General mood fluctuations normally seen in adolescents.
  d Adolescent refusal to cooperate with health care workers.

6 Which one of the following is associated with anorexia nervosa in its *early* stages?
  a Loss of appetite. **c** Amenorrhea.
  b Distorted body image. **d** Binge eating.

7 The bulimic individual is characterized by *all but which one* of the following?
   a Perfectionism.   **c** Severe dieting.
   b Emaciation.   **d** Laxative abuse.

8 Which one of the following nursing diagnoses is *most* specific to a person with bulimia?
   a Extreme weight loss related to fear of fat.
   b Alteration in health maintenance related to ineffective individual coping.
   c Altered nutritional status related to starvation and purging behaviors.
   d Ineffective family coping related to situational or developmental crises.

9 Which one of the following is the *most* appropriate short-term goal for a person experiencing anorexia nervosa?
   a To encourage client's expression of feelings.
   b To restore client's normal nutritional status.
   c To alter client's body image.
   d To promote client's peer alliances.

10 Cues to adolescent suicide include:
   a Giving away valued possessions.
   b Talking about death and suicide.
   c Changing sleep patterns.
   d All of the above.

11 If the nurse suspects that an adolescent client is thinking about suicide, she should do which one of the following?
   a Distract him with cheerful topics of conversation.
   b Avoid mentioning suicide to him to avoid precipitating a suicide attempt.
   c Encourage him to share his feelings and suicidal thoughts with her.
   d Tell him he should not commit suicide because it would hurt his family.

12 The client with a poor body image and low self-esteem would be *best* helped by which one of the following nursing actions?
   a Telling him he is a worthwhile person.
   b Avoiding any form of criticism.
   c Encouraging a daily grooming routine.
   d Giving praise and compliments.

chapter 20

populations at risk

the elderly

INTRODUCTION "Most elderly persons are able to lead active and productive lives, and continue to grow and learn during this developmental period. A person who has successfully completed earlier developmental tasks has a higher possibility of successfully completing the task of aging, and a helpful and supportive environment certainly contributes to their successful resolution."*

However, although people are living longer and healthier lives, problems do arise. A variety of physiological, social, psychological, and environmental stressors, in combination or alone, impinge on the elderly and create difficulties. Diminishing interpersonal and economic resources, decreasing physiological functions, increasing urbanization, accelerating rates of social change, and discriminating practices have increased their vulnerability and have indeed made them a "population at risk."

As the elderly population increases, so does the number of elderly health care recipients. The purpose of this chapter is to increase nurses' understanding of the needs of the aged and to apply selected phases of the nursing process to the care of elderly clients.

OBJECTIVES

1. To differentiate among characteristic responses observed in the elderly.
2. To apply selected phases of the nursing process to the care of elderly clients.

*From Taylor, C.M.: Mereness' essentials of psychiatric nursing, ed. 11, St. Louis, 1986, The C.V. Mosby Co., Chapter 20.

203

1 The life review, with a tendency to reminiscence, appears to be a nearly universal adaptive response in old age, facilitating the satisfactory closure to life. In addition to the life review, there are five other responses or themes associated with, but not unique to, aging: loneliness, loss and grief, suspicion, depression (despair), and confusion. In this exercise read each one of the following 15 statements made by elderly, retired residents of a nursing home. Categorize each one in terms of the characteristic responses to aging by placing a check in the box in the appropriate column. The first one has been filled in to help you get started.

Statements	Life review	Loneliness	Depression	Suspicion	Confusion	Loss—grief
1. "When I was a boy, we used to go fishing every Sunday afternoon after church."	☑	☐	☐	☐	☐	☐
2. "I must get up. Let me up. I have to get dressed or else I will be late for work."	☐	☐	☐	☐	☐	☐
3. "I wish I could hear what they are saying. I'm certain they are talking about me."	☐	☐	☐	☐	☐	☐
4. "My wife died 13 years ago but I still get sad when I talk about her."	☐	☐	☐	☐	☐	☐
5. "I remember our first car. My brothers and I took turns cranking it up to get it started."	☐	☐	☐	☐	☐	☐
6. "There is nothing left to live for. I can't go on like this anymore. Life has no meaning."	☐	☐	☐	☐	☐	☐
7. "I feel so alone. There is no one I can talk to anymore."	☐	☐	☐	☐	☐	☐
8. "Help me shave. I want to look my best when my grandmother visits me tonight."	☐	☐	☐	☐	☐	☐
9. "Why are people laughing at me behind my back?"	☐	☐	☐	☐	☐	☐
10. "My children don't visit anymore. I wish they would bring my grandchildren to see me."	☐	☐	☐	☐	☐	☐
11. "Life is an effort. I might as well be dead."	☐	☐	☐	☐	☐	☐
12. "When I was a girl, my beaus would flock to my porch on a summer's night and serenade me."	☐	☐	☐	☐	☐	☐
13. "What I miss most about being here is not having my old dog. I had to put him to sleep. It still makes me sad."	☐	☐	☐	☐	☐	☐
14. "Bring me my boots and my horse! Get me my bugle. I must sound the charge."	☐	☐	☐	☐	☐	☐
15. "I have no interest in eating. I wish they would stop feeding me and let me die."	☐	☐	☐	☐	☐	☐

Responses to aging

2 "Survival with esteem—not mere physical survival—is the goal of the aged person."* Although stated in the text as the goal of the aged, this statement reflects an appropriate goal for anyone actively involved in the care of the aged. Failure to acknowledge this goal can result in the dehumanization of the client. In the following poem survival with esteem is clearly the goal of the elderly woman who silently admonishes the nurse, "Open your eyes nurse, open and see, not a crabbit old woman, look closer, see me." The nurse, on the other hand, has apparently focused all her attention on meeting the woman's physical needs and has failed to communicate interest in and respect for her client. Read the following poem and complete the exercises as directed:

Look closer†

What do you see nurse, what do you see?
What are you thinking when you look at me?
A crabbit old woman, not very wise
Uncertain of habit, with far away eyes,
Who dribbles her food, and makes not reply,
When you say in a loud voice, "I do wish you'd try!"
Who seems not to notice the things that you do,
And forever is losing a stocking or shoe.
Who, unresisting or not, lets you do as you will
With bathing and feeding, the long day to fill.
Is that what you're thinking, is that what you see?
Then open your eyes, you're not looking at me.
I'll tell you who I am as I sit here so still,
As I move at your bidding, as I eat at your will.
I am a small child of 10, with a father and mother,
Brothers and sisters who love one another.
A young girl at 16 with wings at her feet
Dreaming that soon now a lover she'll meet.
A bride soon at 20, my heart gives a leap
Remembering the vows that I promised to keep.
At 25 now I have young of my own
Who need me to build a secure happy home.
A woman of 30, my young now grow fast,
Bound to each other with ties that should last.
At 40 my young now soon will be gone,
But my man stays beside me to see I don't mourn.

*From Taylor, C.M.: Mereness' essentials of psychiatric nursing, ed. 11, St. Louis, 1986, The C.V. Mosby Co., Chapter 20.
†From McCormack, P.M.: Look closer (Crabbit old woman), J. Gerontol. Nurse. **2:**9, 1976

At 50 once more babies play around my knee,
Again we know children, my loved one and me.
Dark days are upon me, my husband is dead,
I look at the future, I shudder with dread,
For my young are all busy rearing young of their own.
And I think of the years and the love I have known.
I'm an old lady now and nature is cruel,
'Tis her jest to make old age look like a fool.
The body it crumbles, grace and vigor depart,
And now there is a stone where I once had a heart.
But inside this old carcass a young girl still dwells,
And now and again my battered heart swells.
I remember the joys, I remember the pain,
And I am loving and living life over again.
I think of the years all too few, gone so fast,
And accept the stark fact that nothing can last.
So open your eyes nurse, open and see,
Not a crabbit old woman, look closer, see me.

a According to Erikson, the task of the elderly is ego integrity versus despair. Using the assessment phase of the nursing process, analyze the woman's response to aging in terms of her negotiation of the task of old age.

b Using the evaluation phase of the nursing process, identify 3 responses made by the nurse that were nontherapeutic and had a dehumanizing effect on the client.
1. _____
2. _____
3. _____

c List below 3 behavioral responses seen in the elderly client that reflect dehumanization.
1. _____
2. _____
3. _____

d Listed on p. 207 are selected verbal responses made by the elderly woman that reflect the characteristics and themes of aging. The themes are identified in parenthesis. A nursing goal has been entered for each one. In the space provided:

1. Write a rationale statement reflecting the theme identified.
2. List 2 to 3 therapeutic nursing actions that are appropriate to each goal.

Behavioral responses	Nursing goals	Rationale	Nursing actions
1. "What do you see nurse, what do you see, what are you thinking when you look at me? A crabbit old woman, not very wise. . ."	Facilitate communication and validation. (Suspicion)		1. 2. 3.
2. "Who seems not to notice the things that you do, and forever is losing a stocking or shoe."	Provide reality orientation and stimulation. (Confusion)		1. 2. 3.
3. "Dark days are upon me, my husband is dead, I look at the future, I shudder wtih dread."	Encourage expression of feelings. (Grief)		1. 2. 3.
4. "I look at the future, I shudder with dread, For my young are all busy rearing young of their own."	Provide opportunities to relate. (Loneliness)		1. 2. 3.
5. "I'm an old lady now and nature is cruel, 'tis her jest to make old age look like a fool."	Increase self-esteem. (Depression)		1. 2. 3.
6. "I remember the joys, I remember the pain, and I am loving and living life over again."	Support the client in her reminiscences. (Life review)		1. 2. 3.

3 In assessing the elderly client with organic brain disorders the nurse would observe characteristic symptoms and behavior patterns. Listed below are 10 signs and symptoms of Alzheimer's disease, a degenerative brain disease. Read each one and differentiate between them in terms of early versus late signs and symptoms by placing a check in the box in the appropriate column. The first one has been filled in to help you get started.

Signs and symptoms	Early	Late
1. Coma	☐	☑
2. Loss of memory	☐	☐
3. Difficulty communicating	☐	☐
4. Poor attention span	☐	☐
5. Incontinence	☐	☐
6. Poor judgment	☐	☐
7. Diminished energy	☐	☐
8. Confusion	☐	☐
9. Agitation	☐	☐
10. Inability to walk	☐	☐

4 Listed below are 6 nursing diagnoses that are applicable to elderly persons with behavioral disturbances. Using your knowledge of behaviors, signs and symptoms, themes, and dynamics, make a brief statement about how or why each diagnosis applies. The first one has been filled in to help you get started.

a Social isolation related to inadequate personal resources: Loss of friends through illness, death, etc., plus decreased involvement with family, accounts for much of the social isolation experienced by the elderly.

b Potential for self-directed violence related to suicidal behavior:

c Suspicion related to sensory impairment:

d Disturbance in self-concept related to psychosocial factors:

e Confusion related to hospitalization:

f Impaired verbal communication related to organic brain syndrome (Alzheimer's disease):

TEST ITEMS

DIRECTIONS: Select the *best* response. (Answers appear in the Appendix.)

1 Which one of the following factors has contributed to the increased life expectancy and the growing number of elderly in the population?
  a Better preventive measures in health maintenance.
  b More effective treatment measures during illness.
  c Improved treatment of injuries.
  d All of the above.

2 Recent research indicates that mental problems of the elderly are primarily the result of:
  a Alzheimer's disease. **c** Schizophrenia.
  b Anxiety disorders. **d** Loneliness.

3 Which one of the following experiences has the *most* profound affect on the aged person?
  a Decreasing psychomotor abilities.
  b Increasing perceptual difficulties.
  c Diminishing income from retirement.
  d Failing memory for recent events.

4 The life review primarily involves which one of the following?
  a Grief. **c** Depression.
  b Reminiscence. **d** Loneliness.

5 Rather than grieve over interpersonal losses, many elderly people respond by:
  a Experiencing high anxiety.
  b Becoming very depressed.
  c Withdrawing from reality.
  d Developing physical symptoms.

6 In responding helpfully to the elderly client who painfully talks about guilt feelings associated with a significant loss that occurred years before, the nurse would do which one of the following?

    a Validate to the client that it is painful to lose a loved one.

    b Introduce a neutral and less emotional topic to the client.

    c Reassure the client that there is no reason for feeling guilty.

    d None of the above.

7 The nursing diagnosis of fear related to sensory impairment is *most* specific to which one of the following symptoms seen in the elderly?

    a Loss of memory for recent events.

    b Decreased ability to concentrate.

    c Diminished perceptual ability.

    d Poor judgment.

8 Early signs of Alzheimer's disease include which one of the following?

    a Gait disturbances.   **c** Disorientation.

    b Memory impairment.   **d** Restlessness.

9 Which one of the following nursing actions takes *priority* when giving care to a client with advanced Alzheimer's disease?

    a Promoting group social interactions.

    b Encouraging expressions of feelings.

    c Facilitating the life review.

    d Providing safety measures.

10 Major tranquilizers are given to combat agitation in persons with Alzheimer's disease. These medications are given in small amounts because of the:

    a Weight loss commonly seen in the elderly.

    b Delay in drug elimination from the body in the aged.

    c Danger of suicide by overdosing in older people.

    d Potentiation effect when taken by the aged with other drugs.

chapter 21

populations at risk

the physically ill

INTRODUCTION | Individuals confronted with serious physical illnesses and hospitalization face a crisis. They and their families must adjust to a change in roles and life-style. Close, daily supportive relationships are usually disrupted by hospitalization. Self-esteem and body image may be threatened. Dehumanizing experiences are encountered. Privacy is invaded. Feelings of fear, anxiety, helplessness, and hopelessness may be experienced.

One responds to a crisis precipitated by a physical illness in either an adaptive, growth-promoting way or in a dysfunctional, disorganizing way. Personality makeup, early life experiences, previous encounters with illness, and available coping measures all contribute to how the physically ill and their families respond when faced with serious illness, hospitalization, treatment measures, and the threat of possible death. In addition, the nature of the illness itself, whether acute or chronic, whether stigmatizing, disabling, disfiguring, or life-threatening, also plays a critical role in the behavioral outcomes manifested by this population at risk, the physically ill and their families.

"It is a fact that nursing care of physically ill persons is characterized by the execution of an increasing number of highly technical procedures, often to the neglect of attempts to meet the person's emotional needs."* Studies have indicated that growing dissatisfaction with nursing care has not related to physical care but, rather to professional nurses' failure to establish meaningful, caring relationships with their clients. Nurses have been criticized for their impersonal approach and their lack of warmth and empathy. The following excerpt illustrates this point all too well:

*From Taylor, C.M.: Mereness' essentials of psychiatric nursing, ed. 12, St. Louis, 1986, The C.V. Mosby Co., Chapter 21.

211

I am the proud recipient
Of fine intensive care.
Efficient, modern, monitored—
Describe my daily fare.

I cough . . . . I breathe . . . . I move . . . . I turn.
I'm like a small machine.
I've tubes and leads. I'm wired!! I'm tired!!
But God, I cannot sleep.

Will I live or will I die?
My prognosis is unknown.
Inside I'm tense. I ache. I quake.
I'm afraid to be alone.

I hear the sounds of busy feet
And feel the busy hands.
Voices talk and seem concerned,
But do they understand?*

With the exception of life-threatening situations in which physical needs take priority over emotional needs, the skilled nurse can often meet both the physical and emotional needs of the client simultaneously. However, in order to meet the emotional needs of any client, including those of the physically ill, the nurse needs to strive for self-awareness, develop an understanding of clients' emotional reactions to physical illness, and utilize therapeutic communication skills to help clients express their feelings, share their concerns, and work through problems related to their illnesses. Clients' adaptations to the stress of physical illness, hospitalization, treatment measures, and the threat of death often depend on helpful interactions with skilled and sensitive nurses.

The purpose of this chapter is to emphasize nursing measures that can be used to give not only efficient but effective care and to meet not only physical needs but emotional needs as well with this population at risk: the physically ill.

OBJECTIVES

1. To apply selected phases of the nursing process to the care of clients who are physically ill.
2. To review communication skills used to interact therapeutically with the dying client.
3. To discuss the stages of dying.

*From Mezzanotte, E.J.: Efficient care? Nursing '74 **4**:37, 1974.

1 Listed below are 6 nursing diagnoses specific to individuals who are physically ill. Using your knowledge of emotional reactions to physical illness, make a brief statement about how or why each diagnosis applies. The first one has been filled in to help you get started.

a Feelings of dehumanization and low self-esteem related to the use of life-sustaining mechanical devices: Persons who depend on mechanical devices for life often feel that the devices are more important than they are, that they are part of the machine and have lost control over their bodies and their lives.

b Fear related to organ transplants:

c Depression and grief related to loss of a body part:

d Anger related to dependency associated with long-term cardiac pathology and prospective cardiac surgery:

e Guilt related to the birth of an imperfect infant:

f Mixed feelings of relief, remorse, loss, shame, and guilt related to a successful planned abortion:

2 Understanding, emotional support, realistic reassurance, acceptance, caring, empathy, and attentiveness are all general characteristics of therapeutic nursing responses. To be implemented with a client, each response must be expressed behaviorally. Specifically, what can the nurse do to show emotional support and acceptance? What can the nurse say to communicate caring and understanding?

List below 6 nursing approaches that behaviorally illustrate these general characteristics of therapeutic care. An example has been filled in to help you get started.

a Be alert to the client's verbal and nonverbal cues that indicate readiness to talk about themselves, their feelings, and their concerns.

b _____

_____

_____

c _____

_____

_____

d _____

_____

_____

e _____

_____

_____

f _____

_____

_____

g _____

_____

_____

3 Nurses caring for physically ill clients are faced with the possibility that the client may die. A sudden, unexpected death comes as a shock to everyone. The nurse may grieve along with the family. There is no opportunity to prepare for such a death or to work through feelings of loss in advance. A terminal illness in which death is anticipated, however, allows the client, the family, and the nurse to work through these feelings in advance of the death. This process is called anticipatory grief. Clients who are aware that they are dying often respond in a generally predictable pattern, going through five stages in the dying process: denial, anger, bargaining, depression (loss), and acceptance. Others involved with the dying person, including the family and the nurse, may also experience similar stages.

a The following situation consists of segments of interactions occurring over time between a nurse and a dying woman. In the situation a variety of different communication skills are used by the nurse to facilitate the client's progress through the dying process. Each communication skill has been italicized and numbered. Place the number of the examples in the space provided after each communication skill. A communication skill may be illustrated more than once; an example may illustrate more than one skill. The first one has been filled in to help you get started.

Communication skills

a. Clarifying _____   f. Reflecting _____
b. Encouraging _____   g. Refocusing _____
c. Exploring _____   h. Seeking information __1.__
d. Focusing _____   i. Suggesting _____
e. Giving reassurance _____   j. Understanding _____

SITUATION

Stage One: Denial

(After entering the client's room and greeting her, the nurse asks:)

1. **N** *"Have you seen your doctor today, Helen?"*
   C "Yes, Martha. He just left."

2. **N** *"And?"*
   C "Oh, he said something about a tumor. But I don't understand all that technical talk. It's too much for my feeble brain." (Laughingly).

3. **N** *"Are there any questions I can try and answer for you?"*
   C "No. That's OK. You know what they say. What you don't know can't hurt you."

4. **N** *"You don't want to talk about it?"*
   C "Not yet. Why borrow trouble? Anyway, the doctor said I am going to have more tests. No sense worrying until all the results are in."

5. **N** *"It sounds a little like you are worrying now."*
   C "A little. But I'm trying to put those fears out of my head. But it's hard, being in the hospital, surrounded by the sounds and smells of sick people. I keep telling myself that it's happening to them, not me."

215

6. **N** *"Do you want to talk about those fears?"*

   C "No, Martha. I don't think so. Let's wait and see what happens. There will be lots of time for talking later. And, maybe if I'm lucky there will be nothing to talk about."

7. **N** *"I just want you to know that I'm here for you when you need me. I'll be happy to listen when you feel like talking."*

   C "Thank you, Martha." (Whispering.) "I'll remember that. I may need you." (Briskly, loudly.) "Now, let's talk about something else. Let me tell you about my daughter, Janie."

Stage Two: Anger

(The nurse enters the client's room and greets her.)

8. **N** *"How are you today, Helen?"*

   C "Terrible!" (The client sits stiffly in bed, a frown on her face, gripping the bed clothes tightly.)

9. **N** *"What's the matter?"*

   C "Where have you been? You should have been here an hour ago."

10. **N** *"I don't understand. What has happened to make you so upset?"*

    C "I was climbing the walls!"

11. **N** *"You are saying you were in pain?"*

    C "Pain's not the word for it. Why do I have to suffer so? And I was all alone. No one cares what happens to me."

12. **N** *"You sound pretty angry, Helen."*

    C "You bet I'm angry."

13. **N** *"Perhaps you'd like to tell me about it."*

    C "Well, I finally got my medication. The nurse gave it to me early. But what I had to go through to get it! I can take anything except the pain."

14. **N** *"There is no need for you to hurt so. I'll speak with your doctor about shortening the time between your doses. Now, let me rub your back and help ease up those tense muscles. Then we can talk more if you like."*

Stage Three: Bargaining

(When the nurse enters the client's room, the client initiates the conversation.)

   C "Hi, Martha. It's Janie's birthday Saturday."

15. **N** *"Really? She'll be 13, won't she?"*

    C "Yes. My baby is growing up."

16. **N** *"You have two boys besides Janie, don't you?"*

    C "Twin boys. They were 15 when she was born. They are grown and on their own now. I'm not worried about them."

17. **N** *"But you're worried about Janie?"*

    C "She's now a teenager. That's such a difficult time these days. She's just beginning to be interested in boys. I wish I could be home to talk with her. We were just starting to have some good mother-daughter talks when I got sick and had to come to the hospital. I miss them . . . and her." The client continues, "We talk on the phone some, but it's not the same. And she visits. But there is no real privacy here. And even if there was, it wouldn't be the same. She needs a mother's love and constant guidance. I don't want to let her down."

18. **N** *"Let her down?"*

    C "Yes. I wish I could stay around long enough to see that she gets a good education and a good start in life. I think I could rest easy if I saw her married to a good man . . . I've not always been the most cooperative patient. Sometimes I've given the nurses a hard time. I figure that if I do everything I'm told and try to be a good patient, I'll help my chances of getting better. Oh, I don't mean a miracle or anything like that. Just well enough to see Janie grown up and on her own." (Silence.)

    C "Do you know what I got her for her birthday? My sister bought a party dress for me to give her." (Silence.)

19. **N** *"Let's talk more about something you said earlier. You don't think you've been a cooperative patient?"* The nurse continues:

20. **N** *"What do you mean by that?"*

Stage Four: Depression

(The nurse enters the client's room and finds Helen lying in the dark, bed curtains partly drawn. An untouched dinner tray is on the overbed table. Martha checks to see that Helen is awake and then offers to sit with her for a while.)

21. **N** *"You haven't eaten your supper . . . and you've been crying."* (Silence.)

22. **N** *"Perhaps it would help to talk about what you are feeling."*

    C "What's the use of talking? It won't change anything."

23. **N** *"You sound pretty down tonight."*

    C "There's no fight left in me anymore. This is the beginning of the end."

24. **N** *"That's what you've been afraid of all along?"*

    C "Yes. But I couldn't admit it. It's time I faced the truth."

25. **N** *"Go on Helen."*

    C "I did feel better for a bit. The treatments seemed to be helping, and I thought I had it licked. But I'm not better, not really. I'll never get better." (Crying.)
(Silence. The nurse reaches over and takes Helen's hand. The client grips it tightly.)

26. **N** *"It must be frightening for you to be thinking these thoughts. You tried so hard to push them aside."*

    C "It's no use. I'm getting weaker. Even little things I used to do for myself, like comb my hair, are an effort. I'm slipping every day. There is nothing left to live for." (Silence.)

C "The past keeps going through my mind. I remember all the things my husband and I did before he died. And then I think of all the things I wanted to do with my life but will never get to do. It makes me feel so sad."

27. **N** *"What things? Tell me about them."*

C "Well, like raising Janie. There's so much I want to do with her, to tell her, to teach her. . . . At this rate I won't get to see her fourteenth birthday. . . . And I always wanted to paint. I planned to take art classes after Janie was grown and I had more time. You know, I had this fantasy that I would be another Grandma Moses in my old age. Old age! Ha! I won't have to worry about that. It's very depressing to look back on your life and feel so incomplete, to see so many loose ends."

28. **N** *"Have you given any thought as to how you might tie up some of those loose ends?"*

C "Well, yes. But I don't know. Maybe it's silly."

29. **N** *"Silly?"*

C "Yes. I thought about writing a diary or filling a notebook with some of the things I've been thinking and feeling. To share with Janie. Something to leave her when I'm gone. Is that a silly idea? My sister promised to care for her when I'm gone. In fact she's with her now. I know she's in good hands. I don't worry about that anymore. But I want her to have something of me. To remember me by."

30. **N** *"You'd like to write down some of your thoughts and feelings for Janie to read later, when she is older?"*

C "That's right. There is so much I want to share with her." (Excitedly.) "Recollections of when she was a baby, of her father, of the things we did as a family. Also, I want her to know how much I loved her, how much pleasure she gave her father and me, about our hopes for her future. . . . What do you think? Is it silly?"

31. **N** *"It sounds like a very loving thing to do."*

C "I'd like to start right away. I don't have much time left. . . . You know, I feel better now. Would you open my bed curtains and turn on the light? Maybe I'll try some of that applesauce on my tray now."

32. **N** *"Let me get some hot water and I'll fix you a fresh cup of tea before I leave. And would you like me to bring you a notebook and a pen so you can start writing?"*

C "Oh yes. That would be splendid."

33. **N** *"And, I was thinking . . . perhaps you would like some art paper and paints so you could try your hand at painting."*

C "Do you think I could? Really?"

Stage Five: Acceptance

(The nurse enters the room and finds Helen sleeping. She sits down beside the bed and sometime later Helen rouses and sees Martha sitting nearby.)

C "Oh, you're here, Martha. Have you been sitting there long?"

34. **N** "No, just a few minutes. *I thought I would look in on you and see how you were doing before I left for the day. Is there anything I can do for you?*"

C "No, thank you. I'm all right. I've been napping a lot lately."

35. **N** "*How are you feeling?*"

C "Pretty tired. I'm glad I've finished Janie's notebook. I don't think I would have the strength to write anymore. . . . And I've stopped painting too. But I got a lot done, didn't I?" (Pointing with obvious pride and pleasure to the numerous paintings on the walls of her room.) "That was a godsend. I enjoyed painting, but now I'm just content to lie here and look at them. . . . You know, if it hadn't been for you, I would never have fulfilled my dream to paint before I die. Would you like to have one of my pictures? It would please me if you would take one."

36. **N** "I would like that too. Thank you. *I'd enjoy having something you painted. . . . Are you comfortable?*"

C "Yes. The medications keep me free of pain. At this point, that's all I ask. But they do make me sleepy. It's an effort to keep my eyes open."

37. **N** "*It's OK. Close them. I'll be right here with you. I'll stay until you fall asleep and then I'll be back tomorrow.*"

C "Will you hold my hand, Martha?"

(The nurse takes Helen's hand and sits quietly with her. Before she leaves, Martha promises to give Janie the notebook after Helen dies. She also selects the painting she will keep. Helen died the next day. Martha was with her.)

b Complete the following exercises using the grid provided.
1. Describe the general characteristics of each stage of dying.
2. Refer to the previous situation and briefly describe behavioral responses observed in the client that illustrate each of the 5 stages of dying.

Stages of dying	Characteristics	Behaviors
1. Denial		
2. Anger		
3. Bargaining		
4. Depression		
5. Acceptance		

TEST ITEMS

DIRECTIONS: Select the *best* response. (Answers appear in the Appendix.)

1 Which one of the following is the *most* therapeutic nursing response to use with persons who are dealing with emotional reactions precipitated by a physical illness?

   a Reassuring them that they will feel better after a while.

   b Sympathizing with them over their situations.

   c Attending to their fears and concerns.

   d Giving them complete information about their conditions.

2 The experience of dehumanization can *best* be avoided by which one of the following measures?

   a Treating the client at home rather than in the hospital.

   b Including the client in planning the treatment regime.

   c Allowing the client unlimited visiting hours.

   d Introducing the client to persons with similar problems.

3 Emotional reactions precipitated by the loss of a body part are usually related to:

   a Changed perception of self.

   b Concern over disposal of the body part.

   c Inability to cope with feelings of guilt.

   d Unconscious feelings associated with punishment.

4 Immediately following cardiac surgery the client is *most* likely to need help with which one of the following?

   a Guilt feelings.   **c** Sexual urges.

   b Dependency conflicts.   **d** Body image.

5 A young diabetic client who neglected a serious infection in his leg had to have a below-the-knee amputation. After surgery he refused to eat or talk with anyone. Which of the following is the *most* probable explanation of his behavior?

   a Guilt for neglecting to care for himself.

   b Anger at the surgeon who removed his leg.

   c Fear that he might lose his other leg.

   d Grief for loss of a body part.

6 Failing to move into the acceptance stage of dying, the terminally ill client could exhibit which of the following?

   a Anger.   **c** Denial.

   b Bargaining.   **d** All of the above.

7 In the depression stage of dying the client would be *least likely* to manifest:

   a Sad affect.   **c** Sarcasm.

   b Cooperative behavior.   **d** Silence.

8 In order to be truly effective in helping a dying person the nurse must *first:*
  a Identify the five stages of dying.
  b Profess strong religious convictions.
  c Develop greater self-understanding.
  d Accept the inevitability of death.

9 Self-help groups are helpful because the affected individual is:
  a Allowed to replace medical supervision with peer supervision.
  b Encouraged to relate to others with similar problems rather than relate to nonaffected individuals.
  c Helped to decrease dependency on nurses, family members, and close friends.
  d Provided with emotional support and understanding from persons who share the same health problem.

10 The nurse enters the client's room, sits down at the bedside of the dying client, and asks how the client is feeling. The client responds, "Terrible." The nurse's question, "What's the matter?", illustrates which one of the following communication skills?
  a Exploring.   **c** Clarifying.
  b Focusing.   **d** Encouraging.

section IV word games

1 Quote-a-crostic

DIRECTIONS: Using cues on the left, fill in the words in the list on the right. Transfer each letter in the word list to the corresponding numbered square in the puzzle grid. Shaded squares in the grid represent the end of a word. Work back and forth between grid and word list until both are completed. (Note the letters and consecutive numbers that have been entered in the grid to help in location of words.) The completed grid will be a quotation relevant to Section IV of the text. The source of the quote and its author are spelled out in the boxed-in letters in the word list. One word in the list has been filled in to help you get started. (Solution appears in the Appendix.)

Cues

Word list

A Lacking signs of pathology

— — — ☐ — — — — — — —
137 116 71 [8] 106 124 168 186 173 82 117

B Opportunity for socialization

M E A L S
60 [155] 75 139 166

C Schizophrenic's significant other (two words)

— — — — — — ☐
157 1 87 83 192 18 [162]

— — — — — —
108 7 94 107 176 56

D Schizophrenia, affective, somatoform, and substance abuse

— — ☐ — — — — — —
93 84 [98] 118 15 160 47 156 165

E Seclusion (two words)

— — — — — — ☐ — —
149 119 48 55 179 115 [167] 69 79

F Most effective treatment

— — — — — ☐ — — — —
29 88 130 19 39 [190] 113 105 58 159

G Observe

— — — — ☐
104 158 41 140 [13]

H Nonspecific response to stress

— — — — — — — — ☐ —
61 24 30 54 33 45 4 91 [141] 148

I "Peeping Tom"

— ☐ — — — —
101 [2] 199 72 133 177

J To inflict injury, physiological or psychological

— — — — ☐
183 14 150 32 [46]

223

K Major problem of persons with bulimia and
anorexia nervosa

‾‾ ‾‾ ‾‾ ‾‾ ‾‾ ‾‾ ‾‾ ‾‾ ‾‾ ‾‾
198 20 128 70 35 195 50 10 187 97

L _____-compulsive

‾‾ ‾‾ ‾‾ |99| ‾‾ ‾‾ ‾‾ ‾‾ ‾‾
202 12 132 99 205 37 180 44 122

M Given to episodes of depression

‾‾ ‾‾ |27| ‾‾ ‾‾
110 143 27 172 78

N Type of anxiety (two words)

‾‾ ‾‾ ‾‾ ‾‾
57 146 6 96

|125| ‾‾ ‾‾ ‾‾ ‾‾ ‾‾ ‾‾ ‾‾
125 90 194 81 74 129 112 164

O Flat facial expression (two words)

|89| ‾‾ ‾‾ ‾‾ ‾‾   ‾‾ ‾‾ ‾‾ ‾‾ ‾‾ ‾‾
89 9 138 80 40   178 131 28 111 200 64

P Soothe

‾‾ |163| ‾‾ ‾‾
152 163 63 100

Q Quality lacking in a schizophrenogenic mother

‾‾ ‾‾ ‾‾ ‾‾ ‾‾ ‾‾ ‾‾ ‾‾ |203| ‾‾
145 38 73 161 127 59 92 67 203 174

R Disorganized, catatonic, paranoid, residual, of
undifferentiated

‾‾ |85| ‾‾ ‾‾ ‾‾ ‾‾ ‾‾ ‾‾ ‾‾ ‾‾ ‾‾ ‾‾
68 85 95 204 154 193 175 34 126 43 182 23 114

S Overactive

‾‾ ‾‾ ‾‾ ‾‾ ‾‾ |147| ‾‾ ‾‾ ‾‾ ‾‾ ‾‾
201 36 66 196 120 147 134 16 170 188 52

T Disturbances involving somatization

‾‾ ‾‾ ‾‾ ‾‾ ‾‾ ‾‾
197 3 22 191 51 181

‾‾ ‾‾ ‾‾ ‾‾ ‾‾ ‾‾ ‾‾ ‾‾ |77| ‾‾ ‾‾ ‾‾ ‾‾
5 135 65 103 153 109 62 42 77 31 121 11 144

U Restore health

‾‾ ‾‾ ‾‾ |76|
17 102 26 76

V Type of irreversible dementia

‾‾ ‾‾ ‾‾ |151| ‾‾ ‾‾
123 25 171 151 185 169

W Obsolete term for conversion or dissociative
disorder

‾‾ ‾‾ ‾‾ ‾‾ ‾‾ ‾‾ ‾‾ |136|
142 53 86 49 189 21 184 136

	1 C	2 I	3 T	4 H		5 T	6 N	7 C	8 A	9 O	10 K		11 T	12 L	13 G	14 J	15 D		16 S	17 U	18 C		19 F	20 K
21 W	22 T		23 R	24 H	25 V	26 U		27 M	28 O		29 F	30 H	31 T	32 J		33 H	34 R	35 K	36 S		37 L	38 G	39 F
40 O		41 G	42 T		43 R	44 L	45 H	46 J	47 D		48 E	49 W		50 K	51 T	52 S	53 W		54 H	55 E	56 C	57 N	58 F
59 Q	60 B **M**		61 H	62 T	63 P		64 O	65 T	66 S	67 Q	68 R		69 E	70 K		71 A	72 I	73 Q	74 N	75 B **A**	76 U		77 T	78 M
79 E	80 O	81 N	82 A	83 C	84 D	85 R	86 W		87 C	88 F		89 O	90 N	91 H	92 Q	93 D		94 C	95 R	96 N	97 K	98 D	99 L
100 P	101 I	102 U	103 T		104 G	105 F	106 A	107 C		108 C	109 T	110 M	111 O	112 N	113 F	114 R	115 E	116 A		117 A	118 D	119 E	120 S	121 T
122 L	123 V		124 A	125 N		126 R	127 Q	128 K	129 N	130 F	131 O		132 L	133 I	134 S	135 T		136 W	137 A		138 O	139 B **L**	140 G	141 H
142 W	143 M	144 T		145 Q	146 N	147 S	148 H	149 E	150 J	151 V	152 P	153 T	154 R	155 B **E**	156 D	157 C		158 G	159 F	160 D		161 Q	162 C	163 P
164 N	165 D		166 B **S**	167 E	168 A	169 V		170 S	171 V		172 M	173 A	174 Q	175 R	176 C	177 I	178 O	179 E	180 L	181 T	182 R		183 J	184 W
185 V	186 A		187 K	188 S	189 D	190 F		191 T	192 C	193 R	194 N	195 K	196 S		197 T	198 K	199 I	200 O	201 S	202 L	203 Q	204 R	205 L

2 Feelings and fears:

"Emotion turning back on itself, and not leading on to thought or action, is the element of madness."—*John Sterling**

"Fear is implanted in us as a preservative from evil; but its duty, like that of other passions, is not to overbear reason, but to assist it."—*Samuel Johnson**

Basic to existence is the experience of feelings and fears. Feelings can be vitalizing forces in our lives; fears can help mobilize us. However, these affective responses are also overwhelming and incapacitating and underlie many dysfunctions.

DIRECTIONS: In the following grids are hidden affective responses. See how many you can locate. The letters must be connected and a letter cannot be used more than once in a word, but may be used in other words. (Solution appears in the Appendix.)

a Feelings: The feeling of JOY has been identified. At least 20 more feelings are hidden in the grid.

1. Joy	11. _____
2. _____	12. _____
3. _____	13. _____
4. _____	14. _____
5. _____	15. _____
6. _____	16. _____
7. _____	17. _____
8. _____	18. _____
9. _____	19. _____
10. _____	20. _____

*From Edwards, T. editor: The new dictionary of thoughts, New York, 1954, The Standard Book Co., pp. 158 and 195.

A	R	L	O	O	D
N	G	E	W	M	J
U	R	E	T	A	O
A	I	L	P	H	Y
V	E	F	A	T	I
O	L	N	I	C	P

b Fears: Irrational, morbid fears are called phobias. Hidden in the grid are at least 25 fears. Listed below are the scientific names for each of these phobias that may give you hints to the hidden fears.

1. Acarophobia _____
2. Acrophobia _____
3. Aerophobia _____
4. Cynophobia _____
5. Dextrophobia _____
6. Fechtenphobia _____
7. Femellaphobia _____
8. Gatophobia _____
9. Hematophobia _____
10. Hominophobia _____
11. Hydrophobia _____
12. Ichthyophobia _____
13. Mysophobia _____
14. Nyctophobia _____
15. Photophobia _____
16. Pyrophobia _____
17. Rattephobia _____
18. Satanophobia _____
19. Sexesophobia _____
20. Thalassophobia _____
21. Thanatophobia _____
22. Theophobia _____
23. Thermophobia _____
24. Traherophobia _____
25. Werrephobia _____

O	H	F	N	L	B
N	T	E	I	O	U
W	A	R	S	G	O
E	C	T	H	W	D
D	A	R	S	M	O
S	I	N	E	X	F

3 Crosshatch

DIRECTIONS: Fit the words listed below into the proper boxes. The words read left to right or top to bottom, one letter per box. CONSUMERS has been entered to give you a starting point. (Solution appears in the Appendix.)

3 letters
DSM
ECT
EGO
FAT
GAY
LAW
SHY

4 letters
ACID
BODY
CARE
FEAR
HATE
LOSS
MOOD
PLAN
RAGE
RISK

5 letters
ACUTE
ANGER
DYING
FIGHT
GAINS
MANIC
NEEDS
NOT ME
SHOCK

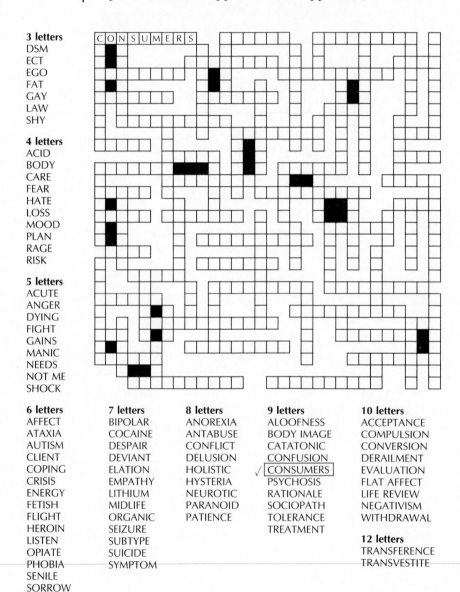

6 letters
AFFECT
ATAXIA
AUTISM
CLIENT
COPING
CRISIS
ENERGY
FETISH
FLIGHT
HEROIN
LISTEN
OPIATE
PHOBIA
SENILE
SORROW

7 letters
BIPOLAR
COCAINE
DESPAIR
DEVIANT
ELATION
EMPATHY
LITHIUM
MIDLIFE
ORGANIC
SEIZURE
SUBTYPE
SUICIDE
SYMPTOM

8 letters
ANOREXIA
ANTABUSE
CONFLICT
DELUSION
HOLISTIC
HYSTERIA
NEUROTIC
PARANOID
PATIENCE

9 letters
ALOOFNESS
BODY IMAGE
CATATONIC
CONFUSION
√ CONSUMERS
PSYCHOSIS
RATIONALE
SOCIOPATH
TOLERANCE
TREATMENT

10 letters
ACCEPTANCE
COMPULSION
CONVERSION
DERAILMENT
EVALUATION
FLAT AFFECT
LIFE REVIEW
NEGATIVISM
WITHDRAWAL

12 letters
TRANSFERENCE
TRANSVESTITE

228

section V

interventions in psychiatric nursing

chapter 22

intervention in a crisis state

INTRODUCTION

In the course of day-to-day living many challenges, changes, and stresses threaten a person's equilibrium. Using problem-solving methods, coping measures, and defense mechanisms, one strives to maintain a healthy personality balance and continue to function effectively. When the usual methods of dealing with problems fail, anxiety increases, disorganization occurs, and crisis results. When helplessness is experienced, the individual is incapable of taking positive action to deal with the situation and is a candidate for crisis intervention.

"Crisis intervention is a subject of interest to all health professionals. It is a technique that is successfully used by persons with a variety of backgrounds to aid individuals and families in understanding and effectively coping with the intense emotions that characterize a crisis."* The goal of intervention in a crisis state is to help solve immediate, seemingly insurmountable problems. Individuals in crisis are helped to face and eventually handle their problems within the framework of their support system, mobilizing coping and defense mechanisms to deal with the critical event. The goal of crisis intervention is based on the belief that persons in crisis possess strengths that have been temporarily overwhelmed. With timely, short-term intervention, persons in crisis are given the support necessary to solve their immediate problems and are helped to emerge from the experience stronger and more confident in their abilities to meet subsequent stresses in growth-promoting ways.

The purpose of this chapter is to review the phases and characteristics of a crisis state and identify nursing actions that can be taken to intervene therapeutically in a crisis state.

---

*From Taylor, C.M.: Mereness' essentials of psychiatric nursing, ed. 12, St. Louis, 1986, The C.V. Mosby Co., Chapter 22.

231

OBJECTIVES

1. To define crisis.
2. To list the general characteristics of a crisis state.
3. To differentiate between developmental and situational events that precipitate crisis states.
4. To identify the phases and characteristics of the phases of crisis.
5. To review communication skills used to interact therapeutically with the individual in crisis.

EXERCISES

1 Define crisis:

2 List below 4 *general* characteristics of a crisis state:

a _____

b _____

c _____

d _____

3 Listed below are 15 events that may precipitate a state of crisis. Read each one and determine whether it illustrates a developmental or situational crisis. Place a check in the box in the appropriate column. The first one has been entered to help you get started.

Events	Crisis	
	Developmental	Situational
1. Birth of a new baby.	☑	☐
2. Retirement from a job.	☐	☐
3. Aging parent moves into nursing home.	☐	☐
4. Moving out-of-state.	☐	☐
5. Death of an aging parent.	☐	☐
6. Mandatory draft registration.	☐	☐
7. Loss of a limb in an accident.	☐	☐
8. Child marries and leaves home.	☐	☐
9. Promotion at work.	☐	☐
10. Vacation or leisure.	☐	☐
11. Stillbirth.	☐	☐
12. Failure to graduate with one's class.	☐	☐
13. Loss of one's home by fire.	☐	☐
14. Onset of menopausal symptoms.	☐	☐
15. Mother has a radical mastectomy.	☐	☐

4 Crisis states generally progress through a series of phases, beginning with denial. These phases, although overlapping, have certain unique characteristics, and as persons progress through a crisis, they demonstrate characteristic behaviors in each phase. The following situation illustrates the 7 phases of crisis observable in the behaviors of Mary Edwards. In the space provided enter the name of each phase of crisis (denial has been filled in to help you get started) and a brief description of the major characteristics of that phase.

Phases of crisis state

a ATTEMPTS TO ESCAPE

b ATTEMPTS TO REORGANIZE

c DENIAL

d DISORGANIZATION

e GENERAL REORGANIZATION

f INCREASED TENSION

g LOCAL REORGANIZATION

Situation	Phases of crisis state and characteristics
①Recently John Edwards was admitted to the hospital for surgical repair of a hernia. During his hospitalization a hurricane developed in the Gulf of Mexico and moved toward his home on the Mississippi coast. John expressed his concerns to his wife Mary. She assured him she would take care of everything. However, she kept putting off the preparations, finding reasons for not taking action. Although she heard the ominous newscasts, she kept thinking that the storm would pass them by. Mary and John's neighbors volunteered to help her, but she dismissed their offers, insisting the house was strong and could withstand any storm.	① DENIAL
②Mary was alone in the house. Both their children were grown and lived out-of-town. On the eve of the day the storm was to hit the mainland, residents were forced to evacuate the area. With the threat of impending disaster, Mary was forced to face reality. She worked relentlessly to make preparations to secure the house, but her efforts were too little and too late. She was forcibly removed to a shelter further inland.	② _____
③At the shelter Mary continued to be active. She occupied herself caring for the children and the aged, serving food, working in the first-aid station. However, as time passed her efforts became more frantic and ineffective. She volunteered for numerous tasks but could not complete anything she started. She was easily distracted and grew increasingly preoccupied with the storm and the fate of her home.	③ _____
④When the hurricane was over, Mary avoided returning to her neighborhood, where widespread devastation was reported. She continued to work at the shelter, insisting she was needed there.	④ _____
⑤When Mary finally visited the site, she found that her home was totally destroyed. She was completely overwhelmed and sat on the ground and wept helplessly. She was found by a neighbor. The weeping had ceased, but she was moaning to herself, her arms wrapped tightly around her chest, rocking gently back and forth. She did not seem aware of the activities going on around her. She did not respond to her name and kept saying: "Why did John have to be in the hospital now? If he hadn't been in the hospital this would never have happened."	⑤ _____
⑥Following the disaster, Mary went to live with her sister who lived nearby in an area not affected by the storm. She helped around the house and functioned fairly effectively as long as she was not reminded of her losses. However, continued TV coverage of the aftermath of the hurricane plus the expressed concerns of friends caused her great anguish. She said, "As long as I don't think about it, I'm OK."	⑥ _____
⑦After John was discharged from the hospital, they moved into temporary housing provided for disaster victims. They were eligible for assistance. Little by little they resumed their normal lives. John returned to work; Mary took a job as a salesperson in a local gift shop. They collected disaster insurance, contacted a real estate broker, and bought a plot of land on which to rebuild their home.	⑦ _____

5 Because persons in crisis are not always aware that they are in crisis and respond with feelings of helplessness and puzzlement, the nurse must often use a very direct, straightforward approach when intervening therapeutically in a crisis state. Passive, nondirective interviewing techniques have limited use in the initial contacts with the client.

Within the framework of the nursing process, the nurse uses a variety of communication skills to interact therapeutically with the individual in crisis. The initial phase of assessment involves collecting data, reviewing the events leading up to the crisis, identifying the event that most probably precipitated the crisis, helping identify the protagonists in the crisis, and helping the client focus on feelings and thoughts relevant to the crisis. The nurse directs the interview so that the client is helped to express the gamut of feelings being experienced: anxiety, fear, pain, loss, anger, depression, helplessness, and frustration. Once this is done, the nurse and the person in crisis can develop a plan of action for coping with the critical situation. This includes helping the client identify resources to reduce the feelings of isolation so often experienced. As the person in crisis feels support, defenses and coping measures are mobilized to deal with the situation.

In the following situation Mary Edwards has been taken to the emergency room of the local hospital where she is interviewed by a nurse skilled in crisis intervention. A variety of therapeutic skills are illustrated. They have been numbered and italicized. Place the number of the examples in the space provided after each communication skill. A communication skill may be illustrated more than once; an example may illustrate more than one skill. The first one has been filled in to help you get started.

Communication skills

a Clarifying _____   **f** Reflecting _____
b Direct questioning _____   **g** Refocusing _____
c Encouraging _____   **h** Seeking information _____
d Focusing __1._____   **i** Suggesting _____
e Giving reassurance _____   **j** Understanding _____

SITUATION

    N "My name is Susan Lamb. I am a nurse. Your name is Mary Edwards. I would like to help you, Mary."

    C (Crying.)

1. **N** *"Let's talk about what you are feeling."*

    C (Mary continued to cry.)

2. **N** *"I understand that you live in a house in the beach area that was hardest hit by the hurricane."*

    C (Nodding.)

3. **N** *"How long have you lived there?"*

    C "Thirty years."

4. **N** *"That's a long time. You must have a lot of memories invested in that house."*

    C "We had a lot of good times there. Oh, what am I going to do? I can't go on. There is no use in going on." (Mary continues to cry.)

5. **N** *"It sounds like you are feeling terribly discouraged right now."*

    C "I don't know what I am going to do. How am I going to face my husband?" (Crying and wringing her hands.)

6. **N** *"Where is your husband now?"*

    C "John is here, upstairs on the surgical ward. He had an operation a few days ago. Oh John, John. . . . If he hadn't gone to the hospital this would never have happened. He left me all alone."

7. **N** *"Do you have any children, Mary?"*

    C "Two. They are grown and on their own. I was pregnant with a third child 6 years ago, but I miscarried. That was terrible." (Mary resumes crying.)

8. **N** *"You were telling me about your children. Your two grown children."*
(Mary tells the nurse about Emma Lou, age 26, and John, Jr., age 24, who are married and living out-of-state. She begins to cry again as she recalls them and the life they all shared in the destroyed home. The nurse reaches over and takes Mary's hand, and the client grips it tightly.)

9. **N** *"I'm here for you. I'm going to help you through this time."*

    C (Nodding.)

10. **N** *"Go on. Tell me more."*

    C "It's the first time I've been alone in my life. Before John, I had my parents. When they died, he was there to help me through it. When the children left home, John and I faced it together. But now . . . ." (Crying.)

11. **N** *"Now you feel as if there is no one you can turn to?"*

    C "He shouldn't have left me. He knows this is the hurricane season. He wanted me to do everything. To take care of the house. What do I know of such things? He has always done it." (Mary releases the nurses's hand and clenches her fists.)

12. **N** *"You sound pretty angry with your husband."*

    C "He's had that hernia for years. Why did he pick this time to go to the hospital?"

13. **N** *"Do you think he could have waited and had the operation later?"*

   C "I guess not. The doctor said it was serious. But it's not fair. We worked hard all our lives. What did we do to deserve this? Oh, what am I going to tell John? What is he going to say?"

14. **N** *"What do you think he will say?"*

   C "I don't know. I don't know. I'm afraid to face him."

15. **N** *"If it would help, I'll be glad to go upstairs with you when you go to see John."*

   C "Oh yes. I think that would help."

16. **N** *"You both have reason to be upset. You've had your home destroyed."*

   C "Thirty years down the drain."

17. **N** *"Are you talking about your home or your life?"*

   C "My life, I guess." (The nurse waits while Mary cries briefly.)

   C "I'm sorry. I can't stop crying. Every time I think about it I feel sort of panicky."

18. **N** *"That must be frightening for you."*

   C (Nodding.)
   (Silence.)

19. **N** *"Are you saying you have lost everything?"*

   C "I guess so. But I really haven't lost everything, have I? I still have John. We are alive. Our children are safe. We have each other. We can start over."

20. **N** *"You can start over."*

21. **N** *"What do you need to do first?"*
   (Client takes a deep breath and then lets it all out.)

   C "I have to talk to John. But what am I going to say to him?"

22. **N** *"Let's think about that. Perhaps it would help for you to think through what you want to say to him."*

   C "It's going to be hard to face him."

23. **N** *"Do you mean he will be angry with you?"*

   C "Oh, no. I don't think so. He's probably going to be angry with himself and blame himself for not being there when I needed him. Oh no. He's a very special person. He's always been very understanding and supportive. I've always been able to count on him."

24. **N** *"You might feel better when you share your feelings with your husband."*

   C "Yes, I believe I will."

25 **N** "All right. *So the first thing you are going to do is talk with John."*

26. **N** *"What about your son and daughter?"*

   C "The children. I must let them know we are safe."

27. **N** *"Have you any other family you need to contact?"*

   C "My sister Clara and her husband Carl. They must be frantic. They live on the other side of town. I must find out how they are."

28. **N** *"So you are going to contact your family."*

29. **N** *"What about where you are going to stay? Could you stay with your sister and brother-in-law for a while?"*

C "Yes. They have room. If they weren't affected by the storm (crying), I know I would have a place with them. The four of us are very close. John and Carl are partners."

30. **N** *"That sounds like a good plan."*
(Silence.)

C "I wonder if we have disaster insurance?"

31. **N** *"Who is your insurance agent?"*

C "I'm not sure. I'll have to ask John. You know I'm just realizing how dependent I am on John. I must find out more about our affairs so I can handle things better in the future."

32. **N** *"Yes? Go on."*

C God forbid, but suppose something had happened to John. Suppose it was John I had lost, not just my house. I don't think I could manage." (Mary cries softly to herself.)

33. **N** *"That must be a frightening thing to realize. But you have time now to do something about that."*

34. **N** *"Review again what you are going to do."*

C "First, I'm going to see John and talk with him. I want to get that over with."

35. **N** *"And then?"*

C "Then I'll call Clara and Carl and the children."

36. **N** *"And you're going to check about your insurance agent."*
(Client nods thoughtfully then says:)

C "Five hours ago, when I saw what was left of our home, I didn't think there was anything left to live for. I wanted to curl up and die. I thought I was losing my mind."

37. **N** *"You had a terrible shock. It's not surprising you were feeling so overwhelmed."*

C "Overwhelmed! That's it. I've never felt so overwhelmed and so alone in all my life. It was terrible. I still feel pretty shaky. I'm trying not to think about what has happened. I'm trying to focus on what I need to do now. But I hope I can remember everything I need to do."

38. **N** *"It wouldn't be too unusual for you to forget. You've been through a lot."*

39. **N** *"Perhaps it would help if you wrote down what you plan to do. Then you could share your plans with your husband when you see him."*

C "Of course! A list. Why didn't I think of that myself? I always make lists. They keep me organized and I feel so accomplished when I cross off everything I've done."

40. **N** *"You seem to feel a little better now that you have a plan in mind."*

C "As a matter of fact, I do feel somewhat better. A little while ago I thought my world was ended. Now I realize that only a small part of it is gone (crying), and I forgot about all that I have left to live for."

N "I'm pleased you feel better. However, you have had a pretty tragic experience and you are bound to have some rough moments. I would like to see you again and find out how you are making out with your plans. Let's make an appointment for tomorrow. In the meantime here is my name and phone number in case you need anything before then. Also, I would like to know your sister's name, address, and phone number in case I need to reach you. Now let's work on your list and then you can go upstairs to visit your husband."

C "Will you still go with me upstairs?"

N "Of course, I'd be glad to."

TEST ITEMS

DIRECTIONS: Select the *best* response. (Answers appear in the Appendix.)

1 A person experiences a state of crisis when the:
   a Feelings of anxiety become particularly intense.
   b Event is perceived as having traumatic proportions.
   c Family members fail to give needed support.
   d Coping measures are used in response to stress.

2 There has been increasing interest in crisis intervention primarily because it is:
   a A short-term, reality-based treatment modality.
   b Less expensive than other forms of treatment.
   c Instrumental in preventing serious mental problems.
   d Providing job opportunities for health care workers.

3 The perception of a crisis as a "catalyst that disturbs old habits, evokes new responses, and becomes a major factor in charting new developments" is based on which one of the following outcomes of a crisis?
   a Reintegration at a less healthy level of functioning.
   b Reintegration at the same level of functioning.
   c Reintegration at a higher level of functioning.
   d None of the above.

4 The *unique* characteristic of a developmental crisis is:
   a Predictability.   **c** Anxiety.
   b Disequilibrium.   **d** Disorganization.

5 Which one of the following events might precipitate a *situational crisis*?
   a Mandatory draft registration.
   b Loss of a limb in an accident.
   c Death of an aging parent.
   d Retirement from a job.

6 Failure to successfully deal with a crisis situation in 4 to 6 weeks usually results in repression of the experience and:
   a Free-floating anxiety.   **c** Pseudoresolution.
   b Increased tension.   **d** Denial.

7 At the loss of her home in a hurricane, Mary Edwards went through a period in which she blamed her husband John for the disaster. At that time she was experiencing which one of the following phases of a crisis state?

   a Attempts to escape.   **c** Denial.

   b Local reorganization.   **d** Disorganization.

8 In the interview between the nurse and Mary Edwards the nurse said, "You might feel better when you share your feelings with your husband." This is an example of which one of the following communication skills?

   a Focusing.   **c** Encouraging.

   b Understanding.   **d** Suggesting.

9 In the phase of local reorganization which one of the following mechanisms is *most* used?

   a Denial.   **c** Projection.

   b Suppression.   **d** Conversion.

10 In a crisis the protagonists are:

   a All persons involved in the crisis.

   b Only the victim's close family members.

   c The victim and the person or persons causing the crisis.

   d Any resource persons who aids in the crisis resolution.

chapter 23

intervention with groups

"A group is not a mere collection of individuals. Rather, a group is an identifiable system composed of three or more individuals who engage in certain tasks to achieve a common goal. Furthermore, to be a group the members must relate to each other, usually around the tasks and goals of the group."*

At the beginning of life, one automatically becomes a member of the family group. As the individual progresses through life's developmental stages, a multiplicity of group contacts are experienced: play and school groups, church affiliations, peer groups, and military, business, community, political, recreational and social associations. Because much of life takes part in group experiences, problems relating to other people are not only distressing but frequently incapacitating as well. Often an interpersonal difficulty is the motivating force behind a person seeking professional help.

Nurses have an excellent opportunity to work with clients in a variety of different types of groups. An increasing number of professional nurses are acquiring the knowledge and developing the skills needed to conduct formal psychotherapy groups in a variety of settings. In addition, the nurse assumes the role of socializing agent and facilitates relatedness and socialization among hospitalized clients in many group situations during a 24-hour period. For example, mealtime provides a good opportunity to promote social interaction between staff and clients. As role models, nurses demonstrate and help clients experience appropriate behaviors associated with food and eating. Similarly, activity groups can promote interaction and group relatedness, exposing clients to new and hopefully positive interpersonal experiences. Because experiences in one group contribute to a person's responsiveness in subsequent groups, the nurse can lay

---

*From Taylor, C.M.: Mereness' essentials of psychiatric nursing, ed. 12, St. Louis, 1986, The C.V. Mosby Co., Chapter 23.

the groundwork for other positive group experiences and help an apparently unrelated individual become more socialized and less isolated. My students generally work with long-term, severely withdrawn individuals. Part of their experience is to promote group interaction among their clients. Initially, because the clients are so resistive to relating, the groups tend to consist of more students than clients. Eventually, however, through persistence and the use of a variety of tools including food, games, music and song, rewards, and recognition, clients join the groups. In some cases clients may only participate in the last week or so of the experience. However, what has been found repeatedly is that the new group of students in the following semester have a much easier task of involving the relatively stable group of clients in group activities. The clients require much less encouragement to participate, supporting the belief that one positive group experience will be instrumental in helping a client participate in other group experiences.

In addition to group work with clients, nurses often participate in meetings with other health care workers. In such groups the health care team engages in a variety of tasks, such as determining clients' needs, planning and evaluating client care, administering agency policies, and engaging in self-assessment. An understanding of the dynamics of group functioning and group process is a useful tool in making group activities at all levels more interesting and more effective. The purpose of this chapter is to increase understanding of the nature of group experiences in general and therapeutic groups in particular.

OBJECTIVES

1. To analyze a hypothetical group interaction in terms of the roles assumed by the members.
2. To speculate on a group's productivity, cohesiveness, leadership qualities, and member interaction from sociograms.
3. To identify the characteristics of the phases of group development.
4. To differentiate between formal psychotherapy groups and socialization groups.

EXERCISES

1 The roles assumed by members of a group as suggested by Robert Bales are identified in the text and are in most cases self-descriptive. Eight group roles are listed in this exercise.

Read the following situation involving members of a community group and identify the roles assumed by each member of the group. In the space provided by each role write in the name of the member assuming that role. Kirby's role has been filled in to help you get started.

Group roles

a Aggressor _____   **e** Information giver _____
b Blocker _____   **f** Information seeker _____
c Coordinator ___Kirby___   **g** Orienter _____
d Harmonizer _____   **h** Recorder _____

SITUATION

Kirby "We need to get started. Tina could not make tonight's meeting and asked that I chair the meeting in her absence."

Jason "That's a mistake. I'm the most qualified person to do the job. I've had lots of experience leading groups."

Paula "Maybe you can lead the meeting next time, Jason. This time Tina asked Kirby and sent him her agenda."

Carol "I missed the last meeting. Could someone please bring me up to date on what happened last week?"

Tom "Sure. We found we needed more information before we could reach a decision. Rob volunteered to check with the town council and report back to us. We agreed to table all decisions until we heard his report."

Kirby "Thanks Tom. That about sums it up and gives us a good place to start. How about it, Rob? Tina had you first on the agenda. Are you ready to give us your report?"

Rob "Yes. I made copies of some data and I'll distribute them to everyone."

Kirby "Good. While Rob is doing that . . . . Let's see . . . . Arthur, I believe it's your turn to take minutes. OK?"

Arthur Nods in agreement and gets out paper to write on.

Helen "Why are we wasting time? There's no use in any of this. We've been through this a hundred times and nothing ever changes."

Jason "I agree with Helen. Now I think we should proceed by . . . ."

Paula "Come on you two. Let's hear Rob's report. Then we can decide our course of action."

Kirby "OK everyone? All right Rob, you're on."

Rob "Well, as you all know I was to speak to the town council Monday. This is what I found out. If you look at the handout I gave you . . . ."

2 The nature of a group, whether a natural group such as a family, a self-help group such as an encounter or sensitivity group, or a formal therapy group such as a psychotherapy group, is readily discernible from the patterns of interaction occurring among the members and the members and the leader(s). Groups, including therapy groups, can be characterized as democratic, authoritarian, or laissez-faire, depending on the leadership structure.

A democratic group is led by a person who is interested in and listens to the responses of the group members. All persons are encouraged to take part and to voice their ideas and opinions. Decision making tends to be a slower process because a decision is generally only reached after everyone has had an opportunity to participate. However, the end result tends to be more satisfying because all members feel involved in the decision-making process.

An authoritarian group, on the other hand, may seem more efficient. Rules governing group functioning are usually set by one or two controlling individuals. Decisions are reached with little or no member input, and as a result there is little member satisfaction in being a part of an authoritarian group, although it may seem more productive than the democratic group.

A laissez-faire group usually has a leader in name only. There is no real structure or direction for operation in this type of group. As a result there is often much anxiety associated with membership in such a group. No leader, no structure, no direction, no decisions, no group relatedness, no output of activity—all these factors contribute to feelings of frustration. The members will disperse unless a leader emerges to provide a structure to hold the group together.

The following exercise consists of a series of sociograms illustrating patterns of interaction commonly found in various types of groups. The letter L in a sociogram stands for leader, an M designates members. Arrows illustrate the direction of the interaction. An arrow pointing in one direction indicates the flow of interaction is unidirectional; an arrow pointing in two directions indicates that a give-and-take interaction is occurring between the individuals.

a In the space provided describe the nature of the interaction that is going on within the group. Identify whether or not the group is democratic, authoritarian, or laissez-faire. An example has been provided to help you get started.

Group interaction	Analysis
1.	In this group there are six members plus a designated leader. However, from the interaction there is no way to differentiate the leader from the other members. There are no silent members. Everyone participates. Interaction is not directed to anyone in particular. It is difficult to tell if anyone is responding to anyone else or merely carrying on a monologue. This is probably a laissez-faire group.
2.	
3.	
4.	
5.	
6.	

b Listed below are several questions about groups that can be answered by referring to the sociograms and your analysis of the group interactions in Exercise 2a. Identify the group or groups referred to in the questions by checking the boxes in the appropriate columns. The first one has been answered in part to help you get started.

Questions	Groups					
	1	2	3	4	5	6
1. Which are the least productive groups?	☑	☐	☐	☐	☐	☐
2. Which groups are dominated by authoritarian leaders?	☐	☐	☐	☐	☐	☐
3. Which groups are dominated by subgroups?	☐	☐	☐	☐	☐	☐
4. Which groups are monopolized by one member?	☐	☐	☐	☐	☐	☐
5. Which are task-oriented groups and will probably get the most accomplished with the least member satisfaction?	☐	☐	☐	☐	☐	☐
6. Which groups have the most passive members?	☐	☐	☐	☐	☐	☐
7. Which groups have little or no intragroup interaction?	☐	☐	☐	☐	☐	☐
8. Which groups are experiencing ineffective leadership?	☐	☐	☐	☐	☐	☐
9. Which are probably democratic-type groups?	☐	☐	☐	☐	☐	☐
10. Which groups are probably effective in terms of leadership, intragroup interaction, and productivity?	☐	☐	☐	☐	☐	☐

3 Every therapy group progresses through four developmental phases: the preaffiliation phase, the intragroup conflict phase, the working phase (also called the intimacy and differentiation phase), and the phase of termination. Listed below are 12 group goals, leader responsibilities, and member behaviors that are characteristic of different phases of a group's life. Differentiate among them by placing a check in the box in the appropriate column. The first one has been filled in to help you get started.

	Phases			
Characteristics	**Preaffiliation**	**Intragroup conflict**	**Working**	**Termination**
1. Members are cautious about developing relationships with each other.	☑	☐	☐	☐
2. Members share feelings of rejection, loss, and abandonment.	☐	☐	☐	☐
3. Leader accepts and supports power-control responses within the group.	☐	☐	☐	☐
4. Leader helps members think and work through problems.	☐	☐	☐	☐
5. Goal is to establish norms to govern group functioning.	☐	☐	☐	☐
6. Members respond positively to suggestions made by fellow members.	☐	☐	☐	☐
7. Goal is to help members examine and alter behavioral patterns.	☐	☐	☐	☐
8. Goal is to become acquainted with other members and the leader.	☐	☐	☐	☐
9. Leader orients members to the group process, to self, and to each other.	☐	☐	☐	☐
10. Members may withdraw and eventually drop out of the group.	☐	☐	☐	☐
11. Goal is to apply what has been learned in the group to other situations.	☐	☐	☐	☐
12. Leader encourages members to express feelings of loss.	☐	☐	☐	☐

4 Listed below are 15 characteristics of formal psychotherapy groups and socialization groups. Differentiate between them by placing a check in the box in the appropriate column. The first one has been filled in to help you get started.

Characteristics	Groups	
	Therapy	Socialization
1. Group size is generally limited to 6 to 10 people.	☑	☐
2. Attendance is variable, depending on the state of the individual at the time of the meeting.	☐	☐
3. Task-oriented activities are the major focus.	☐	☐
4. The ability to verbalize effectively is usually a criterion for membership.	☐	☐
5. Membership is relatively stable.	☐	☐
6. The development of trust is crucial to growth-promoting relationships.	☐	☐
7. Members are helped to deal more effectively with stress.	☐	☐
8. Beginning efforts at communication with others are encouraged.	☐	☐
9. Privacy and a quiet place to meet are essential.	☐	☐
10. A degree of ego strength is appropriate for membership.	☐	☐
11. Members are stimulated to take an interest in reality and in their surroundings.	☐	☐
12. Remotivation techniques are utilized.	☐	☐
13. Encourage the expression of feelings, ideas, and concerns.	☐	☐
14. Provide tangible rewards for participation.	☐	☐
15. Awareness of members' interests and hobbies provide a focus for activities.	☐	☐

TEST ITEMS

DIRECTIONS: Select the *best* response. (Answers appear in the Appendix.)

1 What would be the *least* number of members to constitute a group?

    a Two.   **c** Five.

    b Three.   **d** Ten.

2 Which one of the following roles assumed by group members is essentially a task- or content-oriented role?

    a Elaborator.   **c** Blocker.

    b Compromiser.   **d** Harmonizer.

3 Which one of the following is the *best* example of a group norm?

    a Members are initially strangers.

    b Members assemble weekly to share experiences and concerns.

    c Members decide that everyone would address each other by first names.

    d Members limit group membership to 12 to 15 persons.

4 Every group progresses through developmental phases, each of which is unique and different from the others. The phase of intimacy and differentiation is *best* characterized by:

a Mistrust.   **c** Apathy.
b Competition.   **d** Cohesiveness.

5 Which one of the following phases of group development is experienced *most fully* by all groups?

a Preaffiliation.   **c** Working.
b Intragroup conflict.   **d** Termination.

6 Ten withdrawn and regressed clients have been assembled for a group experience. Which one of the following groups would be *most* suitable to their needs?

a Psychodrama.   **c** Encounter.
b Socialization.   **d** Sensitivity.

7 The method of treatment that helps clients analyze and improve their patterns of interaction by using the child-parent-adult framework is called:

a Insight psychotherapy.   **c** Gestalt therapy.
b Transactional analysis.   **d** Psychodrama.

8 The lessening of emotional trauma by reenacting the situation is a definition of:

a Catharsis.   **c** Abreaction.
b Desensitization.   **d** Ventilation.

9 A person with substantial ego strength would be a candidate for a group with which one of the following goals?

a Emotional support.   **c** Socialization.
b Remotivation.   **d** Emotional insight.

10 An authoritarian group is *most* accurately characterized by which one of the following?

a Efficiency, structure, little member satisfaction.
b Lack of productivity, high anxiety, apathetic membership.
c Member competition, sensitive leadership, task orientation.
d Productivity, member satisfaction, goal direction.

chapter 24

intervention with families

INTRODUCTION

The traditional definition of a family as "two or more people who are related by blood or legal ties"* has become obsolete. Today's family might best be defined as a system composed of human beings of various ages and sexes who are joined together, sometimes by blood or legal ties but often not, for the pursuit of common goals of growth, development, and support of its members.

The view of the family as a system of interrelated parts, one part affecting the others, has implications for nursing. It suggests that care of sick individuals needs to be expanded to include the other family members who may not demonstrate dysfunctional behaviors but who, nonetheless, are affecting the sick individual as well as are affected by him. Intervention would be based on the belief that it is not just one individual who is sick but it is the family system that is experiencing major difficulties functioning. The identified client in the family may be a scapegoat, a victim who helps the other family members maintain a precarious balance. Removing the sick person from the family, even removing the sickness from the individual through treatment measures, may upset the system's homeokinesis and precipitate dysfunctional responses in other members of the family. It seems reasonable, therefore, that all members of the family should be exposed to a therapeutic experience in order to help them deal more effectively with their complex interrelated problems and stressors.

The purpose of this chapter is to review some basic material about the nature of families and their functions, and to develop a beginning understanding of intervention with families.

*From Taylor, C.M.: Mereness' essentials of psychiatric nursing, ed. 12, St. Louis, 1986, The C.V. Mosby Co., Chapter 24.

1. To list the functions of the family.
2. To discuss the goals and family dynamics associated with each of the stages of family development.
3. To identify different types of families.
4. To differentiate between effective and ineffective families.
5. To list the basic goals of family therapy.

1 List 7 functions of the family.

a _____

b _____

c _____

d _____

e _____

f _____

g _____

2 Using the following grid, fill in the goals and family dynamics associated with the stages of family development. Phase one of stage one has been filled in to help you get started.

Stages	Onset	Goal	Family dynamics
I	Phase one: Begins when a childless couple makes a commitment to each other.	To adjust to living together as a married pair.	Stressful period. Couple strives to effect a union and learns to assume the roles of husband and wife without losing their individuality.
	Phase two: Begins with wife's pregnancy.		
II	Begins with birth of first child.		
III	Begins when the eldest child (the firstborn) enters school.		
IV	Begins when the eldest child (the firstborn) becomes an adolescent.		
V	Begins when the children are preparing to or are actually leaving home.		
VI	Begins when all the children have left home and the father and mother have no children to parent.		
VII	Begins with retirement.		

3 Listed below are 15 examples of family groupings and some terms to identify them. Match each grouping with the term that most accurately identifies it by filling in the blanks provided. The first one has been entered to help you get started.

Terms for different types of families

a BLENDED FAMILY*   **b** EXTENDED FAMILY   **c** HOUSEHOLD CONCEPT   **d** NUCLEAR FAMILY

*Also known as reconstituted family.

Family groupings	Family types
1. A man and a woman joined together for the purpose of bearing and raising children.	Nuclear family
2. A union of a man and a woman who bring children from previous marriages into the relationship.	_____
3. A man, his children, and the paternal grandmother living together.	_____
4. A man and a woman living together and raising an adopted child.	_____
5. A gay couple, each divorced, living together with children from their straight marriages.	_____
6. A two-generation family consisting of parents and children.	_____
7. A man and two women, living together in an asexual relationship, for emotional support and financial benefit.	_____
8. A widow living with her parents.	_____
9. Several men and women living together in a group home for the purpose of emotional support.	_____
10. Two or more people living together and building a relationship based on mutual respect and interests rather than procreation.	_____
11. Multiple generations related by blood, living together, pooling resources, sharing labor, and giving affection and support to each other.	_____
12. A divorced man raising his son alone.	_____
13. A group of people bonded together in pursuit of a common goal: growth and development of its members.	_____
14. A widow and widower, retired and unmarried to each other, living together with respect and companionship, collecting separate pensions and Social Security benefits.	_____
15. A couple temporarily raising several foster children, none of whom are related.	_____

4 Listed below are 15 characteristics of effective and ineffective families. Differentiate between them by placing a check in the box in the appropriate column. The first one has been filled in to help you get started.

Characteristics	Families Effective	Ineffective
1. Promotes cohesive patterns of relating.	✓	☐
2. Adapts to changes within and outside the family without loss of stability.	☐	☐
3. Fosters overt hostility between its members.	☐	☐
4. Manifests learning difficulties and antisocial behaviors in its children.	☐	☐
5. Accepts differences between its members.	☐	☐
6. Works together to deal effectively with problems as they arise.	☐	☐
7. Scapegoats the most powerless family member.	☐	☐
8. Exposes its young people to experiences perpetuating the effective family model.	☐	☐
9. Exhibits chronic patterns of dissension.	☐	☐
10. Maintains stability in the face of changes inside and outside the family group.	☐	☐
11. Manifests tensions in domestic violence.	☐	☐
12. Emphasizes material needs over the emotional, physical, and social needs of its members.	☐	☐
13. Strives for power by abusing or neglecting its children.	☐	☐
14. Promotes decision making appropriate to the needs of its members.	☐	☐
15. Provides mutual support and respect for its members.	☐	☐

5 List 4 basic goals of family therapy:

a _____

b _____

c _____

d _____

TEST ITEMS

DIRECTIONS: Select the *best* response. (Answers appear in the Appendix.)

1 *All but which one* of the following individuals was an early proponent of family therapy?
 a Nathan Ackerman.   **c** Clifford Beers.
 b Gerald Caplan.   **d** Don Jackson.

2 One of the *most* significant aspects of the family's function of regulation of sexual activity and reproduction is the:
 a Transmission of cultural heritage.
 b Proliferation of sex education.
 c Promotion of pleasure.
 d Control of venereal disease.

3 The second part of the first stage of family development is characterized by the married couple's:
 a Renewing marriage vows.

b Testing out roles of husband and wife.

c Exploring and discovering each other.

d Adjusting to the wife's pregnancy.

4 The postparental family is faced with which one of the following tasks?

    a Preparing the children to leave home.

    b Adapting to dissolution of the family.

    c Adjusting to the "empty nest syndrome."

    d Retiring from full-time employment.

5 The union of two persons and their children from two previous marriages is an example of which one of the following family types?

    a Nuclear.

    b Reconstituted.

    c Household.

    d Extended.

6 The criterion used by the U.S. Census Bureau to define a family is based on people:

    a Living together under the same roof.

    b United by legal commitment.

    c Related by blood.

    d Having similar interests and goals.

7 *Most* ineffective families are characterized by:

    a Child neglect.

    b Irresolvable stress.

    c Divorce.

    d Violence.

8 Child abuse is more common in which one of the following types of families?

    a Single-parent family.

    b Blended family.

    c Extended family.

    d Nuclear family.

9 The treatment of choice to use with a married couple in the first stage of family development is:

    a Crisis intervention.

    b Conjoint therapy.

    c Group therapy.

    d Family therapy.

10 According to the systems theory approach to intervention with families:

    a Removal of the deviant member of the family will restore family homeokinesis.

    b Exposure of the sick family member to group interaction will interfere with group equilibrium.

    c Treatment of the deviant member separate from the other members is rarely effective.

    d Support of the sick member will sanction dysfunctional responses in other members.

section V word games

1 Fill-in: Interventions
DIRECTIONS: Using the definitions provided, fill in the blanks in the word list with selected INTERVENTIONS. (Solution appears in the Appendix.)

Definitions

A Group focused on relatedness

B Therapy involving marriage partners

C Inpatient intervention

D Therapy with a holistic approach

E Therapy involving several people

F Educative rather than therapeutic group;

G Group aimed at personal growth (two words)

H Goal of this group is self-actualization

I Treatment method focusing on child-parent-adult interactions (abb.)

J Therapy modality used to treat members of the same household

K Therapeutic experience using role-playing as a tool

L Group appropriate for persons with ego strength

M Short-term therapy used in a state of disequilibrium

Word list

_ _ _ <u>I</u> _ _ _ _ _ _ _ _ _

_ _ <u>N</u> _ _ _ _ _

_ _ _ _ _ <u>T</u> _ _ _ _ _ _ _

_ <u>E</u> _ _ _ _ _

_ <u>R</u> _ _ _

_ _ _ _ _ _ <u>V</u> _ _ _

_ <u>E</u> _ _ _   _ _ _ _

_ <u>N</u> _ _ _ _ _ _ _

<u>T</u> _

_ _ _ <u>I</u> _ _

_ _ _ _ _ <u>O</u> _ _ _ _ _

_ <u>N</u> _ _ _ _ _

_ _ _ <u>S</u> _ _

256

2 Crosshatch

DIRECTIONS: Fit the words listed below into the proper boxes. The words read left to right or top to bottom, one letter per box. INTERVENTIONS has been entered to give you a starting point. (Solution appears in the Appendix.)

4 letters
COPE
FEAR
GOAL
ROLE
TASK

5 letters
ANGER
NORMS
RULES

6 letters
ACTION
COPING
CRISIS
DENIAL
FAMILY
GROUPS
LEADER
LOSSES
MEMBER
STATUS
STRESS
TRAUMA

7 letters
BLENDED
GESTALT
NUCLEAR
TENSION
THREATS

8 letters
ANALYSIS
CONFLICT
CONJOINT
DEFENSES
GUIDANCE
INTIMACY
MEETINGS
RECORDER
SELF-HELP

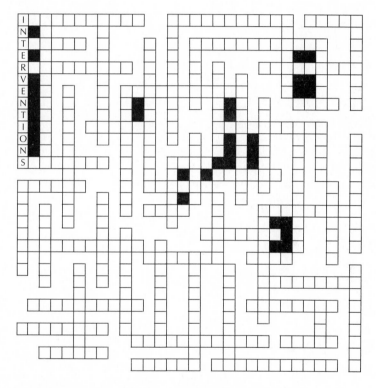

9 letters
AGGRESSOR
CATHARSIS
EMPTY NEST
ENCOUNTER
INITIATOR
SHORT TERM
TREATMENT

10 letters
ABREACTION
ADAPTATION
CHILD ABUSE
ELABORATOR
PREVENTION
RESOLUTION

11 letters
CONSULTANTS
COORDINATOR
INEFFECTIVE
INTERACTION
PREDICTABLE
PROCREATION
PROTAGONIST
PSYCHODRAMA
SITUATIONAL
TERMINATION

12 letters
COHESIVENESS
MENTAL HEALTH
REMOTIVATION

13 letters
√ INTERVENTIONS
SUPPORT SYSTEM
TRANSACTIONAL

section VI

legal and other issues affecting psychiatric nursing

chapter 25

impact of the law on the current practice of psychiatric nursing

INTRODUCTION

"Psychiatric nursing is concerned with assisting individuals, families, and community groups to achieve satisfying and productive patterns of living. The law provides rules for behavioral conduct to facilitate orderly social functioning while simultaneously protecting the rights of the individual. Thus psychiatric nursing and the law impact greatly on each other."* In order to provide optimal care for clients, nurses need to be aware of the guidelines provided by the law as care is implemented. Nurses owe it to their clients to meet their needs consistent with their rights as human beings. Nurses also owe it to themselves to be knowledgeable about the basic principles of the law as they carry out client care. The nurse as a professional person is responsible and accountable for all nursing actions. Failure to carry out an order, administer a medication, take an appropriate action, or, on the other hand, carrying out an action, implementing an order, administering a medication against a client's will or contrary to a client's rights may result in legal action taken against the nurse.

The purpose of this chapter is to identify several basic legal issues that effect the practice of psychiatric nursing and the role of the nurse as a client advocate assisting clients to learn about, protect, and assert their rights within the health care context.

OBJECTIVES

1. To describe the methods of psychiatric admission.
2. To list examples of civil rights.
3. To identify possible legal ramifications to the nurse if client rights are abused.
4. To evaluate selected nursing actions in terms of their respect or violation of clients' rights.

*From Taylor, C.M.: Mereness' essentials of psychiatric nursing, ed. 12, St. Louis, 1986, The C.V. Mosby Co., Chapter 25.

EXERCISES

1 There are two basic methods of psychiatric admission for persons found to be incompetent or dangerous because of mental illness. In the space provided briefly describe what is involved in these admission procedures.

   a Voluntary admission:

   b Involuntary admission:

2 List 10 civil rights that are frequently disrupted when an individual is institutionalized. The first one has been filled in to help you get started.

   a Voting _____   **f** _____
   b _____   **g** _____
   c _____   **h** _____
   d _____   **i** _____
   e _____   **j** _____

3 When a nurse or other staff member interferes with a client's rights, there can be serious legal ramifications. Listed below are 6 clients' rights. What legal action might be taken against a nurse or mental health care worker who interferes with these basic client rights? The first one has been filled in to help you get started.

Client rights/Nursing actions	Legal outcomes
1. Right to habeas corpus/ Client was detained illegally in the hospital.	Charge of false imprisonment.
2. Right to treatment/ Client was diagnosed as having a serious mental illness but received no treatment for the disorder.	
3. Right to informed consent/ Client was not given precise information on the risks involved prior to the administration of psychotropic agents and developed irreversible side effects.	
4. Right to confidentiality and privacy/ Client's confidential conversation was indiscreetly discussed by staff members in the hospital elevator where it was overheard by the client's relative.	
5. Right to refuse treatment/ Client was held down by several staff members and a medication was administered against his will.	
6. Right to least restrictive treatment/ In the absence of sufficient staff, the client was physically restrained when he tried to inflict self-injury.	

4 Listed on p. 264 are 15 nursing actions and 7 rights of clients. Some nursing actions acknowledge and respect the client's rights; others disregard and violate those rights. Categorize and evaluate each action in terms of the client right it most exemplifies by indicating in the appropriate column an *R* if it respects a right and a *V* if it violates a right. The first one has been filled in to help you get started.

Nursing actions	Rights of clients							
	Right to habeas corpus	Right to treatment	Right to least restrictive treatment	Right to refuse treatment	Right to informed consent	Right to confidentiality and privacy	Right to independent psychiatric examination	
1. Withholds the medication and notifies her supervisor when the client refuses his medication.				R				
2. Tells her family about her client, his problems, and her efforts to help him.								
3. Keeps the client under constant and close observation when he threatens suicide.								
4. Identifies clients who are chronically ill and will not profit from therapy.								
5. Describes to the client the action and possible side effects that may occur while he is taking medications.								
6. Listens to the client's expressions of anger at being deprived of his freedom.								
7. Tells the client he will be given his medication in injection form if he refuses to take it by mouth.								
8. Reviews the plan of treatment with the client, including both its positive and negative aspects.								
9. Carries out the physician's order to seclude a violent and resisting client until he regains control.								
10. Mails the client's letters without checking them for any significant or damaging information.								
11. Minimizes the dangers involved in electroconvulsive therapy when answering the client's questions.								
12. Assigns the client to a small group for weekly therapy sessions.								
13. Develops a comprehensive plan of care for the client during team conference.								
14. Answers the client's employees' questions about the client's condition over the telephone.								
15. Reports the client's request to be examined by a different physician other than the one currently caring for him.								

DIRECTIONS: Select the *best* response. (Answers appear in the Appendix.)

1 The person who is primarily responsible for assisting clients to learn about, protect, and assert their rights within the health care context is the:

   a Nursing supervisor.   **c** Criminal lawyer.

   b Client advocate.   **d** Medical doctor.

2 The primary purpose of an *emergency* commitment is to:

   a Prevent mental illness.   **c** Observe the client.

   b Treat the mental disorder. **d** Relieve the family.

3 In a *regular* commitment the client usually:

   a Agrees to being hospitalized.

   b Is examined by one or more physicians.

   c Is tried in a court of law.

   d Understands he is being deprived of his liberty.

4 Civil rights include the right to:

   a Religious freedom.   **c** Vote.

   b Education.   **d** All of the above.

5 The right to habeas corpus provides which one of the following?

   a To establish a humane environment for the care of a hospitalized person.

   b To prohibit the disclosure of material considered to be confidential.

   c To expedite the release of a person who is detained illegally.

   d To arrange for a person to be examined by a physician of his choice.

6 Which one of the following nursing actions would be considered a violation of a client's rights?

   a Assigning the client to a small group for weekly therapy sessions.

   b Reviewing with the client the positive and negative aspects of the treatment plan.

   c Keeping the suicidal client under constant and close observation.

   d Identifying clients who are chronically ill and who will not profit from therapy.

7 Forcefully administering a medication and ignoring a client's refusal to take it could result in which one of the following charges against the nurse?

    a Negligence.   **c** Assault.

    b Malpractice.   **d** None of the above.

8 The majority of lawsuits in psychiatric nursing involve which one of the following?

    a Negligence.   **c** Assault.

    b Malpractice.   **d** Battery.

9 A basic component of the Moral Penal Code is that the offender is found to be:

    a Suspicious.   **c** Dangerous.

    b Depressed.   **d** Suicidal.

10 The M'Naghten rule used in trials involving issues of crime and sanity refers to which one of the following?

    a Test of right and wrong.   **c** Intelligence test.

    b "Irresistible impulse test."   **d** All of the above.

chapter 26

issues affecting the future of psychiatric nursing

INTRODUCTION

"Today's students of nursing will be practicing well into the twenty-first century and will be the nursing leaders of tomorrow. Since it is their nursing practice which will be affected by the way in which current issues are resolved, it is imperative that nursing students become aware of those factors which will shape the nature and scope of psychiatric nursing in the future."*

Therefore it is appropriate that the final chapter in the text should deal with issues that may influence the future of psychiatric nursing. Issues are complex matters created by the interplay of multiple events and conditions that raise questions which do not lend themselves to ready answers or solutions. They are by nature controversial and open to debate. Although this is the last chapter, it is hoped that you are not left with a sense of closure and finality but rather with questions that stimulate you to further thinking and discussion.

The purpose of this chapter is to help you focus on a few of the many critical issues that are open to discussion and may play a role in determining the future of psychiatric nursing.

OBJECTIVES

1. To identify local issues that may affect the care of the mentally ill and the practice of psychiatric nursing in your area.
2. To discuss issues affecting the future of psychiatric nursing.

*From Taylor, C.M.: Mereness' essentials of psychiatric nursing, ed. 12, St. Louis, 1986, The C.V. Mosby Co., Chapter 26.

1 Using local sources such as newspapers, meetings, conferences, and legislation, identify events that may affect the care of the mentally ill and the future of psychiatric nursing in your area. A limited amount of space is provided below for you to list these events.

a _____
_____

b _____
_____

c _____
_____

d _____
_____

e _____
_____

2 Discuss issues affecting the future of psychiatric nursing. Use your own identified list of issues (Exercise 1) or the following list of representative issues that were described in the text.

a Economic issues: Inflation and economic constraints demand the elimination of all health care workers who cannot be accountable for the expenditure of their time in relation to the cost of their services.

b Social issues: Social issues such as the feminist movement have had some possible negative effects on the nursing profession. In an attempt to be involved in occupations with a more even distribution of men and women, fewer women are pursuing nursing as a career because it is still predominantly associated with women.

c Professional issues: The increasing move toward role blurring, in which other persons assume nursing functions, demonstrates that some nursing activities can be implemented by less highly prepared persons.

d Clinical issues: Although prevention of mental illness and promotion of mental health are believed to be more effective long-term goals, many people will only support and allocate funds to the immediate treatment of the mentally ill because the results of short-term goals are more readily visible and measurable.

e Delivery system issues: Although the community mental health movement has merit in the promotion of mental health care practices in community centers, it may be abandoned because these centers tend to cluster in urban areas, meeting the needs of relatively few people, while at the same time drawing off the prepared personnel from inpatient facilities and leaving the care of the greatest numbers of people to the least well prepared.

f Educational issues: As schools of nursing move toward more integrated curricula, few students have specific learning experiences with the mentally ill, and as a result fewer nursing graduates are choosing psychiatric nursing as a field of work, contributing to increased shortages of qualified nurses to work with the mentally ill.

TEST ITEMS

DIRECTIONS: Select the *best* response. (Answers appear in the Appendix.)

1 Which one of the following issues is all-pervasive, directly or indirectly influencing *all* other issues in psychiatric nursing?
  a Clinical.
  b Educational.
  c Social.
  d Economical.

2 The public's increased demand for more accountability in the expenditure of time in the administration of health care is primarily associated with which one of the following issues?
  a The improved educational status of female nurses.
  b The rising incidence of mental illness.
  c The increased cost of health care services.
  d The growing concern with clients' rights.

3 The development of diagnosis related groups (DRGs) is expected to increase the number of persons being cared for in:
  a Hospitals.
  b Communities.
  c Nursing homes.
  d None of the above.

4 A recent social trend that is impacting on the practice of psychiatric nursing is that:
  a Increasing numbers of women are seeking careers not traditionally associated with women.
  b More and more men are replacing women in leadership positions in nursing.
  c Fewer women are pursuing nursing careers because of the influx of men into the profession.
  d Increasing numbers of men entering nursing has favorably affected the status of all nurses.

5 The field of psychiatry has lost some of its mysteriousness with the increased:

   a Use of psychotropic agents.

   b Interest in the self-help phenomenon.

   c Development of self-awareness.

   d Cost of mental health care.

6 The identity of the psychiatric nurse is *most* threatened by which one of the following?

   a Holistic care.   **c** Role blurring.

   b Self-care groups.   **d** Psychotropic drugs.

7 The *most* cost-effective way to impact on the incidence of mental illness is to:

   a Treat mentally ill persons in community mental health centers.

   b Focus on the prevention of mental illness and promotion of mental health.

   c Work with emotionally disturbed people in groups rather than individually.

   d Concentrate on caring for acutely ill rather than chronically ill persons.

8 The "revolving door" syndrome has resulted in which one of the following outcomes among mental health care workers?

   a Feelings of disappointment and failure.

   b Acceptance of the chronic nature of mental illness.

   c Interest in finding alternative treatment methods.

   d All of the above.

9 The fact that it is less costly to maintain mentally ill persons outside of institutions has resulted in which one of the following negative effects?

   a Premature discharge of mentally ill persons into the community.

   b Failure to supervise the discharged person's use of psychotropic medications.

   c Decreased numbers of prepared health care workers to care for discharged persons in the community.

   d All of the above.

10 The fact that fewer nurses are entering the specialty of psychiatric nursing is mainly attributed to the:

a Decreasing number of persons requiring psychiatric care.

b Integration of psychiatric content in undergraduate nursing programs.

c Closing of institutions specific to the care of the mentally ill.

d Increasing efforts to recruit nurses into other specialty areas.

section VI word games

1 Word search

DIRECTIONS: Listed below are 66 words hidden in the puzzle grid. They may be read up or down, forward or backward, or diagonally, but always in a straight line. Some words may overlap and some letters in the grid may be used more than once. All the letters in the grid will not be used. Circle each word as you locate it. ISSUES has been circled to get you started. (Solution appears in the Appendix.)

ACCOUNTABILITY	DETENTION	LEGISLATION
ADMISSION	DISCLOSURE	LIABILITY
ADVOCATES	DUE PROCESS	LITIGATION
AMENDMENTS	ECONOMIC	LOCKED UNITS
ASSAULT	EDUCATION	MALPRACTICE
BILL OF RIGHTS	FORENSIC	MORAL PENAL CODE
CHRONIC	GOALS	NEGLIGENCE
CIVIL RIGHTS	GUARDIAN	PLAINTIFF
CLIENTS RIGHTS	HABEAS CORPUS	PREVENTION
CODE FOR NURSES	HOLISTIC	PRIVACY
COMMITMENT	INCOMPETENT	PROFESSIONAL
COMPETENCY	INFORMED CONSENT	RESEARCH
CONFIDENTIALITY	INJURY	RESTRAINTS
CONSENT	INSANE	REVOLVING DOOR
CONSERVATOR	INSANITY	ROLE BLURRING
CONTRACT	✔ [ISSUES]	SANITY
COST-EFFECTIVE	JAIL	SOCIAL
COURT	JUDGE	STATUTES
CRIME	JURY	TORT
DAMAGES	LAWS	TREATMENT
DEFENDANT	LAWSUIT	VOLUNTARY
DEHUMANIZATION	LEGALITIES	WITNESS
	LEGAL STATUS	

272

```
E V I T C E F F E T S O C O N S E N T E C I T C A R P L A M B A
D R E S E A R C H R W E I Z O P R O S D E C O N O M I C T O L R
O E U F O I B D L E A O T D P G R H O E A F T I U S W A L A I L
C V (I S S U E S) F A G Z S A I T U A L T O O J U R P I L L I A W
L O T T O P F F O T L M I W C R I M E E P R E V E N T I O N B S
A L N H A L I C H M I C L D E O O E O N L E G H D I N Z U J I E
N V E G D G C E J E E I O P M R V N I T O N I V E T E P S U L I
E I T I S I N S A N E V H U O T S D B I D S A C H O S R T R I T
P N E R J L P M I T N I O Y R C A M A O S I S D U V S O C Y T I
L G P F Y U V O L D C L L C T T N E S N O C D E M R O F N I Y L
A D M O L A R S L O E R U N P D I N O W C C I T A I F E G Y T A
R O O L L W I Y U P D I C E L E T T M I I A L L N O S S F A I G
O O C L I E N T S R I G H T S H Y S F N A I D U I T A S F C N E
M R N I H A O B E I O H O E S S R A O C L G E A Z B C I I C A L
S D I B S E I S F V G T H P G U A R D I A N I S A J U O T O S O
E K O W C L T M N A O S P M R O H S T U W Z Y S T A C N N U N C
T E A G I R A C K C L N P O R C O N T R A C T A I S U A I N I K
U L N S A T C A R Y S E F C O N S E R V A T O R O G H L A T I E
T J U I D G U D E F S E N O R O L E B L U R R I N G I N L A T D
A O N L J U D G E L M C G V I O L N E C N E G I L G E N P B O U
T T E D O I E L A B C Y R A T N U L O V D L E G I S L A T I O N
S E S R U N R O F E D O C O M M I T M E N T E F R T S H O L O I
T C H I L E G A L S T A T U S A O P R I T N O I T A G I T I L T
O P L M M C H S S E C O R P E U D Z F N O D E F E N D A N T I S
H A B E A S C O R P U S O A B C O N F I D E N T I A L I T Y M M
```

2 Logic problem

DIRECTIONS: Five clients, Mr. Solo, Miss Low, Mrs. Chin, Mr. Ames, and Mrs. Williams, are all inpatients in a psychiatric hospital. They are assigned to five different nurses, Mr. Mac, Ms. Cobb, Mrs. Eddy, Mr. May, and Miss Todd, who are serving as client advocates to help them with their client rights. Each nurse is working with a different client. None of the male nurses is working with a female client. Each nurse is focusing on a different client right. Using the additional clues and the grid provided below, match the clients with their nurse and the client right being served.

Clues:

a Mr. Solo's right to confidentiality was violated.

b Ms. Cobb's client refused medication and the nurse acknowledged the client's right to least-restrictive treatment.

c The right to habeas corpus involved one of the women clients.

d Before administering a new medication to his client, Mr. Mac gave precise information about the drug's action, side effects, and precautions to the client, acknowledging the client's right to informed consent.

e Mrs. Chin's right to treatment is observed as Miss Todd works closely with her in a nurse-client relationship.

f Mrs. Eddy is no longer working with Miss Low.

(Use an X in the boxes as you eliminate clues and an O in the boxes as you link up a clue with a client, nurse, or client right. For example, clue f indicates that Mrs. Eddy is not working with Miss Low; therefore an X has been inserted in the grid for Eddy/Low. Be sure to refer to the introductory comments in the directions for additional clues.)

	Grid:	Clients					Nurses				
	Client rights	Mr. Solo	Miss Low	Mrs. Chin	Mr. Ames	Mrs. Wms.	Mr. Mac	Ms. Cobb	Mrs. Eddy	Mr. May	Miss Todd
Client rights	Treatment										
	Habeas corpus										
	Confidentiality										
	Informed consent										
	Least restrictive treatment										
Nurses	Mr. Mac										
	Ms. Cobb										
	Mrs. Eddy		X								
	Mr. May										
	Miss Todd										

appendix

answers to exercises

CHAPTER 1

Exercise 1

Prerecorded: 4, 5. Egyptian-Greek: 9, 12. Middle Ages: 1, 13. Fifteenth century: 6. Sixteenth to eighteenth century: 2, 8, 10. Nineteenth century: 14. Twentieth century: 3, 7, 11, 14, 15.

Exercise 2

To serve people residing in catchment area; to assist community to improve its level of mental health; to return hospitalized individuals to community living; to help hospitalized individuals maintain family and community ties.

Exercise 3

2: Provide professional guidance and supervision of paraprofessionals. 3: Acknowledge the blurring of roles and work together collaboratively. 4: Acquire knowledge and skill in consultation and education. 5: Develop relationships within the community.

Exercise 4

1: Carry out basic hygiene care, make simple decisions. 2: Engage in simple, structured, routine tasks. 3: Encourage participation in simple noncompetitive games and group activities. 4: Facilitate relatedness through introductions to other people with similar interests and encourage relatedness at meals, in socialization groups.

CHAPTER 2

Exercise 1

Psychologist: 2, 4, 7, 10. Social Worker: 2, 3, 10. Psychiatrist: 1, 2, 5, 6, 10. Psychiatric Nurse: 2, 4, 6, 10. Activity Therapist: 2, 4, 8, 9, 10.

Exercise 2

a: 1, 4, 7, 9. b: 3, 14. c: 5, 11, 12, 15. d: 2. e: 6 to 10. f: 1, 6 to 10. g: 13.

Exercise 3

2: Sense of security, feelings of safety enhanced; anxiety and insecurity decreased. 3: Participation in group activities; feelings of relatedness and belonging promoted; isolation decreased. 4: Becoming more knowledgeable and skilled in various areas; striving for optimal level of functioning. 5: Feelings of security leading to readiness to assume responsibility for meeting own basic needs. 6: Increased self-awareness; develop ability to assess problems realistically and cope with them more effectively. 7: Increased problem-solving ability; anxiety reduced through ventilation.

CHAPTER 3

Exercise 1

Family: 2, 6, 11. Social: 3, 10, 14. Community: 4, 8, 9, 15. Physiological: 1, 5, 13. Psychological: 7, 12.

Exercise 2

Developmental: 2, 4, 5, 9 to 11, 13. Situational: 3, 6 to 8, 12, 14, 15.

Exercise 3

Open: 1, 2, 5, 8, 9, 12 to 15. Closed: 3, 4, 6, 7, 10, 11. Resources or subsystems: 2, 12: community people. 3: school personnel. 4, 6, 7, 10: family, friends, neighbors. 5, 8: neighbors. 9: family. 11, 14, 15: nurses, doctors. 13: parents, teachers.

CHAPTER 4

Exercise 1a

1: Directs rational, thoughtful behavior; concerned with thoughts, feelings, and sensations; aware of here and now. 2: Storage area for memories that can be recalled at will; keeps disturbing material out of consciousness. 3: Largest storage area for material; cannot be recalled at will.

Exercise 1b

Id: 1: 4, 5, 11 to 13. 2: Innate, primitive, unconscious, selfish, source of libidinal energy and instinctual drives. Ego: 1: 1, 6 to 10, 14. 2: The self; effects compromises between id and superego; rational, reasonable, conscious part of personality. Superego: 1: 2, 3, 15. 2: Two parts—ego ideal (rewarding) and conscience (punishing); incorporates taboos, prohibitions, ideals, standards; mostly unconscious; inhibits id; rigid; source of guilt.

Exercise 2

1: Other pleasurable activities: crying, chewing, swallowing. 2: Anus, urethra: Evacuation of bladder and bowels. 3: Immature genitalia: Manipulation of genitalia (masturbation). 4: None: Stable, dormant stage. Child finds pleasure associating with other children and acquiring skills and knowledge. 5: Mature genitalia: Genital-to-genital activity with partner of opposite sex.

Exercise 3a

Need for satisfaction: biological needs such as food, air, sex. Need for security: emotional needs such as interpersonal intimacy, status, self-esteem.

Exercise 3b

Both needs are met interpersonally. If met in loving, caring ways and the child experiences positive reflected appraisals, he learns to see himself as a person of value (good-me self-concept); if met inconsistently and grudgingly and the child experiences negative reflected appraisals, he learns to see himself as a person of little worth (bad-me self-concept).

Exercise 4

2: Strives for and learns to use power: Child feels beginning sense of power related to attempts to control self and others. 3: Acquires and uses universal language: Child gives up personal language and uses universal language as a tool to promote relationships; able to consensually validate perceptions and feelings with others. 4: Learns to compete and compromise: Child turns away from adults and turns to peers of same sex. Tests out tools of competition and compromise. Peers reinforce or alter child's self-concept. 5: Forms close relationship with chum: Continues group affiliations while developing an intimate relationship with one special friend of the same sex. Significant adults outside the family impact on child's concept of self. 6: Experiences lust: In response to sexual urges, adolescent turns to peers of the opposite sex while continuing to be influenced by peer group of the same sex. 7: Integration of intimacy and lust: Adolescent integrates intimacy and lust into mature adult relationship with person of the oppoxite sex.

Exercise 5a	Good-me: 1, 4, 8, 9, 12. Bad-me: 2, 3, 6, 7, 10. Not-me: 5, 10, 11.
Exercise 5b	Good-me: 2, 8 to 10. Bad-me: 1, 3, 5, 7, 11. Not-me: 4, 6, 12.
Exercise 6	1-h, 2-p, 3-n, 4-j, 5-o, 6-d, 7-l, 8-g, 9-k, 10-a, 11-e, 12-c, 13-m, 14-f, 15-b, 16-i.

CHAPTER 5

Exercise 1	Intrapsychic: 2, 4, 6, 8. Interpersonal: 1, 3, 5, 7, 9, 10.
Exercise 2	Personal examples.
Exercise 3	Coping measures: 1-g, 2-q, 5-v, 8-x, 12-e, 13-d, 15-t, 19-h, 24-j. Ego defenses: 6-k, 7-c, 9-l, 10-u, 11-m, 14-b, 16-s, 17-w, 18-o, 21-n, 22-f. Security operations: 3-i, 4-p, 20-r, 23-a.

CHAPTER 6

Exercise 1	a: 4, 7, 9, 16. b: 2, 5. c: 6, 8, 16. d: 11, 12, 15. e: 1, 3, 10, 12, 15. f: 13, 14, 16. g: 11, 12, 16.
Exercise 2a	Genetic: 2, 4, 11. Physiological: 2, 3, 7. Intrapsychic: 9, 12, 15, 16. Interpersonal: 1, 5, 6, 8, 10, 11, 14, 15. Cultural: 13.
Exercise 2b	Genetic counseling of parents prior to conception; treatment of mother's drug addiction, venereal disease, mental illness; removing Ralph from the home and placing him in a loving foster home; providing Ralph with positive interpersonal experiences at home, in school, in community with peers and other adults; raising Ralph in a less deprived, poverty-ridden community.
Exercise 3	Personal examples.

CHAPTER 7

Exercise 1 and 2	Personal responses.
Exercise 3	a: 4, 8, 13. b: 1, 12, 14, 19. c: 2, 7, 15, 16, 20. d: 3, 11, 17. e: 5, 11. f: 9, 18, 20. g: 6, 11.
Exercise 4	To develop a more positive concept of self; to develop a more harmonious pattern of interpersonal relationships; to assume a more productive role in society.

CHAPTER 8

Exercise 1

Therapeutic: 1: Sitting during conversation, reaching out, touching, nodding head; 2: Quiet, calm, unhurried, mild, soft-spoken manner; 3: Smiling, natural eye contact. Nontherapeutic: 1: Standing during conversation, restlessness, shifting on feet, touching, pointing, shaking finger; 2: Loud, challenging, sharp tone, short responses; 3: Avoiding eye contact, looking around in distracted manner during conversation, frowning, grimacing, smiling. (It should be noted that even therapeutic approaches may have nontherapeutic effects if used inappropriately. For example, a suspicious person may be threatened by touch and reaching out, or a smile may be distorted.)

Exercise 2a

1: f. 2: g, j, w. 3: e, g. 4: b, d, o, q, s, u, v. 5: a. 6: s. 7: h, k. 8: c, l. 9: x. 10: m. 11: r. 12: i, n, p, q, t.

Exercise 2b

1: t, v. 2: l. 3: e, p. 4: j, u. 5: m, p, r. 6: g, q. 7: k, q. 8: a, n. 9: s. 10: b, i. 11: h, x. 12: c, f, o, w. 13: g. 14: d.

Exercise 3

2: Ask specific data. 3: Encourage client to continue without introducing a new idea. 4: Encourage client to elaborate on a topic that is unclear. 5: Express interest in client; establish rapport. 6: Focus on a topic of general interest when initiating a conversation with a client whose problem and need areas have not yet been identified. 7: Encourage client to identify interests and concerns he wishes to discuss. 8: Offer alternative ideas, activities, that might be helpful for the client to consider. 9: Acknowledge client; build self-esteem. 10: Encourage more depth of discussion by asking reality-oriented questions. 11: Return to a topic or area of concern that needs further discussion. 12: Acknowledge client's thoughts and feelings without necessarily agreeing with them.

Exercise 4

2: Focusing on self rather than client suggests lack of interest in the client; allows client to direct attention away from himself and his problems. 3: By giving advice, the nurse attempts to impose values and choices on the client rather than help client make his own decisions. 4: Giving disapproval is a judgmental response which discourages the client from sharing thoughts and feelings. 5: Probing is asking client questions or encouraging a client to talk about a topic before he is ready to do so; tends to create anxiety and client may need to defend. 6: Through persuasion the nurse puts pressure on the client to take a particular action and interferes with client's being self-directive. 7: Disagreeing is a defensive response which cuts off conversation. 8: Reassurance: Although often well-intentioned, reassurance is usually not helpful and communicates to the client that his concerns are not understood and are being dismissed lightly.

CHAPTER 9

Exercise 1

Emergency: 4, 6, 8, 12. Interaction: 2, 5, 9, 14. Relationship: 1, 3, 7, 10, 11, 13, 15.

Exercise 2a	Orientation: 1: Getting acquainted period; nurse and client are strangers to each other. 2: To develop trust; to establish the nurse as significant to the client. 3: Usually initiated by nurse who seeks out client, introduces self and offers to work with the client; accepts testing behaviors; responds with consistency. Maintenance: 1: Working phase characterized by nurse and client actively working together on client's problems. 2: To identify and resolve the client's problems. 3: Nurse focuses on client's problems; sets limits on behaviors as necessary; encourages expression of fears, concerns, hopes, problems. Termination: 1: Concluding phase in which nurse and client prepare for end of the relationship. 2: To help client review learnings that came out of the relationship; to transfer learnings to interactions with others. 3: Nurse deals with client's response to termination: denial, regression, dependency, rebellion; encourages client to express anger, depression, loss associated with ending; nurse deals with own feelings associated with termination.
Exercise 2b	Approaches client; introduces self by name; asks client's name and checks out how she would like to be addressed; suggests working together; identifies purpose of the meetings; suggests time and place to meet; uses communication skills, including introducing a neutral topic until client's needs and problems are identified; responds consistently, adhering to schedule of meetings; accepts testing behaviors; sets limits on behaviors as necessary.
Exercise 2c	Meeting hygiene needs; expressing feelings appropriately; controlling impulses such as eating, masturbation, aggression; relating; weight control.
Exercise 2d	Accepting: 1, 3, 4, 6, 7, 10, 12 to 15. Nonaccepting: 2, 5, 8, 9, 11.
Exercise 2e	Consistent: 1, 5 to 8, 11, 15. Inconsistent (including revisions): 3: The student nurse regularly sought out the client and invited her to return. 4: The student checked with the client and learned what she wanted to be called and used her name consistently. 9: The student began by telling the client to stop the behavior. Only if the approach failed did she seek help. 10: The client was told to go to her room whenever she masturbated in public. 12: The student made an effort to be aware of the client's overt and covert expressions of feelings and encouraged her to talk about them. 13: The student responded matter-of-factly and firmly. 14: The student told the client she would wait 10 to 15 minutes and then would look for her if she had not returned. The student did as she promised.
Exercise 3	Social: 2, 5, 7, 9, 10. Therapeutic: 1, 3, 4, 6, 8.
CHAPTER 10	
Exercise 1a-1	Classification: Antipsychotic, phenothiazine derivative. Other drugs: See Taylor: Table 10-1; Action: Reduce psychotic symptoms, control excited,

overactive individuals, normalize withdrawn, inactive individuals, reduce hallucinations and delusions. Range of dosage/Route: 100 to 800 mg/oral. Client/Dosage: HH/100 mg t.i.d.; HH is hypotensive and drug use should be moderated closely. Contraindications/Precautions: In clients in severe CNS depression, comatose states or psychotic depression; in clients with severe hypotensive or hypertensive heart disease; use cautiously with persons requiring complete mental acuity. Drug idiosyncrasies: Pigmentary retinopathy can occur in persons taking larger than recommended doses; women have greater tendency to orthostatic hypotension than men. Side Effects/Nursing: Dry mouth/ offer fluids, gum, candy; constipation/ offer fluids, balanced diet, roughage, laxatives; orthostatic hypotension/ ambulate gradually; endocrine changes/ diet to regulate weight, reassure client; extrapyramidal changes/ dose adjustment, use of antiparkinsonism drug as ordered; photosensitivity/ protect from rays of the sun; Adverse effects/Nursing: Skin reactions, tardive dyskinesia/ withhold drug only after reporting to doctor and there has been medical evaluation; jaundice/ report to physician, withhold then discontinue drug; agranulocytosis, leukopenia/ check white blood count at regularly scheduled intervals, report signs of sore throat and colds, withhold then discontinue drug; ocular changes/ maintain client on recommended daily dosage, schedule routine eye examinations, report signs of eye problems, withhold then discontinue drug; convulsions/ use anticonvulsants as ordered with persons having history of seizures. Misc. Nursing: Keep medications inaccessible to psychotic clients, administer drugs to one client at a time, observe for and report side effects, adverse effects, effect of drug on behavior. Source: Taylor, PDR.

Exercise 1a-2 See Taylor: Table 10-1.

Exercise 1b-1 See Taylor: Table 10-4.

Exercise 1b-2 Individualized response, depending on medication selected. See Taylor, PDR, etc., for data.

Exercise 1c-1 Classification: Antidepressant, tricyclic. Other drugs: See Taylor: Table 10-5. Action: relief of depression. Range of dosage/Route: 75 to 200 mg/oral. Client/Dosage: FS/50 mg t.i.d.; FS is suicidal and needs close supervision. Contraindications/Precautions: In clients with history of cardiovascular disease, urinary retention, glaucoma, thyroid disease, seizures. Drug idiosyncrasies: Effective more quickly than other tricyclics; drug may be stopped and another in the tricyclic family started with no delay; if an MAO inhibitor is to be started, there should be a delay of at least 2 weeks to allow for complete metabolism of the drug and to avoid the development of hypertensive crisis; abrupt cessation of drug after prolonged use may produce nausea, headache, malaise. Side effects/Nursing: Dry mouth, postural hypotension, perspiration, visual symptoms, tremor, convulsions, twitching, or ataxia/ report to the physician;

can usually be controlled by reduction in dosage. Adverse effects/Nursing: Exacerbation of psychosis, cardiac arrhythmias: report and then discontinue drug. Misc. nursing: Client may require several weeks on drug before effect on depression is noted; observe client closely for suicidal ideation and acts during this period. Source: Taylor, PDR.

Exercise 1c-2

Classification: Antidepressant, monoamine oxidase inhibitor (MAO). Other drugs: See Taylor: Table 10-5; Action: Reduces depression. Range of dosage/Route: 20 to 60 mg/oral. Client/Dosage: FS/Contraindications/ Precautions: In clients with cardiovascular disorders, history of liver disease/ use under close supervision (generally in hospital) when tricyclics have been ineffective. Drug idiosyncrasies: Avoid use with other MAOs or tricyclics, drugs containing epinephrine or ephedrine, and foods containing tyramine or excessive caffeine. Side effects/Nursing.: Dry mouth, postural hypotension, perspiration, visual symptoms, tremor, convulsions, twitching, or ataxia should be reported to the physician; can usually be controlled by reduction in dosage. Adverse effects/Nursing: Hypertensive crisis can be prevented by avoiding specific substances including over-the-counter cold remedies and antihistamines, aged cheese, whiskey, beer, Chianti wine, cream, chocolate, coffee, soy sauce, chicken livers, raisins, yeast products. Misc. Nursing: Observe client for suicidal ideation and acts during time it takes for drug to be effective, check that client swallows pills and does not save them for suicide attempt. Source: Taylor, PDR.

Exercise 1d-1

Classification: Antimanic. Other drugs: None; Action: Normalizes manic behaviors within 1 to 3 weeks; target symptoms include pressure of speech, hyperactivity, flight of ideas, grandiosity, poor judgment, aggressiveness. Range of dose/Route: 900 to 1800 mg/oral; dosage is individualized, according to serum levels and clinical response. Client/Dosage: TW/300 mg t.i.d.; Contraindications/Precautions: in clients with significant renal or cardiovascular disease, in clients who are severely debilitated, dehydrated, or experiencing sodium depletion, in clients taking diuretics/drug may be contraindicated or used cautiously. Drug idiosyncrasies: Lithium toxicity is closely related to serum lithium levels; the ability to tolerate lithium is greater during acute mania and decreases as manic symptoms decrease. Side effects/Nursing.: Fine hand tremor, polyuria, mild thirst, transient mild nausea are sometimes seen in early treatment/often subside without intervention; if persistent, dosage may need to be adjusted. Adverse effects/Nursing.: Diarrhea, vomiting, drowsiness, muscular weakness, lack of coordination, giddiness, ataxia, blurred vision, tinnitus, abdominal cramps, and large output of dilute urine require dosage adjustment; failure to do so may result in renal tubule damage, cardiac toxicity, thyroid imbalance. Misc. nursing: Serum levels should be determined twice a week initially, then may be reduced; desirable range is 1.0 to 1.5 mEq/l; toxicity can often be prevented if serum lithium level is kept below 1.5; to counteract the lag period, antipsychotic agents are sometimes used, however, the combined use of haloperidol with lithium may produce encephalopathic syndrome; clients should be maintained on normal diet, including salt, and a fluid intake of 2500 to 3000 ml; outpatients should be instructed about symptoms of toxicity and the need to discontinue drug and notify physician if they occur. Source: Taylor, PDR.

Exercise 1d-2

Kidneys, heart, thyroid.

Exercise 2a

1-l, 2-i, 3-m, 4-a and k, 5-f, 6-g, 7-i, 8-e, 9-a, 10-l, 11-n, 12-d, 13-a, 14-a, 15-h, 16-c, 17-i, 18-j, 19-b, 20-a.

Exercise 2b

Keep tray of medications inaccessible to group of ambulatory clients; administer medications to one client at a time; observe for side effects, adverse effects, and changes in behavior; use opportunity to interact with client; respond to client's questions about medications; report and record nursing interventions effective in getting resistant client to take medications; teach client about medications preparatory to discharge if he is to be maintained on drugs.

CHAPTER 11

Exercise 1a

Physical: 1 to 5, 8, 9, 16 to 18, 20. Emotional: 6, 7, 10 to 15, 19.

Exercise 1b

Therapeutic: 2, 5, 7 to 10, 12 to 15, 19. Nontherapeutic (including revisions): 1 and 3: Allow, encourage clients to keep pictures, plants, small personal items. 4: Ideally, rooms should be small. Provide partitions for privacy. 6 and 11: Staff needs to be actively involved with clients, encouraging interaction, providing stimulation. 16: Provide suitable seating. 17: Cleaning, repairs. 18: Provide smaller, perhaps round tables for face-to-face interaction at meals. 20: Post current materials.

Exercise 2

Play Ping-Pong with clients; move chairs into conversational circle around the low table and encourage interaction; sit with three clients at the table for four and play a table game from the bookcase; facilitate a sing-along around the pinao; encourage orientation by focusing on the clock, calendar; post schedules of activities, birthdays, news items, art work on the bulletin board; place plants on the window sills, bookcase, and encourage clients to care for them; refer to books and magazines when interacting; form discussion circle under the TV and encourage discussion of a program that has just been viewed.

Exercise 3

Provide favorable climate in which client can: gain self-awareness; try new interpersonal skills; focus more on others and less on self; develop self-esteem; appraise potentially helpful and destructive aspects of behavior; practice decision making; participate in group activities and group decisions.

CHAPTER 12

Exercise 1

1-b: To validate data. Discuss perceptions with others. 1-c: To analyze data. Sort and organize data according to themes. 2-d: To establish a nursing diagnosis. Synthesize all available assessment data. 3-e: To individualize a course of action (plan care). Identify nursing goal, rationale, nursing actions, and anticipated results from care to be given (outcome criteria). 4-f: To carry out course of action (plan of care). Function in a variety of nursing roles while using psychiatric nursing principles. 5-g: To critically assess care. Review assessment data, nursing diagnosis for accuracy and currency. 5-h: To revise or confirm plan of care. Review and revise plan as necessary. 5-i: To engage in self-assessment. Evaluate own responses.

Exercise 2a

Direct observation, client interview, medic alert records, previous hospital records, neighbors, police.

Exercise 2b

Seeing: 1, 3, 4, 7, 8. Hearing: 2, 6, 9. Smelling: 5, 10. Touching: 4, 8.

Exercise 2c

To orient the client to the nurse and the purpose of the interview; to ascertain client's perception of his/her problems; to determine duration of the problem; to obtain factual information about client's ADL, previous health history, etc.

Exercise 2d

2: "What are you frowning about?" 3: "Where is the pain?" "How long does the pain last?" 4: "What do you usually eat for breakfast . . .?" 5: "What is your daughter's name?" "Where does your daughter live?" "When did you see her last?" 6: "How many hours do you sleep at night?" "Do you take pills to help you sleep?" 7: "What has happened to upset you?" 8: "How did you get those bruises on your arms?" 9: "Who are your neighbors?" 10: "How do you feel about returning to the boardinghouse?"

Exercise 2e

Tech. role: 5 to 6, 10, 15. CTE: 1, 11, 15. Social agent: 2, 9. Teacher: 4, 13, 14. Mother surrogate: 4, 12, 14. Nurse therapist: 3, 7. Counselor: 3, 7, 8.

Exercise 3a

Nsg. Dx.: Verbal communication impaired, related to psychologic barriers, psychosis, lack of stimuli. Goal: To help client communicate verbally. Rationale: The client has withdrawn into silence in response to painful past relationships and needs to be actively sought out by the nurse. Nsg. Actions: Seek out client for brief, frequent visits; develop a nurse-client relationship; use variety of therapeutic communication skills, including focusing on client and on neutral topics; use silence and give client time to respond; use games, art, music to stimulate client. Anticipated Results: Within 4 weeks the client will begin to verbalize to the nurse and eventually others.

Exercise 3b

Nsg. Dx.: Potentially violent, directed at others, related to being an abused and battered child. Goal: To develop nurse-client relationship; to help client control violent outbursts; to help client express feelings in more socially acceptable ways. Rationale: The client responds with violence based on her own childhood experiences as a battered child and needs to be exposed to positive IPR. Nsg. Actions: Seek out client when she is not behaving aggressively and initiate a nurse-client relationship; set verbal limits on violent activities; remove client from excessively stimulating situations; encourage client to verbalize rather than act out feelings; identify cues of impending anger, aggression, or violence and channel excess energy into physical activities; acknowledge and reward appropriate behaviors. Anticipated results: In 4 weeks the client will show a decrease in violent behavior and will begin to express anger verbally rather than physically.

CHAPTER 13

Exercise 1

Disorganized: 1, 7, 10. Catatonic: 2, 3, 5. Paranoid: 4, 8, 9. Chronic Undiff.: all behaviors except #6 could be observed. Residual: 6.

Exercise 2a

1: (2) Suspicious, believes she is being poisoned, does not share; (6) sits alone facing door, responds with anger when approached; (12) continues to be suspicious and accuses staff of poisoning her. 2: (4) Wears old clothes and feels different from others; (7) takes no responsibility for her own hygiene, disheveled; (8) negativistic, refuses to follow suggestions and does the opposite of what is expected. 3: (5) Feels guilty and punishes herself for losing job and not helping mother; (7) unable to make decisions; (9) chants "Dear God, Forgive her . . . ." 4: (11) Never completes anything she starts, has difficulty concentrating on tasks, expresses feelings of inadequacy. 5: (9) Refers to herself in the third person; (10) Fails to respond to her name, appears not to know her own name, refers to herself as "Nobody". 6: (3) No friends, pursues solitary activities.

Exercise 2b

Penny experienced a series of rejections beginning in infancy. Her father abandoned her and her mother. The mother gave up Penny to foster homes in order to support herself. Perhaps Penny experienced further rejection, inconsistency, double-bind communication, indifference, predominantly negative reflected appraisals, and high anxiety in these homes. Peers ridiculed her. She learned early in life that relationships are painful, that people cannot be trusted. She defended herself by withdrawing into solitary activities. These early experiences lay the foundation for her subsequent difficulties relating, such is in work situations.

Exercise 2c

1-1, 2-b, 3-h, 4-d, 5-j, 6-c, 7-a, 8-k, 9-i, 10-g, 11-e, 12-f.

Exercise 2d

Rationale: 1 and 2: The client's perception of herself as a "Nobody", her expressions of guilt, shame and doubt, and inferiority, plus her untidy appearance, are all reflections of low self-esteem related to negative IPR and feedback she experienced throughout her life. These cues support the nursing goals to help the client develop a better concept of herself and help her care for her own hygiene needs. Nsg. action: 1: Initiate a positive, corrective nurse-client relationship; communicate respect by calling her by her correct name; introduce her to others, using her name; point out reality when she calls herself "Nobody". 2: Help client with her hygiene and appearance; provide client with privacy when carrying out hygiene; give positive feedback when client appears tidy, takes initiative in meeting her own needs; gradually encourage her to take responsibility for her own care, to make simple decisions about what to wear. Anticipated results: Within 4 weeks the client will: 1: Respond consistently to her correct name and call herself "Nobody" with less frequency. 2: Take increasing responsibility for her own hygiene; make simple decisions; respond with relative comfort to positive feedback.

Exercise 3

Rationale: 1, 2, and 3: Difficulty mastering the developmental task of trust in infancy has interfered with the client's accurate perception of reality, his ability to relate to others, to assume responsibility for his hygiene, and meet his nutritional needs, requiring the nurse to intervene and expose him to a caring, trusting, professional nurse-client relationship in which his needs can be met. Nsg. action: 1: Seek out client; introduce self; communicate honesty and sincerity to client; respond with consistency; listen and, when possible, point out when client's perceptions are false without arguing with him; initially encourage solitary or one-to-one rather than group activities. 2: Provide client with privacy when toileting, bathing, etc.; assist client with hygiene as necessary; give subtle positive appraisals when deserved. 3.: Provide well-balanced diet including, as much as possible, the client's preferred foods; allow client to serve up his own foods; offer self-contained foods such as hard-boiled eggs in the shell, intact fruit, unopened individual containers of milk and juice, etc.; encourage him to eat in the dining room with other clients. Anticipated result: Within 4 weeks the client will: 1: seek out the nurse on his own initiative; begin to give up false beliefs; show interest and receptivity to group interactions and activities. 2: Share toilet facilities with other male clients with minimal anxiety; assume major responsibility for his physical care; accept positive reflected appraisals with minimal anxiety. 3: Begin to give up his beliefs that the food is contaminated; sit in the dining room and eat his meals with other clients; permit his food to be served from the community supply; gain five pounds.

CHAPTER 14

Exercise 1

Self-esteem: 1-10. Love object: 8-10. Independence: 1-4, 7. Freedom: 1-2, 4, 8. Physical integrity: 1, 3, 9. Youth: 1, 3, 5, 9. Autonomy: 1-2, 4. Material poss.: 7, 10.

Exercise 2

Grief: Normal, universal, reaction to real loss of tangible or intangible, highly valued object; adaptive process; self-limiting; generally not incapacitating except in early, acute stage; phases include shock and disbelief, awareness, restitution. Depress.: Disturbance in mood in response to actual, anticipated, or imagined loss; pathological elaboration of grief; goes beyond grief in duration, intensity; loss is often symbolic of other losses; incapacitating; not self-limiting; professional help often required.

Exercise 3a

a: 9, 12, 14. b: 7, 16, 17, 20, 21. c: 12, 16, 17, 20, 21, 28. d: 2, 5. e: 23, 26, 27. f: 1, 24, 30. g: (feelings) 4, 13, 19; (content) 6. h: 12. i: 3, 8, 29. j: 4, 5, 10, 11, 13, 15, 18, 22, 25.

Exercise 3b

Depression occurs as a response to a real or imagined loss. With the loss of a trusted nurse the client experiences a loss symbolic of earlier losses (mother) and loss of self-esteem. If the feelings are not worked through, the depression can increase in intensity and duration and may effect subsequent relationships. The client, with a history of suicide, is also a suicidal risk with this new loss.

Exercise 3c

Rationale: 1: Anticipated loss of the nurse has contributed to the development of depression and possible suicide risk in the client; verbalization of feelings associated with the loss reduces the likelihood of the client acting on them. 2 and 3: Focusing on the positive learnings gained in the nurse-client relationship and helping the client to relate to others will help fill the void left by the ending of a meaningful relationship. Nsg. action: 1: Focus on the client; use a variety of therapeutic communication skills to facilitate the client's expressing feelings; listen to expressions of anger without becoming defensive; sit in silence with client when she does not feel like talking. 2: Use therapeutic communication skills to help the client reflect back on the relationship and its positive aspects; refocus on topics not fully explored. 3: Encourage client to identify other persons on the unit with whom she feels comfortable; introduce her to others, as necessary; join group activities; respond consistently and firmly that the relationship is over if and when the client tries to get the nurse to visit or write.

Exercise 4

b: . . . lack of ego controls. c: . . . hostility towards others and overactivity. d: . . . defense against depression, or situational crisis. e: . . . hyperactivity. f: . . . manic excitement. g: . . . high levels of anxiety interfering with functioning or situational crisis. h: . . . distractability and difficulty focusing on any task for long. i: . . . unacceptable social behavior. j: . . . faulty perceptions and delusions of grandeur. (These statements are not absolutes. Several may be interchanged.)

Exercise 5

Goal: To assist client to control his vulgar language and socially aggressive behaviors that isolate him from others. Rationale: During the manic phase the client's ego is ineffective and is overpowered by id impulses, requiring the nurse to assume ego functions temporarily. Nsg. action: Acceptance; ignore client's vulgar language; set limits on sexual aggressiveness; distract client with socially acceptable activities, such as Ping-Pong, piano playing; encourage participation in supervised group activities; administer lithium as ordered. Anticipated results: Within 4 weeks the client will manifest decreased use of vulgarities; control sexually aggressive behaviors; relate to others more appropriately.

CHAPTER 15

Exercise 1

Displacement: 1, 3, 4, 6 to 8, 10. Symbolism: all. Conversion: 2, 5, 9. Preoccupation: 1, 3, 4, 6 to 8, 10. Undoing: 1, 4, 7, 10. Repression: all.

Example 2a

I° Gains: 3, 6, 7, 9, 10. II° Gains: 1, 2, 4, 5, 8.

Exercise 2b

In general: Respond in a matter-of-fact manner; avoid use of "How are you?" and focusing on client's symptoms; identify and encourage client's involvement in other interests, hobbies; avoid comments emphasizing secondary gains: "Now you can look at your favorite soap opera on TV every day." "You won't have to worry about that final exam in school now." "Look at all those cards! You need to get sick to see how many friends you have."; work with family, teaching them about the illness and have them help you encourage client to become autonomous; limit staff contact to those who understand and accept the client's illness; reflect on own feelings. Also: provide client paralyzed in lower extremities with means of ambulation; encourage client to use unaffected upper extremities for self-care; prepare blind client's food, bath, etc. and orient him so he can do as much for himself as possible.

Exercise 3

Rationale: Physical and emotional needs are interrelated; prevention of anxiety can free the client's energy to deal with his physical problem. Nsg. action: Develop understanding of unconscious nature of the client's conflict; deal with own feelings related to the disorder; provide a light in the client's room; respond with understanding and empathy when the client talks about his fears. Anticipated results: Within 2 days the client will express feelings of security and less anxiety associated with his fear of the dark; focus his attention and energy on his physical problem.

CHAPTER 16

Exercise 1

2: Cold, unfeeling. 3: Disgust. 4: Anger. 5: Courage. 6: Love. 7: Annoyance. 8: Stubbornness. 9: Pleasure. 10: Indifference. 11 to 15: Personal examples.

Exercise 2

Somatization: 2, 6, 8. Conversion: 5, 9. Hypochondriasis: 3, 7. Malingering: 1, 4, 10.

Exercise 3

Physical: 2: Gastrointestinal disorder in which sustained gastric hypermotility and increase in gastric secretions erode stomach lining resulting in epigastric pain 1 to 4 hours after eating. 3: Cardiovascular disorder in which there is sustained elevation of systolic and diastolic arterial blood pressure, leading to organic changes, including renal damage if condition is chronic. 4: Respiratory disorder in which bronchial obstruction interferes with expiration, results in a wheeze, and leads to pulmonary changes and a decreased vital capacity. 5: Musculoskeletal disorder in which there is marked organic damage to joints as well as other tissues. Emotional: 2: Underlying unconscious dependency needs conflict with individual's perception of himself as strong, independent, unemotional, and hard working. Illness precipitated by stress. Brings dependency-independency conflict closer to awareness. 3: Feelings of anger and rage are internalized and the individual maintains a calm, placid, compliant exterior. Tries to conform to expectations of others, demands of authority. 4: Underlying fear of abandonment by mother and mixed feelings of dependency and anger. Represses the anger. Expresses the symbolic "cry for the mother" in the asthmatic wheeze. 5: Masochistic, self-sacrificing individual with a history of maternal deprivation and unmet dependency needs.

Exercise 4

b: Ischemia and ulcer formation in walls of the bowel related to feelings of ambivalence and repressed rage. c: Elevated systolic and diastolic arterial blood pressure related to repressed anger. d: Severe dyspnea related to unconscious fears of being abandoned. e: Immobility and pain in the joints related to conflict over unmet dependency needs.

Exercise 5

Rationale: 1: Although emotionally based, peptic ulcer is life threatening and takes priority over emotional needs. 2: Underlying conflict with dependence and independence necessitating that dependency needs be met in a matter-of-fact way until client can resume independent role. 3: Expression of feelings verbally helps client externalize rather than internalize feelings and conflicts that contribute to the physiological problem. Nsg. action: 1: Provide dietary supervision; administer antacids as ordered; bed rest; work with family and client to try and help client change pattern of living. 2: Acceptance; address client by surname; anticipate needs; gradually allow client to assume some responsibility for care. 3: Use a variety of communication skills to help client talk about his/her feelings; listen; encourage problem solving to find alternative solutions to problems, life-style. Anticipated results: 1: Within 24 hours client will experience relief from pain. 2: Within 2 to 5 days client will accept care being given. 3: Within 7 days client will talk increasingly about his feelings and problems; symptoms of anxiety will decrease.

CHAPTER 17

Exercise 1

Personal responses.

Exercise 2

b: Hallucinatory experiences resulting from impaired sensory perception is often a phenomenon noted in persons with delirium tremens. c: Substance-dependent individuals are often manipulative, passive-aggressive, and a source of embarrassment, and sometimes fear, and hence are often avoided by others. d: With substance abuse, an individual's ego functions of perception and cognition are often impaired and contribute to an inability to meet basic needs, such as self-care, e: Levels of 0.05% alcohol in the blood diminishes inhibitions; a person's ability to make sound judgments and control impulses decreases as the alcohol intake increases. f: Anxiety related to inaccessability to alcohol or drugs reflects an individual's psychological dependence on the substance (habituation). g: Physical, mental, and emotional deterioration occurs insidiously with the prolonged use of alcohol.

Exercise 3a

Goals: 1: To protect the client from self-injury; to orient the client to time, place, and person. 2: To help the client regain physical health. Rationale: 1 and 2: A person under the influence of alcohol can lose touch with reality and be unable to react reasonably, rationally, or responsibly, and requires that the nurse intervene and help him meet his needs on a short-term basis. Nsg. action: 1: Provide dim light in room; stay with the client; consistency; side rails; quiet environment; use clear, simple communication; call client by name; limit number of persons caring for client. 2: Copious fluids—intravenously and/or orally, as indicated; high potency vitamins, anticonvulsants, and sedatives, as ordered; balanced diet; check visitors for contraband sources of alcohol. Anticipated results: 1: Within 24 hours client will become oriented, responding appropriately to his name. 2: Within 5 to 7 days the client's electrolyte balance and nutritional state will be improved.

Exercise 3b

Group experience uses group support; helps alcoholics face the reality of their alcoholism and take steps to change a life pattern; organization assists members to face life without alcohol; members are alcoholics and reformed alcoholics who have understanding and patience for each other; promotes self-esteem by seeking out alcoholics, encouraging their attendance at AA meetings, helping them find jobs.

Exercise 4

Abdominal cramps, vomiting, diarrhea, headache, sweating, pains in muscles and joints.

Exercise 4b

1: Withdrawal symptoms related to heroin dependence. 2: Ineffective individual coping related to inadequate support systems.

Exercise 4c

Advantages: Halting criminal activities; increasing potential for self-support; increasing individual's ability to function; fairly inexpensive; fairly successful. Disadvantages: Another narcotic; maintains addiction; unless highly motivated to give up addiction, individual often returns to it after treatment.

CHAPTER 18

Exercise 1

Personal responses.

Exercise 2

Acceptance, respect, consideration, consistency, firm limits.

Exercise 3a

Cognitive: 1, 3, 5 to 9. Relating: 1, 7, 8, 12. Insight/Judgment: 2, 3, 5, 10, 11. Impulse control: 2 to 4, 6, 10, 11.

Exercise 3b

Rationale: The client's personality is dominated by the primitive demands of the id, and the nurse needs to intervene and support the ego in evolving useful adaptations and controls. Nsg. action: Firm, reasonable, consistent limits and controls on behavior; structured, controlled environment; identify responsibilities client is expected to fulfill and hold client to these obligations; direct client's energies into challenging daily activities; reward acceptable behavior. Anticipated results: Within 2 weeks the client will begin to: accept limits placed on impulsive acts; follow established routine; follow through on obligations; participate in daily activities.

CHAPTER 19

Exercise 1

2: Anxiety, agitation, and violence directed at self and others related to substance abuse. 3: Dehydration and electrolyte imbalance related to periodic binge and purge episodes. 4: Potential for self-directed violence related to suicidal behavior; suicidal thoughts related to loss and feelings of worthlessness and despair. 5: Ritualistic behaviors related to anxiety stemming from unconscious conflicts. 6: Social isolation related to alterations in mental status.

Exercise 2

Rationale: 1 and 2: Anorexia nervosa, a disorder characterized by fear of fat and a distorted body image, is expressed through extreme dieting, bizarre eating habits, excessive exercise, and severe weight loss that can be life threatening. As normal nutritional status is restored, the danger from complications of malnutrition are lessened; as self-esteem is enhanced, the client's body image problem will decrease. Nsg. action: 1: Firm, supportive, consistent, understanding, collaborative approach by staff; intravenous fluids; balanced diet; dietary supplements and vitamins as ordered; allow client to eat in private; routine weighing; limit exercise routine. 2: Involve client in the treatment plans; hygiene care; give deserved praise and compliments for weight gain and improved appearance; encourage peer contacts; focus on client's interests and feelings; listen; be alert to cues of suicidal ideation; referral for psychotherapy. Anticipated results: Within 14 days the client will begin to 1: show weight gain and resumption of more regular eating patterns; 2: verbalize underlying feelings and conflicts; express pride in accomplishments; relate more to others.

Exercise 3

Personal responses.

CHAPTER 20

Exercise 1

Life Review: 1, 5, 12. Loneliness: 7, 10. Depression: 6, 11, 15. Suspicion: 3, 9. Confusion: 2, 8, 14. Loss: 4, 13.

Exercise 2a

Hints of despair: "I look at the future, I shudder with dread", balanced with hope: "But inside this old carcass a young girl still dwells, and now and again my battered heart swells", and acceptance with integrity: "And accept the stark fact that nothing can last."

Exercise 2b

The nurse does not talk or share her thoughts with the client; uses a loud voice unnecessarily, failing to check if client can hear; scolds, gives disapproval rather than acknowledges client's efforts to help; does not allow client to do what she can for herself, promoting unnecessary dependency.

Exercise 2c

"A crabbit old woman, not very wise;" "Who dribbles her food, and makes no reply;" "Who seems not to notice the things that you do;" "And forever is losing a stocking or shoe;" "Who . . . lets you do as you will with bathing and feeding."

Exercise 2d

Rationale: 1: With improved communication and validation, suspiciousness, distortions and use of projection should decrease. 2: With reality orientation and stimulation the client will be kept more in touch with the here and now and confusion will diminish. 3: With the verbalization of emotions, the feelings of loss and grief will be externalized rather than internalized. 4: With increased opportunities to relate in meaningful ways, the client's feelings of loneliness will be reduced. 5: With the increase of self-worth, the depression related to loss of self-esteem and depersonalization will be lessened. 6: With opportunities to reminisce, the client is helped to look back on the past with pleasure and find a satisfactory closure to life. Nsg. action: 1: Develop a nurse-client relationship and have the same nurses work with the client; set up a routine that is predictable; surround client with familiar objects; provide client with hearing aid and eyeglasses as needed; orient the client; be consistent. 2: Orient client; use her name; use touch to make contact; provide adequate light, including a dim night light; provide hearing aid with eyeglasses as needed; have patience. 3: Acknowledge pain associated with loss; use a variety of communication skills to help client focus on and express feelings; listen; use touch to make contact and communicate understanding and reassurance. 4: Develop nurse-client relationship; spend short periods with client regularly rather than long periods irregularly; ambulate client and promote socialization with other clients by having client sit in community areas, eat in dining room, rather than stay alone in own room. 5: Communicate respect by calling client by surname; help with hygiene and appearance; give positive feedback when appropriate; listen with interest to client's conversations; be alert to suicidal ideation. 6: Encourage client to talk about the past; allow client to keep mementoes from the past; listen when client talks about the future, death, etc.

Exercise 3   Early: 1 to 4, 7. Late: 1, 5, 6, 8 to 10.

Exercise 4   b: Elderly persons, especially those with physical illness, may see no alternative except death and, fearing pain, loneliness, the process of dying and lack of control, may attempt suicide. c: With aging may come decreased visual acuity and loss of hearing which may contribute to distortions and suspiciousness. d: Forced retirement and loss of income, family reorganization, and discriminatory practices are commonly experienced by the aged person and contribute to the loss of self-esteem and feelings of depersonalization. e: Removal of the aging individual from familiar surroundings and routines, as through hospitalization, contributes to confusion. f: Organic brain syndrome, an insidious, devastating, and irreversible disorder, is early manifested through impaired verbal communication.

CHAPTER 21

Exercise 1   b: Seriously ill persons realize that without the transplant they will probably die in a short time and, also, that failure of the transplanted organ to be accepted by the body can result in death. c: Many persons go through a period of mourning for the lost body part and experience an altered body image which takes time to accept. In addition, they are concerned that significant others will not accept them. d: A characteristic response to cardiac surgery for persons with long-term cardiac conditions is anger over the dependency role coupled with the anticipation and hope that they will be able to lead more normal, autonomous lives. e: Women who give birth to such infants often feel responsible and guilty and question their own value as women. They may reject the infant or may feel such responsibility that they spend their life punishing themselves for their perceived failure. f: Women who terminate an unwanted pregnancy, a pregnancy resulting from rape, a pregnancy in which genetic counseling detected a severe genetic defect, etc., experience feelings of relief mixed with feelings of loss, shame, and guilt. Society's attitudes and religious values contribute to the conflict associated with an abortion.

Exercise 2   Provide good physical care; anticipate needs before client has to ask; use an unhurried approach; listen to expressions of anger and resentment without getting angry or defensive in return; avoid use of meaningless cliches; explain tests, procedures, and answer questions; spend time with client; involve client in planning care; acknowledge and include family in care.

Exercise 3a   a: 10, 11. b: 2, 25. c: 3, 6, 9, 20, 24, 27, 28, 32, 35. d: 3, 8, 21, 34. e: 7, 14, 31, 34, 36, 37. f: 5, 11, 12, 17, 18, 23, 29. g: 19. h: 1, 15, 16. i: 13, 22, 32, 33. j: 4, 5, 12, 17, 23, 24, 26, 30.

Exercise 3b

Characteristics: 1: Person is unable to deal with reality of impending death. Uses ego defense to defend. 2: Person experiences anger, resentment; feels she is the victim of fate, circumstances, incompetence of others, etc. 3: Individual attempts to bargain or trade off "good" behavior for more time. 4: Individual is no longer able to avoid reality of impending death and is aware that denial, anger, and bargaining are ineffective. Respond to anticipated loss with depression. 5: Person comes to peace with herself about fact she is dying. Characterized by "affective void," she is neither happy nor depressed. Interests are limited. Behaviors: 1: Not wanting to talk about fears; "Why borrow trouble?"; trying to put fears out of mind (suppression). 2: Verbal expressions of anger directed at nurse; nonverbal anger—tense posture, frown, etc. 3: Identifying herself as not very cooperative; offers to try to be "good"; hoping to live long enough to see daughter grow up, get settled. 4: Lying in the dark; alone; not eating; giving up—"What's the use?," "Beginning of the end," "Time I faced the truth." 5: Sense of completion—has finished the diary, the painting; taking pleasure in accomplishments; talks about dying more easily; limited interests—mainly concerned about being free of pain.

CHAPTER 22

Exercise 1

"A state of disequilibrium resulting from the interaction of an event with the individual's or family's coping mechanisms, which are inadequate to meet the demands of the situation, combined with the individual's or family's perception of the meaning of the event." (Taylor, Chapter 22)

Exercise 2

Massive amounts of free-floating anxiety; self-limiting; highly individual threat; effects significant others in the individual's support system.

Exercise 3

Developmental: 1 to 3, 5, 6, 8, 14. Situational: 4, 7, 9 to 13, 15.

Exercise 4

1-c: Of short duration, the individual refuses to accept the reality of the situation. 2-f: The individual remains functional and continues to participate in daily activities. 3-d: The individual ceases to function effectively, becomes preoccupied with the event, and is flooded with anxiety. 4-b: The individual uses coping measures and resumes normal activities. 5-a: The individual defends by using projection, blaming others for the situation. 6-g: Similar to 4-b. Individual resumes normal activities. 7-e: Individual integrates new patterns of behavior and coping into personality and family structure.

Exercise 5

a: 13, 17, 19, 23. b: 3, 6, 7, 14, 21, 26, 27, 29, 31. c: 10, 32, 35. d: 1, 2, 21, 25, 28. e: 9, 15, 20, 30. f: 5, 12, 20, 40. g: 8, 34. h: 3, 6, 7, 27, 29, 31. i: 15, 22, 24, 36, 39. j: 4, 5, 11, 16, 18, 33, 37, 38.

CHAPTER 23

Exercise 1

a: Jason; b: Helen; c: Kirby; d: Paula; e: Rob; f: Carol; g: Tom; h: Arthur.

Exercise 2a

2: This group consists of multiple subgroups relating to each other but not to the group as a whole. The leader is ineffective, uninvolved, or ignored. A laissez-faire group? 3: This group appears to be dominated by a member other than the designated leader. The other members appear passive, silent; the designated leader does not respond to communication directed towards him nor does he attempt to interact with the other members. A laissez-faire group taken over by an authoritarian member? 4: This group is dominated by the designated leader. Communication is directed at individual members, but it is one-way. No feedback is given. An authoritarian group? 5: In this group the leader continues to be dominant, active. The communication is two-way between the leader and the members, but no interaction occurs between the members. An authoritarian group? 6: This is an active group with all members and the leader participating in the discussion. The interaction appears balanced, feedback seems to be occurring. This appears to be a democratic group.

Exercise 2b

Groups.: 1: 1, 8. 2: 1, 3, 8. 3: 1, 4, 6 to 8. 4: 2, 4 to 7. 5: 2, 5. 6: 9, 10. Groups 4 and 5 may also be said to have ineffective leadership (Q-8), depending on criteria for effectiveness.

Exercise 3

Preaffiliation: 1, 8, 9. Intragroup: 3, 5, 10. Working: 4, 6, 7. Termination: 2, 11, 12.

Exercise 4

Therapy: 1, 4 to 7, 9, 10, 13. Socialization: 2, 3, 8, 11, 12, 14, 15.

CHAPTER 24

Exercise 1

Regulation of sexual activity and reproduction; physical maintenance; protection; education and socialization; recreation; conferring of status; giving of affection.

Exercise 2

Goal: I: To adjust to wife's pregnancy. II: To meet needs of infants and preschool children. III: To protect school-aged children from undesirable influences outside the home while enabling to fit into the world. IV: To loosen family ties to permit greater freedom and responsibility for the members. V: To release its members to assume adult responsibilities. VI: To maintain marital relationships. VII: To prepare for dissolution of the family. Family dynamics: I: Wife becomes self-absorbed as she prepares for the birth; husband generally feels increased responsibility. II: Roles of husband and wife expand to include those of father and mother. III: Composition of family may include preschool children as well as school-aged children, the latter of whom need support to deal with societal values that may conflict with family values. IV: Children may overreact to greater freedom causing parents to respond with more rather than less control. V: The "launching stage" in which parents and children all experience difficulty with releasing members and assuming adult responsibility. VI: The "postparental family" in which parents subsume their parental roles into their marital roles; experience the "empty nest" syndrome. VII: The retirement and postretirement years in which the couple prepares for dissolution of the family by death of one of the spouses.

Exercise 3

a: 2, 5. b: 3, 11. c: 7, 9, 10, 13 to 15. d: 1, 4, 6, 8, 12.

Exercise 4

Effective: 1, 2, 5, 6, 8, 10, 14, 15. Ineffective: 3, 4, 7, 9, 11 to 13.

Exercise 5

To resolve pathological conflicts and anxiety within the family; to strengthen the individual member against destructive forces within himself and within the family; to strengthen the family against critical upsets; to influence the orientation of the family identity; to promote a value of health in the family.

CHAPTER 25

Exercise 1a

Individual admits and discharges himself via his own signature.

Exercise 1b

Individual is admitted through actions of others and without his consent. Two types—emergency commitment for purposes of observation from 10 to 60 days and indefinite or regular commitment which may extend for an unspecified period of time for purposes of protection of self or others, treatment.

Exercise 2

Marrying; getting a divorce; making telephone calls; keeping personal belongings; making contracts; writing and mailing letters; making purchases; pursuing an education; making a will, being employed; following religious practices.

Exercise 3

2: Inadequate treatment. 3: Negligence. 4: Invasion of privacy. 5: Cruel and unusual punishment; assault. 6: Battery.

Exercise 4

Habeas corpus: 6-R; Right to treatment: 4-V, 12-R, 13-R. Least restrictive treatment: 3-R, 9-R. Refuse treatment: 1-R, 7-V. Informed consent: 5-R, 8-R, 11-V. Confidentiality: 2-V, 10-R, 14-V. Psych. exam: 15-V.

CHAPTER 26

Exercise 1

Personal examples.

Exercise 2

Discussion.

answers to test items

Chapter 1 1-b 2-a 3-d 4-c 5-c 6-d 7-b 8-c 9-b 10-a
11-b 12-d 13-a 14-a 15-b

Chapter 2 1-d 2-a 3-b 4-a 5-b 6-d 7-d 8-c 9-d 10-d
11-d 12-c 13-b 14-a 15-c

Chapter 3 1-a 2-d 3-b 4-d 5-d 6-d 7-d 8-d 9-c 10-c
11-a 12-a

Chapter 4 1-d 2-c 3-a 4-b 5-a 6-c 7-d 8-a 9-b 10-c
11-d 12-b 13-d 14-b 15-d

Chapter 5 1-a 2-b 3-d 4-a 5-c 6-b 7-a 8-c 9-d 10-b
11-d 12-c 13-a 14-d 15-b

Chapter 6 1-a 2-b 3-c 4-c 5-b 6-c 7-d 8-c 9-d 10-b
11-a 12-b

Chapter 7 1-a 2-b 3-a 4-b 5-c 6-d 7-d 8-b 9-b 10-b
11-c 12-c 13-a 14-d 15-d

Chapter 8 1-b 2-a 3-d 4-d 5-a 6-d 7-d 8-c 9-a 10-c
11-a 12-b 13-b 14-d 15-b

Chapter 9 1-b 2-b 3-d 4-d 5-c 6-a 7-d 8-a 9-c 10-d
11-c 12-a 13-d 14-b 15-a

Chapter 10 1-c 2-b 3-b 4-a 5-c 6-b 7-b 8-d 9-a 10-d
11-c 12-c 13-d 14-b 15-b

Chapter 11 1-a 2-d 3-c 4-c 5-d 6-d 7-c 8-b 9-b 10-b
11-d 12-a

Chapter 12 1-a 2-d 3-a 4-a 5-b 6-c 7-c 8-d 9-b 10-a
11-c 12-b 13-d 14-d 15-d

Chapter 13 1-a 2-c 3-d 4-a 5-d 6-d 7-b 8-b 9-d 10-c
11-a 12-c 13-c 14-b 15-a

Chapter 14 1-a 2-d 3-a 4-b 5-c 6-c 7-d 8-b 9-d 10-d
11-c 12-a 13-a 14-c 15-a

Chapter 15 1-c 2-d 3-a 4-a 5-c 6-d 7-a 8-b 9-c 10-b
11-d 12-b

Chapter 16 1-b 2-a 3-d 4-a 5-c 6-a 7-c 8-a 9-c 10-d
11-b 12-a

Chapter 17 1-c 2-a 3-d 4-b 5-d 6-b 7-d 8-b 9-d 10-c
11-a 12-c

Chapter 18	1-d	2-c	3-b	4-c	5-a	6-b	7-d	8-a	9-d	10-d
Chapter 19	1-b	2-b	3-d	4-a	5-c	6-b	7-b	8-c	9-b	10-d
11-c	12-c									
Chapter 20	1-d	2-a	3-c	4-b	5-d	6-a	7-c	8-b	9-d	10-b
Chapter 21	1-c	2-b	3-a	4-b	5-d	6-d	7-c	8-c	9-d	10-a
Chapter 22	1-b	2-c	3-c	4-a	5-b	6-c	7-a	8-d	9-b	10-a
Chapter 23	1-b	2-a	3-c	4-d	5-a	6-b	7-b	8-c	9-d	10-a
Chapter 24	1-c	2-a	3-d	4-c	5-b	6-a	7-b	8-d	9-b	10-c
Chapter 25	1-b	2-c	3-b	4-d	5-c	6-d	7-c	8-a	9-c	10-a
Chapter 26	1-d	2-c	3-b	4-a	5-b	6-c	7-b	8-d	9-a	10-b

solutions to word games

FEELINGS AND FEARS (Section IV)

a Feelings: anger, apathy, awe, doom, fear, glee, gloom, grief, guilt, hate, ire, joy, love, pain, panic, pity, rage, regret, relief, woe.

b Fears: 1-bugs, 2-heights, 3-air, 4-dogs, 5-right, 6-fights, 7-women, 8-cats, 9-blood, 10-men, 11-water, 12-fish, 13-dirt, 14-night, 15-light, 16-fire, 17-rats, 18-Satan, 19-sex, 20-sea, 21-death, 22-God, 23-heat, 24-trains, 25-war.

FILL-IN

Ego Defenses (Section II): a-compensation, b-regression, c-symbolization, d-denial, e-conversion, f-fixation, g-projection, h-rationalization, i-displacement, j-repression, k-isolation.

Nursing Process (Section III): a-planning, b-evaluation, c-observation, d-assessment, e-validate, f-client, g-goals, h-hypothesis, i-intervention, j-actions, k-chart, l-theme, m-revision, n-results.

Interventions (Section V): a-socialization, b-conjoint, c-hospitalization, d-gestalt, e-group, f-sensitivity, g-self-help, h-encounter, i-TA, j-family, k-psychodrama, l-insight, m-crisis.

LOGIC

Therapies (Section I): Sue-GT-Thur., June-MT-Tues., Marion-RT-Wed., Walter-ADL-Fri., David-OT-Mon.

Client Rights (Section VI): Treatment-Chin-Todd, Habeas Corpus-Williams-Eddy, Confidentiality-Solo-May, Informed Consent-Ames-Mac, Least Restrictive Treatment-Low-Cobb.

QUOTE-A-CROSTIC

Section II: *Second Heaven*- Judith Guest. "Nearly all her life she had read for escape . . . newspapers, magazines, bad novels, good novels, billboard signs, cereal boxes. She read all her junk mail, putting words, tons of words, between her and the thing that had happened to her." (New York, New American Library, A Signet Book, 1983, pp. 82-83.)

A-Wellness	M-Jahoda
B-He	N-Shame and doubt
C-Phallic phase	O-Bad
D-Stressors	P-Nipple
E-Strength	Q-Interpersonal
F-Friend	R-Behavior
G-Wholism	S-Growth and
H-General _____ theory	T-Freud
I-Brawl	U-Anal zone
J-Negative feedback	V-Doodles
K-Sex	W-Health
L-Aged person	

Section III: *Nurse*- Peggy Anderson. "I love to think about what goes on in people's minds. I love to watch their eyes and watch the way they react to things. . . . I've learned a lot from patients about human beings." (New York, Berkley Publishing Corp., 1979, p. 41.)

A-Nonverbal
B-The amount
C-Therapy
D-Beliefs
E-Teach
F-Problem solving
G-Seethe
H-Acting out
I-Agent

J-Empathy
K-Akathisia
L-One-to-one
M-Attitudes
N-Shove
O-Withdrawn
P-Holistic
Q-Toy
R-Window

Section IV: *Personhood*- Leo F. Buscaglia. "Most people abhor the very idea of pain. . . . They seek to evade it. . . . They perform all types of mental gymnastics . . . or blind themselves with momentary sources of relief such as alcohol, tranquilizers and drugs. Some, in desperation, will even choose psychosis. . . ." (New York, Fawcett Columbine, 1982, p. 123.)

A-Symptomless
B-Meals
C-Smother mother
D-Disorders
E-Quiet room
F-Prevention
G-Watch
H-Adaptation
I-Voyeur
J-Wound
K-Self-esteem
L-Obsessive

M-Moody
N-Free floating
O-Blank affect
P-Lull
Q-Tenderness
R-Schizophrenia
S-Hyperactive
T-Psychophysiological
U-Heal
V-Senile
W-Hysteria

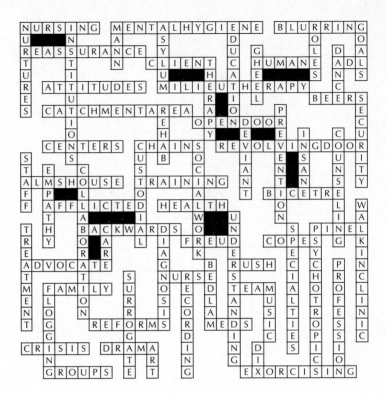

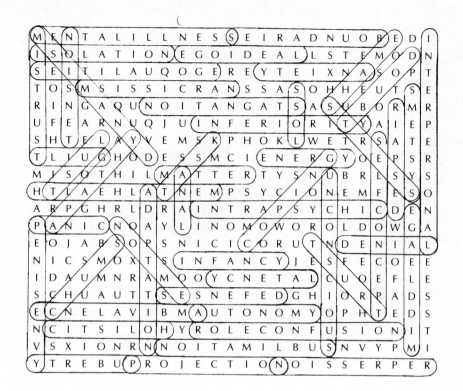

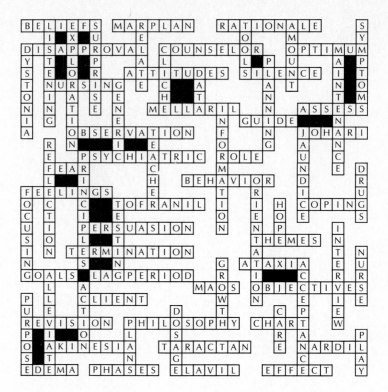

Section IV

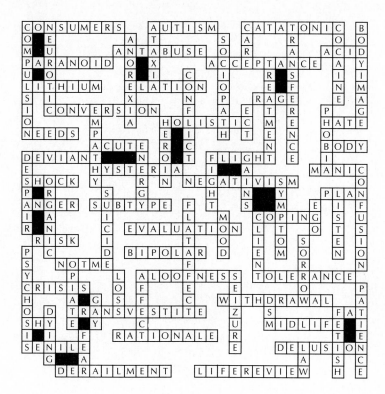

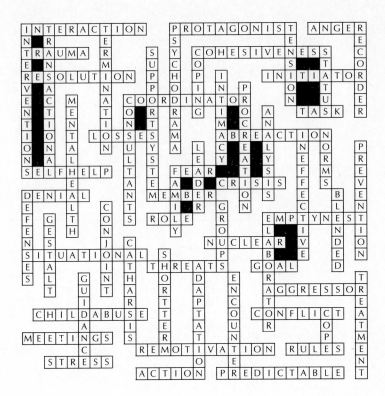

308

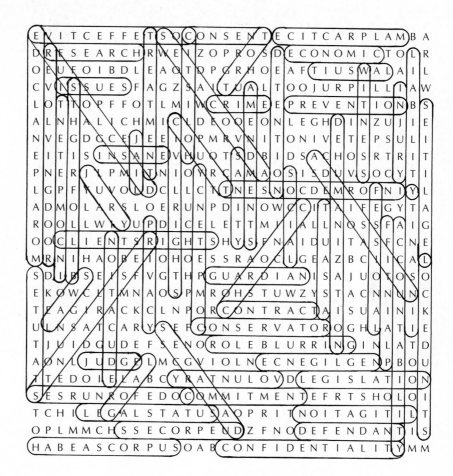

Index

Behavior—cont'd
 sexual
  aggressive, 160
  deviant, 192, 194, 195
  promiscuous, 197
Bipolar affective disorder
 manic type, 159-160
 mixed, 154
Body image, 211; *see also* Self-concept
 adolescent and, 202
Bronchial asthma, 174, 177, 178, 180
Bulimia, 197, 202

C

Card, drug, 98-99
Care
 history of, 3-4
 plan of, 186-187
Chlorpromazine, 97
Civil rights, 262-264, 265
Clarification, 74
Client
 perception of, 65
 rights of, 262-264, 265
Clinical issues, 268
Closed human system, 27
Cocaine, 190
Commitment, consistent, 90
Communication
 crisis intervention and, 235-239
 double-bind, 139
 effective, 73-84
 nontherapeutic, 75-79, 82
 nonverbal, 173
 physically ill and, 212
 therapeutic; *see* Therapeutic communication
Community mental health, history of, 3-4
Conceptual framework, 23-29
Confusion, 204, 208, 209
 alcohol and, 185-186
Consciousness, 31
Consistency
 limits and, 196
 nursing approach and, 91-93
 relationship and, 90
Control, impulse, 194
Conversion, 164, 165, 166, 170, 175-176

Conversion—cont'd
 body part to reflect feeling and, 174-175, 180
Coping
 alternative method for, 191
 anxiety and, 41-42
 substance-abuse and, 191
Counselor-therapist role, 11-12
Crisis intervention, 231-240
Crisis state, 232-233
 phases of, 233-234
Cultural theory of development, 140
Custodial care, 3
Cyclical depressive and manic episodes, 153; *see also* Bipolar affective disorder

D

Death
 of loved one, 153, 154
 threat of, 211, 214-215
Defense mechanism; *see also* specific defense mechanism
 anxiety and, 42, 164, 165
 drug addiction and, 191
Degenerative brain disease, 208
Dehumanization, 206
Delirium tremens, 190
Delivery system
 issues and, 268-269
 mental health, 3-10
Democratic group, 244
Denial, 215-216
 anxiety and, 42
Dependence
 alcohol and, 186-187
 psychological, 189
Dependency-independency conflict, 179
Depression, 153, 154, 155, 204, 217-218
Desipramine, 104-106
Development
 crisis of, 232, 239
 cultural theory of, 140
 interpersonal learning and, 35
 personality, 30-38
 stressor and, 25
 task of, 37
Diagnosis, nursing process and, 121, 128

Psychosexual theory, 33-34
Psychotherapy group, 241, 243
Psychotic disorder, 197, 198
Psychotropic medication, 97-112
  history of, 3

R

Rationalization, 42
Reaction-formation, 42
Reality orientation, 164
Reclusiveness, 6-7
Reflected appraisal, 36
Regression, 42
Regulation, hospital environment and, 114
Relatedness, 144
Relationship, interpersonal, 85-96
  developmental task and, 37
Repetitive pattern of behavior, 164, 165, 170,
    171
Repression, 164, 165, 166
  anxiety and, 42
Revision, interview approach and, 125
Rheumatoid arthritis, 174, 177, 178
Rights, clients', 262-264, 265
Ritual, 164, 165, 170, 171
Role
  counselor-therapist, 11-12
  in group, 242-243, 248
  mental health team, 11-20
  nurse and
    nursing process and, 127
    purpose and action in, 15
  in psychotherapy, 242-243, 248
Routine, 90
Rule, hospital environment and, 114

S

Schizophrenia, 139-151
Secondary gain
  after acute stage of illness, 179-180
  from illness, 167, 172
Selective inattention, 42
Self-assessment, 122; *see also* Self-awareness
  adolescent and, 199-200
Self-awareness, 44, 56; *see also* Self-assessment
  nurse and, 65-72

Self-concept; *see also* Body image
  elderly and, 209
  reflected appraisal and, 36-37
Self-destructive behavior, 197, 198, 202
Self-esteem, 211-213
  adolescent and, 202
  loss of, 154
Sexual behavior
  aggressive, 160
  deviant, 192, 194, 195
  promiscuous, 197
Side effect, drug, 108
Significant other, 35
Situational crisis, 232, 239
Situational stressor, 25, 26
Skill
  assessment; *See* Assessment
  communication, 73-84, 81
Social isolation, 208
Social issues, 268
Social relationship, 37, 85-96
Social worker, psychiatric, 11
Socialization
  group and, 241
  nursing role and, 11-12
Socially disruptive behavior, 192-196
Sociogram, 244-245
Somatic disorder, 197, 198
Somatization, 173-174, 175-176, 180
Somnolent detachment, 42
Stages in dying process, 215-220
Stress, 25-26
  and adaptation theory, 23-29
  anxiety and, 41-50
Stressor, 25-26
  anxiety and, 41
Structure
  environment and, 196
  personality, 30-38
Sublimation, 42
Substance dependence, 182-191; *see also* Drug
    and alcohol abuse
Suicide, 153, 154, 197, 202
  attempted, 155
  elderly and, 208
Sullivan, H.S., 43
  anxiety and, 45